What People are saying about this book:

"A readable, practical, and entertaining book about a challenging, original, and promising new discipline. I recommend it."—**Dan Goleman,** Associate Editor of *Psychology Today.*

"NLP represents a huge quantum jump in our understanding of human behavior and communication. It makes most current therapy and education totally obsolete."—**John O. Stevens,** author of *Awareness* and editor of *Gestalt Therapy Verbatim* and *Gestalt is.*

"This book shows you how to do a little magic and change the way you see, hear, feel, and imagine the world you live in. It presents new therapeutic techniques which can teach you some surprising things about yourself."—**Sam Keen,** Consulting Editor of *Psychology Today* and author of *Beginnings Without End, To a Dancing God,* and *Apology for Wonder.*

"How tiresome it is going from one limiting belief to another. How joyful to read Bandler and Grinder, who don't believe anything, yet use everything! NLP wears seven-league-boots, and takes 'therapy' or 'personal growth' far, *far* beyond any previous notions."—**Barry Stevens,** author of *Don't Push the River,* and co-author of *Person to Person.*

"Fritz Perls regarded John Stevens' *Gestalt Therapy Verbatim* as the best representation of his work in print. Grinder and Bandler have good reason to have the same regard for *Frogs into Princes.* Once again, it's the closest thing to actually being in the workshop."—**Richard Price,** Co-founder and director of Esalen Institute.

frogs into PRINCES

Neuro Linguistic Programming ™

by

Richard Bandler

and

John Grinder

edited by
Steve Andreas
(formerly John O. Stevens)

Copyright © 1979
Real People Press
Box F
Moab, Utah 84532

ISBN: 0-911226-18-4 clothbound $10.00
ISBN: 0-911226-19-2 paperbound $6.50

Cover Artwork by Elizabeth Malczynski, Brooklyn, NY

Library of Congress Cataloging in Publication Data:

```
Bandler, Richard.
     Frogs into princes.

     "Edited entirely from audiotapes of introductory
NLP training workshops conducted by Richard Bandler
and John Grinder."
     Bibliography: p.
     1. Psychotherapy. 2. Nonverbal communication.
3. Psycholinguistics. 4. Imagery (Psychology)
I. Grinder, John, joint author. II. Title.
RC480.5.B313     616.8'914     79-13255
ISBN 0-911226-18-4
ISBN 0-911226-19-2
```

Other excellent NLP books available from Real People Press:

Using Your Brain—for a CHANGE, by Richard Bandler. 165 pp. Illustrated 1985. Cloth $10.00, paper $6.50.

Reframing: Neuro-Linguistic Programming and the Transformation of Meaning, by Richard Bandler and John Grinder. 203 pp. 1981. Cloth $10.00, paper $6.50.

Trance-formations: Neuro-Linguistic Programming and the Structure of Hypnosis, by John Grinder and Richard Bandler. 250 pp. 1981. Cloth $10.00, paper $6.50.

7   8   9   Printing   90   89   88   87

Contents

Foreword by Steve Andreas (formerly John O. Stevens)   i–iv

A Challenge to the Reader   1–2

Note   3

I   *Sensory Experience*:   5–78
Representational Systems and Accessing Cues

II   *Changing Personal History and Organization*:   79–136
Anchoring

III   *Finding New Ways*:   137–193
Reframing

Bibliography   194

Foreword

I have been studying education, therapies, growth experiences, and other methods for personal change since I was a graduate student with Abe Maslow over twenty years ago. Ten years later I met Fritz Perls and immersed myself in gestalt therapy because it seemed to be more effective than most other methods. Actually all methods work for *some* people and with *some* problems. Most methods claim much more than they can deliver, and most theories have little relationship to the methods they describe.

When I was first introduced to Neuro Linguistic Programming I was both fascinated and *very* skeptical. I had been heavily conditioned to believe that change is slow, and usually difficult and painful. I still have some difficulty realizing that I can usually cure a phobia or other similar long-term problem painlessly in less than an hour—even though I have done it repeatedly and seen that the results last. Everything written in this book is explicit, and can be verified quickly in your own experience. There is no hocus-pocus, and you will not be asked to take on any new beliefs. You will only be asked to suspend your own beliefs long enough to test the concepts and procedures of NLP in your own sensory experience. That won't take long; most of the statements and patterns in this book can be tested in a few minutes or a few hours. If you are skeptical, as I was, you owe it to your skepticism to check this out, and find out if the outrageous claims made in this book are valid.

NLP is an explicit and powerful model of human experience and

i

communication. Using the principles of NLP it is possible to describe *any* human activity in a detailed way that allows you to make many deep and lasting changes quickly and easily.

A *few* specific examples of things you can learn to accomplish are: (1) cure phobias and other unpleasant feeling responses in less than an hour, (2) help children and adults with "learning disabilities" (spelling and reading problems, etc.) overcome these limitations, often in less than an hour, (3) eliminate most unwanted habits—smoking drinking, over-eating, insomnia, etc., in a few sessions, (4) make changes in the interactions of couples, families and organizations so that they function in ways that are more satisfying and productive, (5) cure many physical problems—not only most of those recognized as "psychosomatic" but also some that are not—in a few sessions.

These are strong claims, and experienced NLP practitioners can back them up with solid, visible results. NLP in its present state can do a great deal, but it cannot do everything.

> ... if what we've demonstrated is something that you'd like to be able to do, you might as well spend your time learning it. There are lots and lots of things that we cannot do. If you can program yourself to look for things that will be *useful* for you and learn those, instead of trying to find out where what we are presenting to you falls apart, you'll find out where it falls apart, I guarantee you. If you use it congruently you will find lots of places that it won't work. And when it doesn't work, I suggest you do something else.

NLP is only about four years old, and many of the most useful patterns were created within the last year or two.

> We haven't even begun to figure out what the possibilities are of how to use this material. And we are very, very, serious about that. What we are doing now is nothing more than the investigation of how to use this information. We have been unable to exhaust the variety of ways to put this stuff together and put it to use, and we don't know of any limitations on the ways that you can use this information. During this seminar we have mentioned and demonstrated several dozen ways that it can be used. It's the structure of experience. Period. When used

systematically, it constitutes a full strategy for getting any behavioral gain.

Actually, NLP can do *much* more than the kinds of remedial work mentioned above. The same principles can be used to study people who are unusually talented in any way, in order to determine the structure of that talent. That structure can then be quickly taught to others to give them the foundation for that same ability. This kind of intervention results in *generative* change, in which people learn to generate and create new talents and behaviors for themselves and others. A side effect of such generative change is that many of the problem behaviors that would otherwise have been targets for remedial change simply disappear.

In one sense nothing that NLP can accomplish is new· There have always been "spontaneous remissions," "miracle cures," and other sudden and puzzling changes in people's behavior, and there have always been people who somehow learned to use their abilities in exceptional ways.

What *is* new in NLP is the ability to systematically analyze those exceptional people and experiences in such a way that they can become widely available to others. Milkmaids in England became immune to smallpox long before Jenner discovered cowpox and vaccination; now smallpox—which used to kill hundreds of thousands annually—is eliminated from human experience. In the same way, NLP can eliminate many of the difficulties and hazards of living that we now experience, and make learning and behavioral change much easier, more productive, and more exciting. We are on the threshold of a quantum jump in human experience and capability.

There is an old story of a boilermaker who was hired to fix a huge steamship boiler system that was not working well. After listening to the engineer's description of the problems and asking a few questions, he went to the boiler room. He looked at the maze of twisting pipes, listened to the thump of the boiler and the hiss of escaping steam for a few minutes, and felt some pipes with his hands. Then he hummed softly to himself, reached into his overalls and took out a small hammer, and tapped a bright red valve, once. Immediately the entire system began working perfectly, and the boilermaker went home. When the steamship owner received a bill for $1,000 he complained that the boilermaker had only been in the engine room for fifteen minutes, and requested an itemized bill. This is what the boilermaker sent him:

For tapping with hammer:	.50
For knowing where to tap:	$ 999.50
Total:	$1,000.00

What is really new in NLP is knowing exactly what to do, and how to do it. This is an exciting book, and an exciting time.

Steve Andreas (formerly John O. Stevens)

A Challenge to the Reader

In mystery and spy novels, the reader can expect to be offered a series of written clues—fragmentary descriptions of earlier events. When these fragments are fitted together, they provide enough of a representation for the careful reader to reconstruct the earlier events, even to the point of understanding the specific actions and motivations of the people involved—or at least to reach the understanding that the author will offer at the conclusion of the novel. The more casual reader is simply entertained and arrives at a more personal understanding, of which s/he may or may not be conscious. The writer of such a novel has the obligation to provide enough fragments to make a reconstruction possible, but not obvious.

This book is also the written record of a mystery story of sorts. However, it differs from the traditional mystery in several important ways. This is the written record of a story that was *told,* and story-telling is a different skill than story-writing. The story-teller has the obligation to use feedback from the listener/watcher to determine how many clues s/he can offer. The kind of feedback s/he takes into account is of two types: (1) the verbal, deliberate conscious feedback—those signals the listener/watcher is aware that s/he is offering to the story-teller, and (2) the non-verbal, spontaneous, unconscious feedback: the glimpse, the startle, the labored recollection—those signals the listener/watcher offers the story-teller without being aware of them. An important skill in the art of story-telling is to use the unconscious feedback so as to provide just enough clues that the

1

unconscious process of the listener/watcher arrives at the solution before the listener/watcher consciously appreciates it. From such artistry come the desirable experiences of surprise and delight—the discovery that we know much more than we think we do.

We delight in creating those kinds of experiences in our seminars. And while the record that follows may have contained enough clues for the participant in the seminar, only the more astute reader will succeed in fully reconstructing the earlier events. As we state explicitly in this book, the verbal component is the least interesting and least influential part of communication. Yet this is the only kind of clue offered the reader here.

The basic unit of analysis in face-to-face communication is the feedback loop. For example, if you were given the task of describing an interaction between a cat and a dog, you might make entries like: "Cat spits, ... dog bares teeth, ... cat arches back, ... dog barks, ... cat—" At least as important as the particular actions described is the *sequence* in which they occur. And to some extent, any particular behavior by the cat becomes understandable *only* in the context of the dog's behavior. If for some reason your observations were restricted to just the cat, you would be challenged by the task of reconstructing what the cat was interacting with. The cat's behavior is much more difficult to appreciate and understand in isolation.

We would like to reassure the reader that the non-sequiturs, the surprising tangents, the unannounced shifts in content, mood or direction which you will discover in this book had a compelling logic of their own in the original context. If these otherwise peculiar sequences of communication were restored to their original context, that logic would quickly emerge. Therefore, the challenge: Is the reader astute enough to reconstruct that context, or shall he simply enjoy the exchange and arrive at a useful unconscious understanding of a more personal nature?

John Grinder
Richard Bandler

Note

It is a common experience with many people when they are introduced to Neuro-Linguistic Programming and first begin to learn the techniques, to be cautious and concerned with the possible uses and misuses of the technology. We fully recognize the great power of the information presented in this book and whole-heartedly recommend that you exercise caution as you learn and apply these techniques of a practitioner of NLP, as a protection for you and those around you. It is for this reason that we also urge you to attend only those seminars, workshops and training programs that have been officially designed and certified by Richard Bandler and John Grinder. These will be most often presented under the auspices of Grinder, DeLozier & Associates or Richard Bandler and Associates.

Writing both the following addresses is the only way to insure both Richard Bandler and John Grinders' full endorsement of the quality of services and/or training represented as NLP.

Richard Bandler
2912 Daubenbiss Ave #20
Soquel, CA 95073

Grinder, DeLozier & Associates
1077 Smith Grade
Bonny Doon, CA 95060

I

Sensory Experience

There are several important ways in which what we do differs radically from others who do workshops on communication or psychotherapy. When we first started in the field, we would watch brilliant people do interesting things and then afterwards they would tell various particular metaphors that they called theorizing. They would tell stories about millions of holes, or about plumbing: that you have to understand that people are just a circle with pipes coming from every direction, and all you need is Draino or something like that. Most of those metaphors weren't very useful in helping people learn specifically what to do or how to do it.

Some people will do experiential workshops in which you will be treated to watching and listening to a person who is relatively competent in most, or at least part, of the business called "professional communications." They will demonstrate by their behavior that they are quite competent in doing certain kinds of things. If you are fortunate and you keep your sensory apparatus open, you will learn how to do some of the things they do.

There's also a group of people who are theoreticians. They will tell you what their *beliefs* are about the true nature of humans and what the completely "transparent, adjusted, genuine, authentic," etc. person *should be,* but they don't show you how to *do* anything.

Most knowledge in the field of psychology is organized in ways that mix together what we call *"modeling"*—what traditionally has been called "theorizing"—and what we consider *theology.* The descriptions

5

of what people *do* have been mixed together with descriptions of what reality "*is*." When you mix experience together with theories and wrap them all up in a package, that's a psychotheology. What has developed in psychology is different religious belief systems with very powerful evangelists working from all of these differing orientations.

Another strange thing about psychology is that there's a whole body of people called "researchers" who will *not associate* with the people who are practicing! Somehow the field of psychology got divided so that the researchers no longer provide information for, and respond to, the clinical practitioners in the field. That's not true in the field of medicine. In medicine, the people doing research are trying to find things to help the practitioners in the field. And the practitioners respond to the researchers, telling them what they need to know more about.

Another thing about therapists is that they come to therapy with a set of unconscious patternings that makes it highly probable that they will fail. When therapists begin to do therapy they look for what's wrong in a *content*-oriented way. They want to know what the problem is so that they can help people find solutions. This is true whether they have been trained overtly or covertly, in academic institutions or in rooms with pillows on the floor.

This is even true of those who consider themselves to be "process-oriented." There's a little voice somewhere in their mind that keeps saying "*The process. Look for the process.*" They will say "Well, I'm a process-oriented therapist. I work with *the* process." Somehow the process has become an event—a thing in and of itself.

There is another paradox in the field. The hugest majority of therapists believe that the way to be a good therapist is to do everything you do intuitively, which means to have an unconscious mind that does it for you. They wouldn't describe it that way because they don't like the word "unconscious" but basically they do what they do without knowing how they do it. They do it by the "seat of their pants"—that's another way to say "unconscious mind." I think being able to do things unconsciously is useful; that's a good way to do things. The same group of people, however, *say* that the ultimate goal of therapy is for people to have conscious understanding—*insight* into their own problems. So therapists are a group of people who do what they do without knowing how it works, and at the same time believe that the way to really get somewhere in life is to consciously know how things work!

When I first got involved with modeling people in the field of psychotherapy, I would ask them what outcome they were working toward when they made a maneuver, when they reached over and touched a person this way, or when they shifted their voice tone here. And their answer was "Oh, I have no idea." I'd say "Well, good. Are you interested in exploring and finding out with me what the outcome was?" And they would say "Definitely not!" They claimed that if they did specific things to get specific outcomes that would be something bad, called "manipulating."

We call ourselves *modelers.* What we essentially do is to pay very little attention to what people *say* they do and a great deal of attention to what they *do.* And then we build ourselves a model of what they do. We are not psychologists, and we're also not theologians or theoreticians. We have *no* idea about the "real" nature of things, and we're not particularly interested in what's "true." The function of modeling is to arrive at descriptions which are *useful.* So, if we happen to mention something that you know from a scientific study, or from statistics, is inaccurate, realize that a different level of experience is being offered you here. We're not offering you something that's *true,* just things that are *useful.*

We know that our modeling has been successful when we can systematically get the same behavioral outcome as the person we have modeled. And when we can teach somebody else to be able to get the same outcomes in a systematic way, that's an even stronger test.

When I entered the field of communication, I went to a large conference where there were six hundred and fifty people in an auditorium. And a man who was very famous got up and made the following statement: "What all of you need to understand about doing therapy and about communication is that the first essential step is to make contact with the human you are communicating with as a person." Well, that struck me as being kind of obvious. And everybody in the audience went "Yeahhhh! Make contact. We all know about that one." Now, he went on to talk for another six hours and never mentioned *how.* He never mentioned one single specific thing that anybody in that room could *do* that would help them in any way to either have the experience of understanding that person better, or at least give the other person the illusion that they were understood.

I then went to something called "Active Listening." In active listening you rephrase what everyone says, which means that you

8

distort everything they say.

Then we began to pay attention to what really divergent people who were "wizards" actually do. When you watch and listen to Virginia Satir and Milton Erickson do therapy, they *apparently* could not be more different. At least I couldn't figure out a way that they could appear more different.

People also report that the experiences of being with them are profoundly different. However, if you examine their behavior and the essential key patterns and sequences of what they do, they are similar. The patterns that they use to accomplish the rather dramatic things that they are able to accomplish are very similar in our way of understanding. What they accomplish is the same. But the way it's *packaged*—the way they come across—is profoundly different.

The same was true of Fritz Perls. He was not quite as sophisticated as Satir and Erickson in the number of patterns he used. But when he was operating in what I consider a powerful and effective way, he was using the same sequences of patterns that you will find in their work. Fritz typically did not go after specific outcomes. If somebody came in and said "I have hysterical paralysis of the left leg," he wouldn't go after it directly. Sometimes he would get it and sometimes he wouldn't. Both Milton and Virginia have a tendency to go straight for producing specific outcomes, something I really respect.

When I wanted to learn to do therapy, I went to a month-long workshop, a situation where you are locked up on an island and exposed every day to the same kinds of experiences and hope that somehow or other you will pick them up. The leader had lots and lots of experience, and he could *do* things that none of us could do. But when he *talked* about the things he did, people there wouldn't be able to learn to do them. Intuitively, or what we describe as unconsciously, his behavior was systematic, but he didn't have a conscious understanding of *how* it was systematic. That is a compliment to his flexibility and ability to discern what works.

For example, you all know very, very little about how you are able to generate language. Somehow or other as you speak you are able to create complex pieces of syntax, and I know that you don't make any conscious decisions. You don't go "Well, I'm going to speak, and first I'll put a noun in the sentence, then I'll throw an adjective in, then a verb, and maybe a little adverb at the end, you know, just to color it up a little bit." Yet you speak a language that has grammar and syntax—

rules that are as mathematical and as explicit as any calculus. There's a group of people called transformational linguists who have managed to take large amounts of tax dollars and academic space and figure out what those rules are. They haven't figured out anything to *do* with that yet, but transformational grammarians are unconcerned with that. They are not interested in the real world, and having lived in it I can sometimes understand why.

When it comes to language, we're all wired the same. Humans have pretty much the same intuitions about the same kinds of phenomena in lots and lots of different languages. If I say "You that look understand idea can," you have a very different intuition than if I say "Look, you can understand that idea," even though the words are the same. There's a part of you at the unconscious level that tells you that one of those sentences is well-formed in a way that the other is not. Our job as modelers is to do a similar task for other things that are more practical. Our job is to figure out what it is that effective therapists do intuitively or unconsciously, and to make up some rules that can be *taught* to someone else.

Now, what typically happens when you go to a seminar is that the leader will say "All you really need to do, in order to do what I do as a great communicator, is to pay attention to your guts." And that's true, *if* you happen to have the things in your guts that that leader does. My guess is you probably don't. You *can* have them there at the unconscious level, but I think that if you want to have the same intuitions as somebody like Erickson or Satir or Perls, you need to go through a training period to *learn* to have similar intuitions. Once you go through a conscious training period, you can have therapeutic intuitions that are as unconscious and systematic as your intuitions about language.

If you watch and listen to Virginia Satir work you are confronted with an overwhelming mass of information—the way she moves, her voice tone, the way she touches, who she turns to next, what sensory cues she is using to orient herself to which member of the family, etc. It's a really overwhelming task to attempt to keep track of all the things that she is using as cues, the responses that she is making to those cues, and the responses she elicits from others.

Now, we don't know what Virginia Satir *really* does with families. However, we can describe her behavior in such a way that we can come to any one of you and say "Here. Take this. Do these things in this sequence. Practice until it becomes a systematic part of your unconscious behavior, and you will end up being able to elicit the same responses that Virginia elicits." We do not test the description we arrive at for accuracy, or how it fits with neurological data, or statistics about what should be going on. All we do in order to understand whether our description is an adequate model for what we are doing is to find out whether it works or not: are you able to exhibit effectively in your behavior the same patterns that Virginia exhibits in hers, and get the same results? We will be making statements up here which may have no relationship to the "truth," to what's "really going on." We *do* know, however, that the model that we have made up of her behavior has been effective. After being exposed to it and practicing the patterns and the descriptions that we have offered, people's behavior changes in ways that make them effective in the same way that Satir is, yet each person's style is unique. If you learn to speak French, you will still express yourself in your own way.

You can use your consciousness to decide to gain a certain skill which you think would be useful in the context of your professional and personal work. Using our models you can practice that skill. Having practiced that consciously for some period of time you can allow that skill to function unconsciously. You all had to consciously practice all the skills involved in driving a car. Now you can drive a long distance and not be conscious of any of it, unless there's some unique situation that requires your attention.

One of the systematic things that Erickson and Satir and a lot of other effective therapists do is to notice unconsciously *how* the person they are talking to thinks, and make use of that information in lots and lots of different ways. For example, if I'm a client of Virginia's I might go:

> "Well, man, Virginia, you know I just ah ... boy! Things have been, they've been heavy, you know. Just, you know, my wife was ... my wife was run over by a snail and ... you know, I've got four kids and two of them are gangsters and I think maybe I did something wrong but I just can't get a grasp on what it was."

I don't know if you've ever had the opportunity to watch Virginia operate, but she operates very, very nicely. What she does is very magical, even though 1 believe that magic has a structure and is available to all of you. One of the things that she would do in her response would be to join this client in his model of the world by responding in somewhat the following way:

> "I understand that you feel certain weight upon you, and these kinds of feelings that you have in your body aren't what you want for yourself as a human being. You have different kinds of hopes for this."

It doesn't really matter what she says, as long as she uses the same kinds of words and tonal patterns. If the same client were to go to another therapist, the dialogue might go like this:

"Well, you know, things feel real heavy in my life, Dr. Bandler. You know, it's just like I can't handle it, you know ..."

"I can see that, Mr. Grinder."

"I feel like I did something wrong with my children and I don't know what it is. And I thought maybe you could help me grasp it, you know?"

"Sure. I see what it is you're talking about. Let's focus in on one particular dimension. Try to give me *your* particular perspective. Tell me how it is that you see your situation right now."

"Well, you know, I just ... I'm ... I just feel like I can't get a grasp on reality."

"I can see that. What's important to me—colorful as your description is—what's important to me is that we see eye to eye about where it is down the road that we shall travel together."

"I'm trying to tell you that my life has got a lot of rough edges, you know. And I'm trying to find a way...."

"It looks all broken up from ... from your description, at any rate. The colors aren't all that nice."

While you sit here and laugh, we can't even get as exaggerated as what we've heard in "real life." We spent a lot of time going around to mental health clinics and sitting in on professional communicators. It's very depressing. And what we noticed is that many therapists mismatch in the same way that we just demonstrated.

We come from California and the whole world out there is run by electronics firms. We have a lot of people who are called "engineers," and engineers typically at a certain point have to go to therapy. It's a rule, I don't know why, but they come in and they usually all say the same thing, they go:

"Well, I could see for a long time how, you know, I was really climbing up and becoming successful and then suddenly, you know, when I began to get towards the top, I just looked around and my life looked empty. Can you see that? I mean, could you see what that would be like for a man of my age?"

"Well, I'm beginning to get a sense of grasping the essence of the kinds of feelings that you have that you want to change."

"Just a minute, because what I want to do is I'm trying to show you my perspective on the whole thing. And, you know—"

"I feel that this is very important."

"And I know that a lot of people have a lot of troubles, but what I want to do is to give you a *really* clear idea of what I see the problem is, so that, you know, you can show me, sort of frame by frame, what I need to *know* in order to find my way out of this difficulty because quite frankly I could get very depressed about this. I mean, can you see how that would be?"

"I feel that this is very important. You have raised certain issues here which I feel that we have to come to grips with. And it's only a question of selecting where we'll grab a handle and begin to work in a comfortable but powerful way upon this."

"What I'd really like is your point of view."

"Well, I don't want you to avoid any of those feelings. Just go ahead and let them flow up and knock the hell out of the picture that you've got there."

"I ... I don't see that this is getting us anywhere."

"I feel that we have hit a rough spot in the relationship. Are you willing to talk about your resistance?"

Do you happen to notice any pattern in these dialogues? We watched therapists do this for two or three days, and we noticed that Satir did it the other way around: *She matched the client.* But most therapists don't.

We have noticed this peculiar trait about human beings. If they find something they can do that doesn't work, they do it *again.* B. F.

Skinner had a group of students who had done a lot of research with rats and mazes. And somebody asked them one day "What is the real difference between a rat and a human being?" Now, behaviorists not being terribly observant, decided that they needed to experiment to find out. They built a huge maze that was scaled up for a human. They took a control group of rats and taught them to run a small maze for cheese. And they took the humans and taught them to run the large maze for five-dollar bills. They didn't notice any really significant difference. There were small variations in the data and at the 95% probability level they discovered some significant difference in the number of trials to criterion or something. The humans were able to learn to run the maze somewhat better, a little bit quicker, than the rats.

The really interesting statistics came up when they did the extinguishing part. They removed the five-dollar bills and the cheese and after a certain number of trials the rats stopped running the maze.... However, the humans never stopped! ... They are still there! ... They break into the labs at night.

One of the operating procedures of most disciplines that allows a field to grow and to continue to develop at a rapid rate is a rule that if what you do doesn't work, *do something else.* If you are an engineer and you get the rocket all set up, and you push the button and it doesn't lift up, you alter your behavior to find out what you need to do to make certain changes to overcome gravity.

However, in the field of psychotherapy, if you encounter a situation where the rocket doesn't go off, it has a special name; it's called having a "resistant client." You take the fact that what you do doesn't work and you blame it on the client. That relieves you of the responsibility of having to change your behavior. Or if you are slightly more humanistic about it, you "share in the guilt of the failure" or say he "wasn't ready."

Another problem is that the field of pschotherapy keeps developing the same things over and over and over again. What Fritz did and what Virginia does has been done before. The concepts that are used in Transactional Analysis (TA)—"redecision" for example—are avail- able in Freud's work. The interesting thing is that in psychotherapy the knowlege doesn't get transferred.

When humans learned to read and write and to communicate to one another somewhat, that knowledge began to speed up the rate of development. If we teach someone electronics, we train them in all the things that have already been discovered so that they can go on and discover *new* things.

What happens in psychotherapy, however, is that we send people to school instead. And when they come out of school, *then* they have to learn to do therapy. Not only do they have to learn to do therapy, but there's *no way* to learn to do therapy. So what we do is we give them clients, and we call what they do "private practice"so they can practice privately.

In linguistics there's a distinction called nominalization. Nominalization is where you take a process and you describe it as if it's an event or a thing. In this way you utterly confuse those around you, and yourself—unless you remember that it is a representation rather than experience. This can have positive uses. If you happen to be a government, you can talk about nominalizations like "national security" and you can get people to worry about those words. Our president just went to Egypt and changed the word "imperative"to the word "desirable" and suddenly we're friends with Egypt again. All he did was change a word. That's word magic.

The word "resistance" is also a nominalization. It's describing a process as a thing without talking about *how it works*. The earnest, concerned, authentic therapist in the last dialogue would describe the client as being callous and insensitive, so totally out of touch with his feelings that he could not communicate effectively with him. That client was really resistant.

And the client would be out looking for another therapist because that therapist needed glasses. He had absolutely no perspective at all. He couldn't see eye to eye with him at all!

And they would *both* be right, of course.

Now, is there anyone here who hasn't yet identified the pattern that we're talking about? Because it really was the beginning point for us.

Woman: Ah, in the last dialogue the client was using visual words like "look, see, show, focus, perspective." And the therapist was using feeling words like "grasp, handle, feel, smooth, rough."

Right. And there are also some people who use mostly auditory words: "I hear what you're saying," "That rings a bell,""I can resonate with that," etc. What we noticed is that different people actually think differently, and that these differences correspond to the three principal senses: vision, hearing, and feeling—which we call kinesthetics.

When you make initial contact with a person s/he will probably be thinking in one of these three main *representational systems*. Internally s/he will either be generating visual images, having feelings, or talking to themselves and hearing sounds. One of the ways you can know this is by listening to the kinds of process words (the predicates: verbs, adverbs and adjectives) that the person uses to describe his/her experience. If you pay attention to that information, you can adjust your own behavior to get the response you want. If you want to get good rapport, you can speak using the same kind of predicates that the other person is using. If you want to alienate the other person, you can deliberately *mis*match predicates, as we did in the earlier client-therapist dialogues.

Let me talk a little about how language works. If I look at you and say "Are you comfortable?" you can come up with a response. The presupposition of your being able to respond congruently to my question is that you understand the words that I am speaking. Do you know *how* you understand the word "comfortable" for example?

Woman: Physically.

You understand it physically. You sense some change in your body which is distinctive. That shift in your feeling state is distinctive from "terrified." That's a different response.

She senses a change in her body as a way of understanding the meaning of the word "comfortable." Did anybody else notice how they understand it? Some of you will see visual images of yourself in a comfortable position: lying in a hammock, or lying on the grass in the sunshine. And a few of you may even hear the sounds which you associate with comfort: the babbling of a brook, or wind blowing through some pine trees.

In order for you to understand what I am saying to you, you have to take the words—which are nothing more than arbitrary labels for parts of your personal history—and *access* the meaning, namely, some set of images, some set of feelings, or some set of sounds, which *are* the meaning for you of the word "comfortable." That's a simple notion of how language works, and we call this process *transderivational search*. Words are triggers that tend to bring into your consciousness certain parts of your experience and not other parts.

Eskimos have some seventy words for snow. Now, does that mean that people who are raised in a tribe called Eskimos have different sensory apparatus than we do? No. My understanding is that language is the accumulated wisdom of a group of people. Out of a potentially infinite amount of sensory experience, language picks out those things which are repetitive in the experience of the people developing the language *and* that they have found useful to attend to in consciousness. It's not surprising that the Eskimos have seventy-some words for snow in terms of where they live and the kinds of tasks they have to perform. For them, survival is an issue closely connected with snow, and therefore they make very fine distinctions. Skiers also have many different words for different kinds of snow.

As Aldous Huxley says in his book *The Doors of Perception,* when you learn a language, you are an inheritor of the wisdom of the people who have gone before you. You are *also a victim* in this sense: of that infinite set of experiences you could have had, certain ones are given names, labeled with words, and thereby are emphasized and attract your attention. Equally valid—possibly even more dramatic and useful—experiences at the sensory level which are unlabeled, typically don't intrude into your consciousness.

There is always a slippage between primary and secondary representation. There's a difference between experience and the ways of representing experience to yourself. One of the least immediate ways of representing experiences is with words. If I say to you "This particular table right here has a glass of water partially filled sitting on top of it," I have offered you a string of words, arbitrary symbols. We can both agree or disagree about the statement because I'm appealing directly to your sensory experience.

If I use any words that don't have direct sensory referents, the only way you can understand those—unless you have some program to demand more sensory-based descriptions—is for you to find the counterpart in your past experience.

Your experience will overlap with mine to the degree that we share a culture, that we share certain kinds of backgrounds. Words have to be relativized to the world model of the person you are talking to. The word "rapport" for a ghetto person, "rapport" for a white middle-class person, and "rapport" for someone in the top one hundred families in this country, are *very, very* different phenomena. There's an illusion that people understand each other when they can repeat the same words. But since those words internally access different experiences— which they must—then there's always going to be a difference in meaning.

There's a slippage between the word and the experience, and there's also a slippage between *my* corresponding experience for a word and *your* corresponding experience for the same word. I think it's extremely useful for you to behave so that your clients come to have the illusion that you understand what they are saying verbally. I caution you against accepting the illusion for yourself.

Many of you probably have intuitions about your clients when you first meet them. There may be a certain type of client that comes into your office and even before they speak you look up and you *know* that one's going to be hard, that one's going to be really difficult. It's going to be a rather tedious and long-range project for you to assist that person in getting the choices they want, even though you don't know what those are yet. At other times, before a new client even speaks, you know it will be interesting, it will be a delight. There will be a spark there, there will be a sense of excitement and adventure as you lead this person to some new behavior patterns to get what it is that they came for. How many of you have intuitions like that? Let me have a volunteer. Do you know when you have the intuition that you are having it?

Woman: Umhm.

What is that experience?...

We'll help you. Start by listening to the question. The question I'm asking you is one that I'd like to train you all to ask. The question is "*How do you know* when you are having an intuition?" (She looks up and to her left.) Yes, that's how you know.

She didn't *say* anything; that is the interesting thing. She just went through a process non-verbally in responding to the question that I asked her. That process is a replica of the process she actually goes through when she has the intuition, and it was the answer to the question.

If you take nothing else away from this workshop, take away the following: *You will always get answers to your questions insofar as you have the sensory apparatus to notice the responses.* And rarely will the verbal or conscious part of the response be relevant.

Now let's go back and demonstrate again. How do you know when you are having an intuition?

Woman: Well, let me take it back to the dialogue here earlier. . . . I was trying to put that into some form. And what it was for me was the symbol of—

What kind of a symbol? Is this something you saw, heard, or felt?

I saw it in my head as just—

Yes. You saw it in your head. It was a picture.

Now, all the information that she just offered us verbally is wholly redundant if you were in a position to be able to watch her non-verbal response to the initial question. Everything that she just presented verbally was presented in a much more refined way non-verbally. If you clean up your sensory channels and attend to sensory experience, when you make a statement or ask a human being a question they will always give you the answer non-verbally, whether or not they are able to consciously express what it is.

The information about representational systems comes through in lots and lots of different ways. The easiest way to begin to train your senses is this: people make movements with their eyes which will indicate to you which representational system they are using. When somebody walks into your office, they are planning what they are going to do. They are either visualizing, or they are telling themselves what they are going to say, or they are paying attention to the feelings that they want to describe to you. When they do that, they go inside and they *access* that information, and they make typical gestures that every one of you knows about unconsciously, and yet through the whole history of psychology no one has ever explicitly described.

For example, I'll name a standard one. You ask somebody a question. They say "Hm, let's see," and they look up and to their left, and tilt their head in the same direction. When people look up, they are making pictures internally.

Do you believe that? It's a lie, you know. Everything we're going to tell you here is a lie. All generalizations are lies. Since we have no claim on truth or accuracy, we will be lying to you consistently throughout this seminar. There are only two differences between us and other teachers: One is that we announce at the beginning of our seminars that everything we say will be a lie, and other teachers do not. Most of them believe their lies. They don't realize that they are made up. The other difference is that most of our lies will work out really well if you act *as if* they are true.

As modelers, we're not interested in whether what we offer you is true or not, whether it's accurate or whether it can be neurologically proven to be accurate, an actual representation of the world. We're *only* interested in *what works*.

Let me have three volunteers to come up here....

What I'm going to do next is to ask Fran and Harvey and Susan up here some questions. All I want you out there to do is to clear your sensory apparatus. You could sit there and make images about what something is reminding you of, or you could talk to yourself about such things, or you could have feelings about what's going on.

This is what I am proposing you adopt as a learning strategy for the next few minutes: simply clear all your internal experience. Quiet the internal dialogue, check and make sure that your body is in a comfortable position so that you can leave it there for a while, and don't make internal images. Simply notice with your sensory apparatus what relationship you can discover between the questions I'm going to ask of these three people and the responses they make non-verbally. I would like you to pay particularly close attention to the movements and changes in their eyes. There are lots of other things going on which will be useful for us to talk about at some other time. At this time we simply want you to pay attention to *that* part of their non-verbal response.

I'll just ask the three of you up here some questions. I'd like you to *find* the answers to those questions, but don't verbalize the answers. When you are satisfied that you know what the answer is, or you've decided after searching that you don't know what the answer is, stop. You don't have to give me any verbal output; you keep the answers to yourself.

In the United States there's an interesting phenomenon called "traffic lights." Is the red or the green at the top of the traffic light?... When you came here today, how many traffic lights did you pass between where you started your trip and arriving here at the hotel?...What color are your mother's eyes?... How many different colored carpets did you have in the last place you lived? (Fran stares straight ahead in response to each question; Harvey looks up and to his left; Susan looks up and to her right, or sometimes straight ahead.)

Now, have you noticed any movements in their eyes? Do you see systematic shifts there? OK. Store that information for a moment. These are complex human beings, and they are giving more than one response. However, notice what is *common* about the responses they gave to that set of questions.

I'm going to shift the questions a little bit and I want you to notice if there is a systematic difference in the way they respond.

Think of your favorite piece of music.... What is the letter in the alphabet just before R?... Can you hear your mother's voice? (Fran and Harvey look down and to their left as they access information after each question; Susan looks down and to her right.)

Now, there was a difference between the last set of responses and the previous set.

Now I'm going to shift my questions again.

Do you know the feeling of water swirling around your body when you swim?... What happens in winter when you are in a nice, warm, cozy house, and you walk out into the cold air outside?... (Fran and Harvey look down and to their right while accessing the answer to each question; Susan looks down and to her left.)

Can you make a connection between the classes of questions I was asking and the kind of movements that you were seeing? What did you actually see in your sensory experience when I asked the questions?

Man: I noticed especially that when it seemed like Susan was picturing something, she would look up. And then there were times when she would look straight ahead.

OK. I agree with you. How do you know when she was picturing something? That's an assumption on your part. What were the questions that I was asking that those movements were responses to?

Man: The color of eyes. How many lights—like she was picturing the intersections.

So the questions I was asking demanded visual information by presupposition. And the responses you noticed were a lot of up movements. Did you notice any preference as to side?

Woman: Susan looked to her right. She looked to her right because she is left-handed.

Because she's left-handed Susan looks to her right? She doesn't always look to her right. Watch this.

Susan, do you know what you would look like with long flaming red hair?... Do you know what you would look like if you had a beard?... Do you know what you look like sitting right here?... (Her eyes move up and to her left.) Which way did her eyes go that time? Distinguish left and right with respect to her. You said that she typically went up to her right in answering the previous visually-oriented questions. What movement did you see with her eyes just now, in response to the last questions? This time her eyes dilated and moved up to her *left* and back. So she doesn't always look up and to her right. She sometimes looks up and to her left. There's a systematic difference between the kind of questions I asked just now, and the kind of visual questions I was asking before. Can you describe the difference?

Woman: The first questions had to do with experiences she was remembering, and the second group she had not experienced and was trying to visualize.

Excellent. The first set of pictures we call *eidetic* or *remembered* images, and the second set we call *constructed* images. She's never seen herself sitting here in this chair in this room. It's something she has had no direct visual experience of, therefore she has to *construct* the image in order to see what it is that she would look like.

Most "normally organized" right-handed people will show the *opposite* of what we've seen with Susan here. Susan is left-handed and her visual accessing cues are reversed left to right. Most people look up and to their left for visual eidetic images and up and to their right for constructed visual images.

However, lots of normally organized right-handers will look up and to their right as they respond to questions about visual memory. Barbara, here in the audience, looked up and to her right to recall something a few moments ago. Do you remember what it was you saw up there?

Barbara: No.

Do you remember one of the houses you lived in as a child?

Barbara: Yes, I do.

She just went up and to her right again. What did you see, Barbara? Name one thing you saw.

Barbara: I saw the living room.

I'm going to predict that the living room that you saw was peculiar in a specific way. I want you to check this and let me know whether my statements are accurate. The living room you saw was suspended in space. It wasn't bounded in the way it would be bounded visually if you were actually inside of that living room. It was an image which you had never seen before because it was a fragment of a set of images you'd seen lots of times in the past. It was not a visual input that you've ever had directly. It was literally extracted, a piece of a picture extracted from some part of your experience and displayed separately. Is that accurate?

Barbara: Yes.

When you ask visual memory questions and a person looks up to their right, you cannot conclude that they are left-handed or that their accessing cues are reversed. All you can conclude is that they looked up and to their right. If you want to explore it further, there are a couple of possibilities. One is what's true of Susan—namely, that she has reversed cerebral organization. The other possibility is that they could be constructing images of the past, as is true of Barbara. If that is so, the images will not have the color, the detail, the contextual markers, or the visual background that an actual eidetic remembered image has. That is an important difference.

When Barbara recalls images, she recalls them outside of context, which is characteristic of constructed images. By the way, she will argue about the past with people a lot—especially with someone who remembers eidetically.

Sally: I didn't see Fran's eyes going up or down, just straight.

OK. Was there any marked difference between the way she was looking straight at me before I asked a question and the way she continued to look straight at me after I'd asked the question? Did you notice any change?

Sally: Yes. She looked more pensive then.

"Pensive." What looks like "pensive" to you and what looks like "pensive" to me may be *totally* different kinds of experiences. "Pensive" is a complex judgement about experience; it's not in your sensory experience. I'm sure that "pensive" has appropriate meaning for you, and that you can connect it with your sensory experience easily. So could you describe, so that we could agree or disagree, what you actually *saw,* as opposed to the judgement that she was being "pensive"?

As we said before, all these questions are being answered before the verbalization. So if you have the opportunity to watch anyone we're communicating with directly, you will always get the answer before they offer it to you verbally. I just asked Sally to describe something, and she demonstrated non-verbally what she saw. She mirrored in her own movements what Fran was doing.

Sally, do you remember the feeling of what you just did?

Sally: My eyes kind of closed a little.

So your eyelids dropped a little bit. Is there anything else that you could detect either from what you felt your eyes doing or from remembering what Fran was doing?...

Have you ever had the experience in a conversation that the other person's eyes are still resting on your face but somehow suddenly you are all by yourself? You are all alone? That's what was going on here. In both of these cases the pupils dilated and the facial muscles relaxed.

If you have trouble seeing pupil dilation, I believe that's not a statement about pupil dilation; it's a statement about your own perceptual programs. And I'm not talking about whether you have 20/20 vision or 20/2000 vision with corrective lenses. Your ability to perceive is something that is *learned* and you can learn to do it better. Most people act as if their senses are simply passive receptacles into which the world dumps vast amounts of information. There is a vast amount of information, so vast that you can only represent a tiny fraction of it. You learn to actively select in useful ways.

So what we'll ask you to do in a few minutes is to change your perceptual programs to determine (1) whether the patterns we're talking about exist, and (2) whether they can be useful. We're going to proceed in that step-wise fashion. We're going to rely on whatever rapport we have with you to get you to do an exercise in which you discover for yourself, using your own sensory apparatus, whether in fact these things we're talking about are there. Then we'll talk about how to *use* them because that's the really important thing. The ultimate question is whether this is worth knowing about.

Let me reassure you that if you have patterns of communication that work for you now in therapy or education or business, those skills will still be available to you when we finish this seminar. I guarantee you that much. We're not going to do anything to take choices away. We would like you to consider a new approach. My guess is that some of you are quite effective and competent communicators therapeutically. You get results and you're pleased with them, and it's a challenge, and you like your job, at least some of the time. But even in the cases where you do very, very well indeed, you get bored from time to time. There's a tendency for you to repeat some set of interventions that you've made in the past which were successful, hoping for success again in the present. I think one of the most dangerous experiences human beings can have is success—especially if you have success early in your career—because you tend to become quite superstitious and repetitious. It's the old five-dollar bill at the end of the maze.

For example, say you once had somebody talk to an empty chair and visualize their mother in that chair and they dramatically changed. You might decide that every therapist in the country ought to do that, when in fact that's only one of a myriad ways of going about accomplishing the same result.

For those of you who are doubtful, and those who have skeptical parts, we would like to ask you—and this is true for all of the lies we are going to tell you—to do the following: accept our lie for a limited period of time, namely during the exercise that follows our description of the pattern we claim exists. In this way you can use your own sensory experience—not the crazy verbalizations we offer you—to decide whether in fact the things we describe can be observed in the behavior of the person you're communicating with.

We're making the claim right now that you've missed something that was totally obvious. We're claiming that you have been speaking to people your whole life and they've been going "Well, the way it looks to me ..." (looks up and to his left), "I tell myself ..." (looks down and to his left), "I just feel ..." (looks down and to his right)—and you haven't consciously noticed that. People have been doing this systematically through a hundred years of modern psychology and communication theory and you've all been the victims of a set of cultural patterns which didn't allow you to notice and respond directly and effectively to those cues.

Accessing Cues Exercise:

Find someone you don't know, or you know minimally. One of you is going to be A and one of you is going to be B. A will begin asking questions. Make the task of learning this relatively simple for yourself by organizing your questions into sets the way I did. Start out by asking visual eidetic questions: What color are the carpets in your car? What color are your mother's eyes? What shape are the letters on the sign on the outside of this building? All of those are questions about things that people here have seen before.

Then ask questions about things that the person has not seen and will have to construct: How would you look from my point of view? How would you look with purple hair?

Then ask auditory questions: What's your favorite kind of music? Which door in your house sounds the loudest when it's slammed? Can you hear somebody very special that you are close to saying your name in a particularly delightful way? Can you hear yourself sing "Mary Had a Little Lamb"?

Those are all ways of accessing auditory experience. The cues that the person will offer you non-verbally will be systematically different from the cues they offer you to the previous sets of questions. Then ask a set of kinesthetic questions: How do you feel early in the morning? What does cat fur feel like?

Visual accessing cues for a "normally organized" right-handed person.

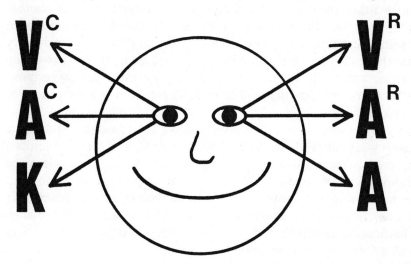

V^c Visual constructed images. V^r Visual remembered (eidetic) images.

(Eyes defocused and unmoving also indicates visual accessing.)

A^c Auditory constructed sounds or words. A^r Auditory remembered sounds or words.

K   Kinesthetic feelings (also smell and taste).   A   Auditory sounds or words.

Woman: Is there a difference between the eye movements people make when they are remembering something that they've heard in the past, and when they are trying to imagine what something would sound like?

When you say "imagine" that presupposes images or pictures. Ask them to *create* a sound they haven't heard before. There will be a difference, yes. Discover that for yourself.

I'd like to warn you of two pitfalls. You may *think* that the word "think" is one representational system. It's not. The words "think, understand, be aware of, believe, sense, know," are all *unspecified*. Do not use those words because the response you get will be random.

You will also get confusing responses if you say "Do you remember the last time you felt the feeling of swimming through the water?" You've asked them to do two things. You've asked them to *remember* and then to *feel*. They may remember visually; that is, they may search or scan visually, they may repeat it auditorily, or they may do it directly kinesthetically. However they do it, you are going to get a two-step process. One will be the remembering portion, following your instructions, and the other will be actually recovering those feelings of swimming.

If you get responses which do not make any sense to you, *ask* the person what they did internally. Your job is to correlate what you can observe on the outside with the questions you ask. Correlate the relationship between the kind of information you are asking for and the non-verbal eye movement responses you're getting from your partner. If you don't understand it, ask. "I saw this on the outside. What does that correspond to in your internal processing?" If they don't know, ask them to guess.

If you're not getting the kinds of eye movements we were talking about, make the question more difficult. "What color shoes was your mother wearing the last time you saw her?" If you ask "What color are your mother's eyes" and you don't see any movement, make the question more complex. "Your eyes are blue, too. Is the color of your eyes brighter or deeper in color than your mother's eyes?" That's a more complex, comparative question. She will then have to form an image of the color of her eyes and her mother's eyes and then make a visual comparison.

After four or five minutes of asking your partner these sets of questions, you should have an idea about what eye movements you can see which indicate unequivocally which of the internal representational systems that person is utilizing at that moment. Switch roles, so that both of you have the opportunity to ask questions and observe responses. If you run into things you don't understand, we will be wandering through the room—wave to us. We will come over and assist you in making sense out of it. We are offering you generalizations, and every single generalization anyone has ever offered you is going to be false at some time and some place. The generalizations are only tricks—as most of what we will do here is—to get you to pay attention to your experience, to notice a certain dimension of sensory experience which culturally you've been trained not to notice. Once you notice it, it constitutes a really powerful source of information about the other person's unconscious processes.

You will find people who are organized in odd ways. But even somebody who is organized in a totally different way will be systematic; their eye movements will be systematic for *them*. Even the person who looks straight up each time they have a feeling and straight down each time they have a picture, will remain consistent within themselves. The important thing is that you have the sensory experience to notice who is doing what. Go ahead now and discover what, if any, patterns you can discover.

*   *   *   *   *

OK. How did the exercise go? Many of you are nodding. Some of you had difficulties, or questions, or were perplexed by some of the things you saw. Let's have those. Those are more interesting.

Woman: We found that we could learn as much by watching the questioner as the listener. By watching the questioner's eyes we could predict what kind of question we were about to be asked.

Man: When I asked my partner, Chris, an auditory question, she went up and visualized.

Do you remember the question you asked?

Man: "What are the first four notes of Beethoven's Fifth Symphony?"

OK. Now, did other people have the same experience? Some of you asked people auditory questions, or kinesthetic questions, and you noticed them visually accessing and then giving you auditory or kinesthetic information. Do you have an understanding of what was happening? Chris, what did you do? Did you read it off the score? Did you see a record player or did you see an album?

Chris: I heard it.

You heard it. OK. Were you aware of starting with any kind of picture whatsoever? If the rest of you are watching, this is one of those interesting discrepancies between her consciousness and what she's offering us non-verbally.

Chris, do you know what the second four notes of Beethoven's Fifth are? OK, you know what they are.

Woman: Ah, that might be a spatial thing for her.

Can you give us a sensory correlate for the word "spatial"? Whether it's the notion of looking "pensive" or that's a "spatial" thing, what we're going to ask you to do, since we all have different understandings of those words, is to use words either before or after the judgements that you make which we can agree or disagree with. What is it you saw or heard or felt?

Woman: Well, when I did it, I went "da da da DUM," you know, and I looked at the spatial interval. I wasn't seeing the notes.

Those of you who had partners who had this kind of experience, check with them. I will guarantee the following was going on. They searched and found a visual image which somehow represented the experience they were looking for. From that image, by simply imitating the image or stepping into it, they then had the feelings or sounds which were appropriate for that particular visual experience.

We've got to make a distinction now. The predicates, the words a person chooses to describe their situation—when they are specified by representational system—let you know what their consciousness is. The predicates indicate what portion of this complex internal cognitive process they bring into awareness. The visual accessing cues, eye-scanning patterns, will tell you literally the whole *sequence* of accessing, which we call a *strategy*. What we call the "*lead system*" is the system that you use to go after some information. The "*representational system*" is what's in consciousness, indicated by predicates. The "*reference system*" is how you decide whether what you now know—having already accessed it and knowing it in conscious-ness—is true or not. For example. What's your name?

Ted: Ted.

Ted. How do you know that? Now, he's already answered the question, non-verbally. It's an absurd question. Ted understands this, but he also answered it. Do you know how you know? Right now, sitting in this room, if I call you "Jim," you don't respond. If I call you "Ted," you do respond. That's a kinesthetic response. Now, without me supplying any stimuli from the outside, when I simply ask you the question "Do you know what your name is?" do you have an answer?

Ted: Yes, I have.

Do you know what to say before you actually say it?

Ted: No, I don't.

So if I say "What's your name?" and you don't answer, you don't know what your name is?

Ted: I know what my name is because when someone says "Ted" I have a certain feeling, a response because that's me.

Are you saying "Ted" on the inside and getting that feeling as a way of verifying when I ask you that question?

Ted: Yeah.

So you have a strategy to let you know, when supplied input from the outside, which is an appropriate response to which, right? "Ted" but not "Bob." But when I ask you "What's your name?" how do you know what to say to me?

Ted: I don't think of it.

So you have no consciousness of any process that you use at that point? . . . OK. Now, did anybody else notice a cue that would tell you the answer to the question even though Ted at this point doesn't have a conscious answer to the question we asked him? . . . Each time we asked the question, his eyes went down to his left and came back. He heard his name. I don't know whose tonality he heard it in, but it was there. And he knows that the name "Ted" is correct because it feels right. So in this case his lead system is auditory: that's how he goes after the information, even though he's not aware of it. He becomes conscious of his name auditorily; in this case his representational system is the same as his lead system. His reference system is kinesthetic: when he hears the name "Ted" either outside or inside, it *feels* right.

One of the things that some people do when you ask them questions is to repeat them with words inside their head. Lots of people here are doing that. I say "Lots of people repeat words" and they go inside and say to themselves "Yeah, people repeat words."

Have any of you had the experience of being around somebody whose second language is the one you're speaking? Typically the first eye movement they will make as they hear something is to translate it internally, and you'll see that same auditory cue.

Some people take forever to answer a question. What they usually have is a complex strategy *in consciousness*. For example, one guy had a fascinating strategy. I asked him "When was the first time you met John?" And he went inside and said "When was the first time I met John? Hmmm. Let's see," and his eyes went up and he made a constructed picture of John. Then he looked over to his left and visually flipped through all the possible places he remembered, until he found one that gave him a feeling of familiarity. Then he named the place auditorily, and then he saw himself telling me the name of that place, and imagined how he would look when he did that. He had the feeling that it would be safe to go ahead and do it, so he told himself

"Go ahead and do it."

There's a whole set of advanced patterns we call streamlining which you can use to examine the structure of a strategy and streamline it so that all the unnecessary or redundant steps are taken out. It involves examining strategies for loops and other kinds of restrictions and problems, and then streamlining those out so that you have efficient programs to get you the outcomes you want.

Let's take an example from therapy. Somebody comes in with the problem that they're very jealous. They say "Well, you know, I just ... (looking up and to his right) well, I just (looking down and to his right) really *feel* jealous and (looking down and to his left) I tell myself it's crazy and I have no reason to, but I just have these feelings." He starts leading visually; he constructs an image of his wife doing something nasty and enjoyable with someone else. Then he feels the way he would feel if he were standing there actually observing it occurring in the room. He has the feelings that he would have if he were there. That's usually all he is aware of. Those feelings have the name "jealousy" and that's the representational system, kinesthetic. He leads visually, represents kinesthetically, and then he has an auditory reference system check which tells him that his feelings are invalid. So all three different systems are used in different ways.

Woman: So in that situation you're suggesting that if you were working with that person you would tie in with the feeling system, the representational system?

It depends on what outcome you want. Our claim is that there are no mistakes in communication; there are only outcomes. In order for us to respond to your question you have to specify what outcome you want. If you want to establish rapport, then it would be useful to match the representational system, indicated by the predicates. The client comes in and says "Well, I feel really jealous, man, you know, and it's hard on me and I don't know what to do." You can say "Well, I'm going to try to help you get a handle on it because I feel you are entitled to that. Let's come to grips with this and really work to have some solid understanding about this." That would be a first step which would help you to establish rapport. If instead you said to that person "Well, I'm going to try to help you get a perspective on your feelings," you would not get conscious rapport. You might or might not get *un*conscious rapport, which is the most important one anyway.

When this man comes in with his jealousy problem and you can see the accessing cues, you have all the information you need to understand the process he goes through. Even when people begin to get an idea that this kind of stuff is going on, they don't teach people *new* ways to do it. If your therapist just tries to assist you in making more realistic pictures, he's working with content, and still leaving the structure intact. Most of the time people don't try to change the actual structure of the process. They try to make it "more realistic" or workable. This means that as long as the revised content remains the same they'll be fine, but when they switch content they will get into trouble again.

The way you motivate yourself may have the same structure as jealousy: you make a picture of what you want that feels good and then tell yourself how to make that picture come true. If that's so, then until you have another way to motivate yourself you are going to keep that way no matter how unpleasant it is sometimes. Even the crummiest strategy is better than none at all.

Man: What's the difference in the cerebral hemispheres as to the dominant hand and dominant eye?

Each time we do a seminar someone asks us that question. As far as I can tell, there is no research to substantiate the idea that there is eyedness. You won't find any research that is going to hold up. Even if there were, I still don't know how it would be relevant to the process of interpersonal communication, so to me it's not a very interesting question. Your eyes are split so that half of each eye is connected to each hemisphere. The tendency to look in a microscope with one eye or another has been noted as statistically significant; however, I don't know of any *use* for that information right now.

Man: What about a situation where one eye is measurably much better visually? One is practically blind and the other one is OK. Is there any correlation there with the handedness?

I don't know. I have no idea. Again, I've never found that a useful organizing principle in communication. If you know of something in that area, let me know about it.

Man: At what age do you assume that human beings establish hand dominance?

I don't. No assumptions. Linguists claim that it occurs somewhere around four and a half. I have no basis on which to substantiate that. Handedness is a dimension of experience which I know exists in the world. I have never found any useful connection to communication.

There is an infinite amount of sensory experience available right here in this room. We consistently make unconscious choices about what we sample. If we didn't, we'd all be "*idiot savants,*" who can't forget things; they can't *not* know things. When you ask them about anything, they have to give you a complete "dump" of all the information they have ever had on that particular topic.

Most therapy is founded on the presupposition that if you know how things came about, the roots where it all originated, that will give you a basis from which to change it. I believe that that's an accurate *and* limiting assumption. Yes, that is *one* way to go about changing, but it is only *one* out of an *infinite number of ways* to understand behavior. When people achieve handedness is in no way significant, as far as I can tell, in the process of doing therapy and communication *unless* what you really want to do is to teach children to be differently handed.

The only thing I've ever used handedness in is stuttering. That's the only time I've ever used it face-to-face, experientially with a kid to assist him in getting more choices. I simply noticed that if he were given a task in which it was specified he do it with this hand as opposed to that hand—and it didn't matter which hand—and he didn't have to talk simultaneously, he could do the task and then describe it. If he had to talk at the same time, or if the task involved both hands, so that there was hemispheric switching, he had difficulty.

Children do have accessing cues at a very young age, and that *is* relevant information to notice. There is something now that they are imposing upon children called "learning disabilities." Many of these "learning disabilities" are really functions of the educational system. For example, I was given a bunch of children who fell into the classification of "crossed hemispheres" and they told me that this was something that existed in the world. They wanted me to find out if there was any difference between these children and the rest of them, given accessing cues and so on. What I discovered is that they were all children who were trying to spell auditorily. When I said "How do you spell the word 'cat'?" they went inside and their eyes moved down and to their left. I asked the children what they were doing and they said "Sounding the word out," because they were taught to spell phonetically. You can't even spell "phonetics" phonetically!

Who here is a good speller? Somebody who used to win spelling bees? How do you spell the word "phenomena"?

Woman: I read it.

She sees it, she reads it, whichever word you use to describe it. Now, as you visualized the word "phenomena" you somehow knew that was correct. Now, change the "ph" to an "f" and tell me what changes in your experience as you see it with an "f" instead of a "ph."

Woman: It stops being a word.

It stops being a word. How do you know that it stops being a word? What experience do you have?

Woman: It makes the whole rest of the word fall apart in my visual—

The letters literally drop off and fall?

Woman: Yeah, they sort of fuzz out and disappear.

There are two steps to spelling. One is being able to visualize the word, and the other is having a system by which to check the accuracy. Try something for me. Can you see the word "caught"? OK, go ahead and leave it up there and change the "au" to "eu" and tell me what happens.

Woman: It became "cute," and it's changed its spelling.

Did anybody who was near her notice what her response was? What did she do?

Woman: She winced.

I said change it to "eu" and her shoulders rolled forward, her head tipped back, and she winced. There was a change in her feelings right here at the mid-line of the torso. No matter what language we've operated in, what country we've been to, no matter what the language is, good spellers have exactly that same formal strategy. They see an eidetic, remembered image of the word they want to spell, and they know whether or not it's an accurate spelling by a kinesthetic check at the mid-line. All the people who tell us they are bad spellers *don't* have that strategy. Some bad spellers make eidetic images, but then they check them auditorily. Others make constructed visual images and spell creatively.

Knowing this, a question we could then ask is "Well, how is it that some children learn to spell visually with a kinesthetic check, and other children learn to spell in other ways?" But to me that's not nearly as interesting a question as "How do you take the child who is a bad speller and teach him to use the same strategy that a good speller uses?" When you do that, you will never need to teach children to spell. They will learn automatically if you teach them an appropriate *process,* instead of content.

Man: How about adults? Can you teach adults?

No, it's hopeless. (laughter) Sure you can. Let me address that question in a slightly different way. How many here now see clearly that they are visually oriented people? How many people see that? How many people here feel that they are really kinesthetically oriented people in their process? Who tell themselves that they are auditory? Actually *all* of you are doing *all* of the things we're talking about, *all the time.* The only question is, which portion of the complex internal process do you bring into awareness? All channels are processing information all the time, but only part of that will be in consciousness.

At seminars like this, people always go out at lunch time and try to figure out what they "are," as if they are only one thing, thereby stabilizing everything pathologically. People try to figure out what they "are" instead of using that information to realize that they have other choices. People will come up to me and say "I'm really confused about this representational stuff because I really *see* myself as being a very *feeling* person." That's a profound utterance, if you think about it. I've heard that maybe a hundred and fifty times. How many people have heard something like that already this morning? Rather than thinking of yourself as being visually oriented, kinesthetically oriented, or auditorily oriented, take what you do best as a statement about which system you already have well-developed and refined. Realize that you might put some time and energy into developing the other systems with the same refinement and the same fluidity and creativity that you already have in your most developed system. Labels are traps, and one way that you can stabilize a piece of behavior in an unuseful way is to label it. Instead, you can take the fact that you notice most of your behavior falls into category X, to let yourself begin to develop your skills in Y and Z.

Now, I'd like to caution you about another thing. In psychotherapy one of the major things that Freud made fashionable, and that has continued unconsciously as a presupposition of most therapists' behavior, is the phenomenon known as introspection. Introspection is when you learn something about behavior, you apply it to yourself. I would like to caution you *not* to do this with most of the material we are presenting you, because you will simply go into a loop. For example: How many people here who can visualize easily know what they would look like if they weren't visualizing? ...

If you do that, you get a spinning sensation. How many of you during the exercise were paying attention to the feeling of your own eyes moving up and down? That's an example of introspection and it is *not* useful to do it to yourself in this context. These tools are mostly for *ex*trospection, sensory experience. They are things to detect in *other* people. If you use it on yourself, all you will do is confuse yourself.

Man: How well does this pattern of accessing cues hold up in other cultures?

There is only one group that we know of that is characteristically organized differently: the Basques in the Pyrenees of northern Spain They have a lot of unusual patterns, and that seems to be genetic rather than cultural. Everywhere else we've been—the Americas, Europe, Eastern Europe, Africa—the same pattern exists in most of the population. It may be a neurological bias that is built into our nervous system as a species.

Woman: Do people who are ambidextrous have any different patterns?

They will have more variation from the generalization that we have offered you. For example, some ambidextrous people have the visualization reversed and *not* the auditory and the kinesthetic, or vice versa.

It's really interesting to me that the percentage of left-handed and ambidextrous people in the "genius" category in our culture is much higher than the percentage in the general population. A person with a different cerebral organization than most of the population is automatically going to have outputs which are novel and different for the rest of the population. Since they have a different cerebral organization, they have natural capabilities that "normally organized" right-handers don't automatically have.

Woman: You talked earlier about children who spelled badly because they did it auditorily, and that you could teach them how to do it visually. And now you just talked about the auditory or ambidextrous person having something different that makes him unique. I'm wondering if it's worth the energy it takes to make those kids be able to do what other people do more easily if it's taking away from other things that they can do?

If I teach a child how to spell easily, I'm not taking anything away. Choices are not mutually exclusive. Many people close their eyes in order to be in touch with their feelings, but that's just a statement about how they organize themselves. There's no necessity to that. I can have all the feelings that I want with my eyes open. Similarly, if I have an ambidextrous or left-handed person with a different cerebral organization, I don't have to destroy any choices they presently have to *add* to that. And that's our whole function as modelers. We assume since you all managed to scrape up whatever amount of money it cost you to come here, that you are competent, that you already are succeeding to some degree. We respect all those choices and abilities. We're saying "Good, let's *add* other choices to those choices you already have, so that you have a wider repertoire" just as a good mechanic has a full tool box.

Our claim is that you are using *all systems all the time.* In a particular context you will be *aware* of one system more than another. I assume that when you play athletics or make love, you have a lot of kinesthetic sensitivity. When you are reading or watching a movie, you have a lot of visual consciousness. You can shift from one to the other. There are contextual markers that allow you to shift from one strategy to another and use different sequences. There's nothing forced about that.

There are even strategies to be creative, given different forms of creativity. We work as consultants for an ad agency where we psychologically "clone" their best creative people. We determined the strategy that one creative person used to create a commercial, and we taught other people in that agency to use the same structure at the unconscious level. The commercials they came up with were then creative in the same way, but the content was totally unique. As we were doing the process, one of the people there even made a change in the strategy that made it better.

Most people don't have a large number of strategies to do anything. They use the same kind of strategy to do everything and what happens is that they are good at some things and not good at others. We have found that most people have only three or four basic strategies. A really flexible person may have a dozen. You can calculate that even if you restrict a strategy to four steps there are well over a thousand possibilities!

We make a very strong claim. We claim that if any human can do anything, so can you. All you need is the intervention of a modeler who has the requisite sensory experience to observe what the talented person actually *does*—not their report—and then package it so that you can learn it.

Man: It occurs to me that in your work, the therapeutic goal of bringing clients to awareness is being replaced by giving the client a new pattern of response that they may choose to use.

If you include unconscious choice, I agree with you. There are several presuppositions in our work and one of them is relevant in responding to you: that choice is better than non-choice. And by choice I mean unconscious as well as conscious choice. Everybody knows what conscious choice is, I guess. Unconscious choice is equivalent to variability in my behavior, such that all of the variations get me the outcome I'm after. If I'm presented with the same real world situation a number of times, and I notice that my response varies but that each response gets the outcome I'm after, I have unconscious choice.

However, if each time you go into a similar context you find yourself responding in the same way and you dislike the response, you probably do not have choice. The important question to me is what structure—and there are lots of different ones—produces the state in which you don't have choice? And then what steps can you take to alter that structure? We're going to give you lots of different ways to go about that.

We're offering you classes of information which are universal for us as a species, but which are unconscious for other people. You need those as tools in your repertoire, because it's the unconscious processes and parts of the person you've *got* to work with effectively in order to bring about change in an efficient way. The conscious parts of the person have already done the best they can. They are sort of useful to have around to pay the bill, but what you need to work with are the other parts of the person.

Don't get caught by the words "conscious" and "unconscious." They are not real. They are just a way of describing events that is useful in the context called therapeutic change. "Conscious" is defined as whatever you are aware of at a moment in time. "Unconscious" is everything else.

You can make finer distinctions, of course. There are certain kinds of unconscious data which are immediately available. I say "How's your left ear?" Until you heard that sentence, you probably had no consciousness of your left ear. When you hear me say that, you can shift your consciousness to the kinesthetics of your left ear. That is easily accessible from unconscious to conscious. If I say "What color shoes did your kindergarten teacher wear on the first day that you went to school?" that's also represented somewhere. However, getting at it will take a lot more time and energy. So there are degrees of accessibility of unconscious material.

Typically a person arrives in your office and says "Help! I want to make a change here. I'm in pain. I'm in difficulty. I want to be different than I am presently." You can assume that they have already tried to change with all the resources they can get to consciously, and they have failed utterly. Therefore, one of the prerequisites of your being effective is to have patterns of communication which make good rapport with their *un*conscious resources to assist them in making those changes. To restrict yourself to the conscious resources of the person who comes to you will guarantee a long, tedious, and probably very ineffective process.

By the way, here in this seminar there is no way that you will be able to consciously keep up with the rapid pace of verbalization that will be going on. That is a systematic and deliberate attempt on our part to overload your conscious resources. We understand that learning and change take place at the unconscious level, so that's the part of you we want to talk to anyway. The part of your functioning which is responsible for about ninety-five percent of your learning and skill is called your unconscious mind. It's everything that's outside of your awareness at a point in time. I want to appeal directly to that part of you to make a complete and useful record of anything that happens here, especially the things we don't comment on explicitly, which it believes would be useful for you to understand further and perhaps employ as a skill in your work as a professional communicator— leaving you free at the conscious level to relax and enjoy your experience here.

The point we're at now is "So what?" You have all had some experience identifying accessing cues and representational systems. What do you use it for?

One way I can use this information is to communicate to you at the unconscious level without any awareness on your part. I can use unspecified words like "understand" and "believe" and indicate to you non-verbally in which sensory channel I want you to "understand." For example, I could say to you "I want to make sure you *understand* (gesturing down and to the audience's left) what we've done so far." My gesture indicates to you unconsciously that I want you to understand auditorily.

You can also use this information to interrupt a person's accessing. All of you make a visual image, and see what happens when I do this.

(He waves both arms over his head in a wide arc.) My gesture knocks all your pictures out of the air, right?

Thousands of times in your life you said something or asked a question of someone and they said "Hm, let's see," and they went inside to create a visual image. When they go inside like that, they can't simultaneously pay attention to input from outside. Now let's say that you and I are on opposite sides about some issue at a conference or a corporate meeting. I begin to talk, and I'm forceful in presenting my material and my system in the hope that you will understand it. After I've offered you a certain amount of information, at some point you will begin to access your internal understanding of what's going on. You'll look up and begin to visualize, or look down and begin to talk to yourself or pay attention to how you feel. Whichever internal state you go into, it's important that I pause and give you time to process that information. If my tempo is too rapid and if I continue to talk at that point, I'll just confuse and irritate you.

What often happens is that when I notice you look away, I think that you aren't paying attention, or that you are avoiding me. My typical response in stress during a conference is to *increase* the tempo and the volume of my speech because I'm going to *make* you pay attention and *drive* that point home. You are going to respond as if you are being attacked, because I'm not allowing you an adequate amount of time to know what I'm talking about. You end up quite confused, and you'll never understand the content. If I am facilitating a meeting, I can notice whenever a listener goes inside to access, and I can interrupt or distract the speaker at those times. That gives the listener adequate processing time so that he can make sense of what is going on, and decide whether he agrees or disagrees.

Here's another example: If you can determine what a person's lead and representational systems are, you can package information in a way that is irresistible for him. "Can you see yourself making this new change, and as you see yourself in this process, do you have those feelings of accomplishment and success and say to yourself 'This is going to be good.'?" If your typical sequence happens to be constructed images, followed by feelings, followed by auditory comment, that will be irresistible for you.

I once taught a mathematics course at the University of California to people who were not sophisticated mathematically. I ended up teaching it as a second language. The class was a group of linguistic students who had a good understanding of how language systems work, but did not have an understanding of mathematical systems. However, there is a level of analysis in which they are exactly the same. So rather than teach them how to talk about it and think about it as a mathematician would, I simply utilized what was already available in their world model, the notion of translation, and taught them that these symbols were nothing more than words. And just as there are certain sequences of words which are well-formed sentences, in mathematics there are certain sequences of symbols which are well-formed. I made my entire approach fit *their* model of the world rather than demanding that they have the flexibility to come to mine. That's one way to go about it.

When you do that, you certainly do them a favor in the sense that you package material so it's quite easy for them to learn it. You also do them a *disservice* in the sense that you are supporting rigid patterns of learning in them. It's important for you to understand the outcomes of the various choices you make in presenting material. If you want to do them a really profound favor, it would contribute more to their evolution for you to go to their model and then teach them to overlap into another model so that they can have more flexibility in their learning. If you have that kind of sensitivity and capability, you are a very unusual teacher. If you can offer them that experience, then they can have two learning strategies. They can now go to some other teacher who doesn't have that sensitivity of communication, and because they are flexible enough they will be able to adapt to that teaching style.

A lot of school children have problems learning simply because of a mismatch between the primary representational system of the teacher and that of the child. If neither one of them has the flexibility to adjust, no learning occurs. Knowing what you now know about representational systems, you can understand how it is possible for a child to be "educationally handicapped" one year, and to do fine the next year with a different teacher, or how it is possible for a child to do really well in spelling and mathematics, and do badly in literature and history.

You can also translate between representational systems with couples. Let's say that the husband is very kinesthetic. He comes home after working hard all day and he wants to be comfortable. He sits down in the living room, kicks his boots off here, throws a cigarette down there, gets a beer from the icebox, grabs the paper, and sprawls all over his chair, and so on. Then the wife, who's very visual, walks in. She's worked hard all day cleaning house so it will look good, as a way of showing respect for him. She sees his stuff scattered all over the living room and gets upset. So the complaint from him is "She doesn't leave me enough space to be comfortable, man. It's my home. I want to be comfortable." What she says to him at this point is "You're so sloppy. You leave stuff lying all over and it looks cluttered, and when it looks cluttered like that I know that you don't respect me."

One of the things Virginia Satir does is to find the kinesthetic counterpart of her visual complaint, and vice-versa. So you can look at the husband and say:

"You don't understand what she said, do you? You really have no idea what she experiences. Have you ever had the experience that she went to bed first, and she's been sitting there watching TV in bed, eating crackers? And you come in and get into bed and feel all those cracker crumbs all over your skin. Did you know that's what she experiences when she walks in and sees your stuff lying all over the front room?"

So there's no fault, no blame. You don't say "You're bad" or "You're stupid" or anything like that. You say "Here's a counterpart that you can understand in your system."

He says "Well, when we're in public, and I want to express affection, she's always standing back, always pushing me away." And she says "He's always making scenes in public. He's pawing me all the time!" That is his way, of course, of simply being affectionate, but she needs to see what is going on. He complains that she moves away and he falls flat on his face. He reaches out toward her and nothing happens. So you find a counterpart and say to her:

"Have you ever had the experience of wanting and needing help, really seeing the need for companionship and assistance, and it's like you're standing in the middle of the desert and you look around in all directions and there's no one there? You don't see anybody and you are all alone. Do you know that's what he feels when he comes toward you and reaches out and you back up?"

The point is not whether those are actually accurate examples or not The point is that you can use the principle of sorting people by representational systems, and then overlapping to find counterparts between them. That establishes something that even the major insurance companies in this country have adopted, "no-fault" policies. Family and couple therapists ought to at least have that, and have a way of demonstrating it.

As I stand back and give her space to see what I'm saying, and I get in close to him and make good solid contact with him, the teaching at the unconscious meta-level is this: *I can get responses from her that he would love to get, and I can get responses from him that she would love to get.* That's never mentioned; that's all at the unconscious level. So they will model and adopt my kinds of behavior to make their communications more effective. That's another way of making contact and establishing rapport with each individual member and then translating between representational systems, as a way of teaching them how to communicate more effectively.

Reference systems are also important. What if someone comes in and tells you "I don't know what I want." They are saying that they don't have a reference system. We taught a seminar just recently and a woman there said that she had a very difficult time. She could not decide what she wanted from a menu. She had no basis on which to make that decision. She said her whole life was like that; she could never decide things, and she was always dissatisfied. So we literally made up a decision strategy for her. We said OK, when you are faced with a decision, go inside and tell yourself what it is you have to decide, no matter what it is. Let's say you are in a restaurant. Tell yourself "You must choose food." Then go back to sensory experience and find out what your choices are. In other words, read the menu. As you read "hamburger" on the menu, make a picture of a hamburger in front of you, taste what it would taste like, and check whether that feels positive to you or not. Then read "fried eggs," see fried eggs in front of you, taste what they would be like, and check whether that feels positive to you or not. After she went through the process of trying that a few times, she had a way of making decisions, and started to make them quickly and unconsciously for all kinds of things in her life.

As she went through that process a number of times, it became streamlined in the same way that learning to drive a car does. It drops into unconsciousness. Consciousness seems to be occupied by things we don't know how to do too well. When we know how to do things really well, we do them automatically.

Man: We were wondering about accessing smells. We played with that a little bit and discovered that they went visual to see the object and then to the smell.

Not necessarily. *You* used the sequence you described. You said "What we discovered *they* do is..." and then you described yourself. That is a common pattern in modern psychotherapy, as far as I can tell. Thomas Szasz said "All psychology is either biography or auto-biography." Most people are doing therapy with themselves instead of other people. To respond more specifically to your statement, people can access olfactory experience in many different ways. One of the things you can notice, however, is that when people access smells, they will flare their nostrils. That's a direct sensory signal, just as the eye movements we've been talking about are direct sensory signals, to let you know what experience the person is having. They may or may not precede that with a visual, kinesthetic, or auditory access, but you can see the nostril flare.

Turn to somebody close by; one of you decide to be A and the other to be B. I'm going to ask A to watch B respond to the question I'm going to ask. A, clear your sensory channels and watch your partner's nose. B, when was the last time you took a good whiff of ammonia?... Now is there any doubt about that? It's an involuntary response. Usually the person will breathe in at the moment the nostrils flare.

Let me ask you all to do something else which is along these lines to give you another demonstration. As a child, you had lots of experiences. Maybe you had a grandmother who lived in a separate house that had special smells. Maybe it was some special food, or a blankie, or a little stuffed toy animal, or something else special to you. Pick some object from your childhood and either feel it, talk to yourself about it, or see it in your hands. When you have it in any of those systems, breathe in strongly and let that take you where-ever it takes you. Try that for a minute. That's one way of accessing smells.

There are as many ways to use this information as your ingenuity permits. If you use visual guided fantasy with your clients, there are some clients you use it with automatically and it works fine. Other people you wouldn't even try it with. What's the criterion you use to decide that, do you know? If they can visualize easily, you use visual guided fantasy, right? We're suggesting that you *reverse* that. Because for people who do not normally visualize in consciousness, visual guided fantasy will be a mind-blowing, profound change experience. For those who visualize all the time, it will be far less useful. The only thing you need to do in order to make it work for people who *don't* normally visualize is to join their system wherever they are—wherever their consciousness is—establish rapport and then slowly *overlap* to lead them into the system you want to engage them in fantasy with. It will be extremely powerful, much more powerful than with someone who already visualizes.

If you have any fragment of any experience, you can have it all. Let me ask you to do the following: Roll your shoulders forward and close your eyes and feel as though something or someone is pushing down on your shoulders. And then take those feelings, intensify them, and let them come up into a picture. Who or what do you find there? As you get the picture, I want you to notice some dimension of the picture that is connected with some sound that would be occurring if that were actually happening. And now hear the sound.

That's the principle of *overlap*. You can always go to the state of consciousness a person indicates by their predicates, and from there you can overlap into any other dimension of experience and train a person to do any of these things.

Richard: I know. I did it myself. Four years ago I couldn't see an image; in fact I didn't know that people did. I thought people were kidding when they did visual guided fantasies. I had no idea that they were actually seeing images. And when I figured out what was going on, I realized that there were these differences between people. Then I began trying to make images. Of course, the way I first tried to make images was by talking to myself and having feelings, which is the way people who have trouble making images usually go about it. They say to themselves "Gee, I should look at this even harder!" and then feel frustrated. Of course, the more I talked to myself and the more I had feelings, the less I could see images. I had to learn to do it by overlap: by taking a feeling or a sound and then adding the visual dimension.

You can use overlap to train a client to be able to do all systems, which I think is a benefit for any human to be able to do. You yourself can notice which of the representational systems you use with refinement and sophistication, and which you have difficulty with. Then you can use overlap as a way of training yourself to be as sophisticated in any system as you are in your most advanced.

Let's say you have good kinesthetics but you can't visualize. You can feel yourself reach out with your hand and feel the bark of some tree. You explore tactually until you have a really good kinesthetic hallucination. You can visualize your hand, and then you look past your hand inside your mind's eye and *see* what the tree looks like, based on the feelings—as you feel the roughness, the texture, the temperature of the bark. If you visualize easily and you want to develop auditory, you can see the visual image of a car whirling around a corner and then hear the squeal of the tires.

Man: Would a congenitally blind therapist be at a disadvantage?

Visual accessing cues are only one way to get this information. There are other things going on equally as interesting, that would give you the same information and other information as well. For instance, voice tone is higher for visual access and lower for kinesthetic. Tempo speeds up for visual and slows down for kinesthetic. Breathing is higher in the chest for visual and lower in the belly for kinesthetic. There are *lots* and *lots* of cues. What we are doing is giving one little piece at a time. Your consciousness is limited to seven—plus or minus two—chunks of information. What we are doing is saying "Look, you normally pay attention to other dimensions of experience. Here's another class of experience we'd like you to attend to, and notice how you can use it in a very powerful way."

I can get the same information by voice tone, or tempo changes, or by watching a person's breathing, or the change in skin color on the back of their hand. Someone who is blind can get the same classes of information in other ways. Eye movement is the easiest way that we've discovered that people can learn to get access to this class of information called "representational system." After they have that, we can easily teach them other dimensions.

You might think that a blind therapist would be at a disadvantage. However, blindness is a matter of degree in all of us. The non-sighted person who has no chance of seeing has an advantage over most other communicators: he *knows* he is blind, and has to develop his other senses to compensate. For example, a few weeks ago in a seminar there was a man who is totally blind. A year ago, I had taught him how to be able to detect representational systems through other means. Not only was he able to do it, but he was able to do it every bit as well as every sighted person in that room. Most of the people I meet are handicapped in terms of their sensory ability. There is a tremendous amount of experience that goes right by them because they are operating out of something which to me is much more intense than just "preconceived notions." They are operating out of their own internal world, and trying to find out what matches it.

That's a good formula for being disappointed, by the way. One of the best ways to have lots of disappointment in your life is to construct an image of how you would like things to be, and then try to make everything that way. You will feel disappointed as long as the world doesn't match your picture. That is one of the best ways I know of to keep yourself in a constant state of disappointment, because you are never going to get the world to match your picture.

There is another vast source of process information in observing the motor programs that are accessed when a person thinks about an activity. For example, Ann, would you sit in a "normal" position with your legs uncrossed? Thank you. Now let me ask you a preparatory question. Do you drive a car? (Yes.) Is there a single one you drive typically? (Yes.) OK, now, this is a question I don't want you to answer out loud, but just go ahead and access the answer internally. Is it a stick shift or is it an automatic shift? ... Did anyone else get the answer? Would you like to guess about the answer and check it out?

Man: Stick shift.

OK. How do you know that?

Man: She shifted. I saw her move her right hand.

Can you tell by the shift whether it was a manual or automatic?

Man: It's manual.

Now, is that true, Ann? (No.) No, it's an automatic. Now, did anybody else have that answer?

Woman: Yeah, because I figured she was little and she wouldn't want to drive a stick shift.

OK. Did anybody use *sensory experience* to get the answer? ... Well, let me answer the question directly. If you had been watching Ann's feet, you would have gotten the answer to that question. One of the differences in the motor program between an automatic and a stick shift is whether you have a clutch to work. If you had been watching, you could have seen muscle tension in her right leg and not in her left, which would have given you the answer.

If you ask a person a question that involves a motor program, you can observe the parts of their body they will have to use in order to access the information. Information doesn't come out of a vacuum in human beings. In order for a human being to get information to answer a question, they have got to access some representation of it. And although they may only bring one of those systems into consciousness, they are going to access all systems unconsciously to gather the information.

Ann: We have both kinds of car and I drive both. You said "Which one do you drive usually?" If you had asked me "Do you have a different car?" and then asked me about that specific car, would my motor programs have been different? If I was thinking of driving the other car, would my legs have moved differently?

Yes. You use your left foot only if there is a clutch. Consider how you answer the following question. You all have front doors to the homes or apartments that you live in, whether they are long-term homes or apartments. As you walk into your apartment or home, does the first door open to the right or the left? Now, how do you decide that question? . . . All the hands are moving.

Let me ask you another question. When you come home in the evening and your house is locked, which hand do you use to actually open the door? . . . Watch the hands.

People have always tried to turn body language into a content vocabulary, as if holding your head back *meant* that you were reserved and crossing your legs *meant* that you were closed. But body language doesn't work like words work; it works differently. Eye movements and body movements will give you information about *process.*

The proper domain, in our opinion, of professional communicators is process. If you indulge in content, you are going to unavoidably impose part of your belief and value system on the people you communicate with.

The kinds of problems that people have, usually have nothing to do with content; they have to do with the *structure,* the *form* of how they organize their experience. Once you begin to understand that, therapy becomes a lot easier. You don't have to listen to the content; you only have to find out how the process works, which is really much simpler.

There's an important pattern that we'd like to talk about next. If I'm your client and you ask me "Well, how did it go this week?" and I respond to you by going (sighs heavily, head down, low tonality) "Ah, everything worked just great this week. (sighing, shaking head "no," slight sneer) No problems." Now, the laughter indicates that there are a number of people here who recognize that there is some unusual communication being offered. The name that we have adopted for that is *incongruity*. What I offer you in my voice tone, my body movements, and my head movements does not match my words. Now, what responses do you have to that as professional communicators? What choices do you have to respond to that situation?

Woman: If I knew you really well, I'd say "I don't believe you." Or I might say "Well, you don't *look* very happy because things are going well."

So you would meta-comment on the discrepancy that you've been able to perceive, and confront the person with it. Does anybody else have other ways of responding?

Man: I would try to help you express *both* messages, maybe exaggerate the non-verbal components....

OK, the gestalt technique: amplify the non-verbal message until it accesses the appropriate experience, right? OK, that's another choice. Does everybody understand the choices we're talking about so far? Our job is choice. The notion of incongruity is a choice point which is going to be repetitive in your experience if you are in the business of communication. It makes sense for you to have a varied repertoire, a range of possible responses, and to understand—I hope at the unconscious level rather than consciously—what the outcome will be when you select one of these maneuvers or techniques.

Meta-commenting is one choice, and I think it's a good choice. However, it is only *one* choice. When I watch and listen to therapists communicate, I often notice that that's the *only* choice that a lot of them have when presented with incongruity—that the people who are in the business of choice *don't have any*. You want to have a lot of choices in responding to incongruity. You want to have the choice of exaggerating the non-verbal, or of calling them a liar and attacking them, or of ignoring it, or of simply mirroring back and saying incongruently "I'm so glad!" (shaking head and sneering)

Or you can "short-circuit" them by reversing the verbal and non-verbal messages: "That's too bad" (smiling and nodding head). The response you get to that is fascinating, because most people have no idea what they verbalized. Either they will enter a confusion state, or they will begin to explicitly verbalize the message that was previously non-verbal. It's almost as if they take all the conscious material and make it unconscious and vice-versa.

Or you might choose to respond with an appropriate metaphor: "That reminds me of a story my grandfather O'Mara told me once. He was Irish himself, but he told about this Baltic country that he had spent some time in as a youth when he was traveling in Europe—poor, destitute, but nevertheless out having experience. And the duke that ruled this little principality—this was before the Second World War, when there were a lot of small countries—had a problem. The Minister of the *Interior* did not have good communication with the Minister of the *Exterior*. And so some of the things that the Minister of the *Exterior* could see needed to be attended to in order for a judicious trade arrangement to be made with other entities—other neighboring, surrounding people—came into conflict somehow with some of the needs that the Minister of the *Interior* felt ..."

Now how do people learn to be incongruent? Think of a young child who comes home and hands a piece of homework to his parents. The parents look at the homework and the father says (scowling face and shaking head "no," with harsh tonality) "Oh, I'm so glad you brought that home, son!" What does the kid do? Does he lean forward and meta-comment? "Gee, Dad! I hear you say you're glad, but I notice..." Not if you're a kid. One thing that children do is to become hyperactive. One hemisphere is registering the visual input and the tonal input, and the other hemisphere is registering the words and their digital meaning, and they don't fit. They don't fit maximally where the two hemispheres overlap maximally in kinesthetic representation. If you ever watch a hyperactive kid, the trigger for hyperactivity will be incongruity, and it will begin here at the midline of the torso, and then diffuse out to all kinds of other behavior.

Let me ask you to do something now. I want you to raise your right hand.... Did anybody notice any incongruity?

Man: You raised your left hand.

I raised my left hand. So did many people out there! Some of you raised your left hand. Some of you raised your right hand. Some of you didn't notice which hand I lifted. The point is that when you were all children, you had to find a way of coping with incongruity. Typically what people do is to distort their experience so that it is congruent. Is there anyone in here that actually heard me say "Raise your left hand"? Many of you raised your left hand. Some of you raised your left hand

and probably thought you raised your right hand. If you didn't notice the incongruity, you somehow deleted the relationship between your own kinesthetic experience and my words, in order to make your experience coherent.

If there are mixed messages arriving, one way to resolve the difficulty is to literally shut one of the dimensions—the verbal input, the tonal input, the body movements, the touch, or the visual input—out of consciousness. And you can predict that the hyperactive child who shuts the right hemisphere out of consciousness—it's still operating, of course, it's just out of awareness—will later be persecuted by visual images: dead babies floating out of hot dogs in the air above the psychiatrist's desk. The ones who cut off the kinesthetics will feel insects crawling all over them, and that will really bug them. And they will tell you that. That is a straight quote from a schizophrenic. The ones that cut off the auditory portion are going to hear voices coming out of the wall plugs, because literally they are giving up consciousness of that whole system and the information that is available to them through that system, as a way of defending themselves in the face of repeated incongruity.

In this country, when we have gone into mental hospitals we have discovered that the majority of the hallucinations are auditory, because people in this culture do not pay much attention to the auditory system. In other cultures, hallucinations will tend to cluster in other representational systems.

Woman: I'd like you to comment some more because I stumbled into some of this out of talking with people about hallucinatory phenomena.

Hallucinatory phenomena in my opinion are the same thing you've been doing here all day. There's no formal difference between hallucinations and the processes you use if I ask you to remember anything that happened this morning, or what happened when I said "Ammonia" and all of you went "uhhhrrrhhh!" As far as I can tell, there are some subtle differences between people who are in mental hospitals and people who are not. One is that they are in a different building. The other is that many of them don't seem to have a strategy to know what constitutes shared reality and what doesn't.

Who has a pet? Can you see your pet sitting here on the chair? (Yes.) OK. Now, can you distinguish between the animal that you have here, and the chair that it is sitting on? Is there anything in your experience that allows you to distinguish between the fact that you put the visual image of the pet there, and the fact that the image of the chair was there before you deliberately put it there? Is there any difference? There may not be.

Woman: Oh, yes, there is.

OK. What is the difference? How do you know that there is a real chair and there's not a real dog?

Woman: I really can see that chair in my reality here and now. But I can only picture the dog in my head, in my mind's eye....

You don't see the dog over here sitting in the chair?

Woman: Well, only in my mind's eye.

What's the difference between the image of the chair in your mind's eye and the image of the dog in your mind's eye? Is there a difference?

Woman: Well, one's here and one isn't.

Yes. How do you *know* that, though?

Woman: Well, I still see the chair even when I look away and look back. But if I stop thinking about the dog in the chair, the dog isn't there anymore.

OK. You can talk to yourself, right? Would you go inside and ask if there is a part of you at the unconscious level that is capable of having the dog there when you look back? Would you make those arrangements and find out if you can still tell the difference? Because my guess is there are other ways you know, too.

Woman: The image of the dog isn't as clear.

OK, so that's one way that you make a reality check. Would you go inside and ask if there is a part of you that can make it as clear?

Woman: Not while I'm awake.

I know your conscious mind can't do it. I'm not asking that question. Can you talk to yourself? Can you go "Hi, Mary, how are you?" on the inside? (Yes.) OK. Go inside and say "Is there any part of me at the unconscious level which is capable of making that image of the dog as clear as the chair?" And be sensitive to any response you get. It may be verbal, it may be a feeling, it may be something visual. While she's doing that, does anyone else know how they know the difference?

Man: Well, earlier when you hit the chair I could hear a sound. When you hit the dog, I couldn't.

So essentially your strategy consists of going to another representational system and noticing whether there is a representation that corresponds in that system to what you detected in another system.

Woman: I know I put the dog there.

How do you know that?

Woman: Because I can remember what I did.

OK, *how* do you remember putting the dog there? Is that a visual process? Do you talk to yourself? OK. Now I want you to do that *same* process for putting the chair there. I want you to put the chair here, even though it's already here. I want you to go through the same process you used to put the dog here to put the chair here and then tell me what, if any, difference there is.

Does anybody know the point of all this?

Woman: We're all schizophrenic.

Of course we're all schizophrenic. In fact, R. D. Laing is far too conservative when he talks about schizophrenia being a natural response. Evolutionarily the next step, which we're all engaged in, is multiple personality. You're all multiple personalities. There are only two differences between you and an officially diagnosed multiple personality: (1) the fact that you don't have to have amnesia for how you are behaving in one context; you can remember it in another context, (2) you can choose how to respond contextually. Whenever you *don't* have a choice about how you respond in context, you are a robot. So you have two choices. You can be a multiple personality or a robot. Choose well.

The point that we're trying to make is that the difference between somebody who doesn't know their hallucination is a hallucination and yourselves is only that you have developed some strategy by which you know what is shared reality and what is not. And if you are going to have hallucinations, you probably have them about *ideas* instead of about *things*.

If one of you in the audience said "Well, wait a minute, there really is a dog there, anybody can see that!" then probably one of the other people in this room would take you away.

Now, when Sally used the word "pensive" earlier, she was halucinating with exactly the same formal process that a schizophrenic does. For example, there was a mental patient who looked at us and said "Did you just see me drink a cup of blood?" He was doing exactly the same thing. He was taking input from the outside, combining it in an interesting way with a response he was making internally, and then assuming it all came from the outside.

There are only two distinctions between anybody in this room and an institutionalized schizophrenic: (1) whether you have a good reality strategy and you can make that distinction, and (2) whether the content of your hallucination is socially acceptable or not. Because you all hallucinate. You all hallucinate that somebody's in a good mood or a bad mood, for example. Sometimes it really is an accurate representation of what you are getting from the outside, but sometimes it's a response to your own internal state.

And if it's not there, sometimes you can induce it. "Is something wrong?" "What's bothering you?" "Now I don't want you to worry about anything that happened today while you were gone."

Drinking blood in this culture is not acceptable. I've lived in cultures where that's fine. The Masai, in Eastern Africa, sit around and drink cups of blood all the time. No problem. It would be weird in their culture for somebody to say "I can see that you are feeling very bad about what I just said." They would begin to wonder about you. But in this culture it's reversed.

When we trained residents in mental hospitals we used to go up early and spend time in the wards because the patients there had problems we never had the opportunity to encounter before. We would give them the task of determining for themselves which parts of their experience were validated by other people, and which were not. For instance, with the cup-of-blood guy, we immediately joined his reality. "Yeah, warm this one up for me, will you?" We joined his reality so much that he came to trust us. And then we gave him the task of discovering which parts of his reality other people in the ward could validate for him. We didn't say this was really here and that wasn't, but simply asked him to determine which parts of his reality other people could share. And then he learned—as most of us have as children—to talk about those parts of reality which are either socially acceptable hallucinations, or that other people are willing to see and hear and feel, too. That's all he needed to get out of the hospital. He's doing fine. He still drinks cups of blood, but he does it by himself. Most psychotics just don't have a way of making distinctions between what's shared reality and what's not.

Man: Many psychiatrists do not have that, when working with those people.

Many do not have it, period, as far as I can tell! The only difference is that they have other psychiatrists that share that reality, so they at least have a shared reality. I've made lots of jokes about the way humanistic psychologists treat each other when they get together. They have many social rituals that did not exist when I worked at an electronics corporation. The corporation people didn't come in in the morning and hold each other's hands and look meaningfully into each other's eyes for five and a half minutes. Now, when somebody at the corporation sees somebody do that, they go "Urrrrhhh! Weird!" And the people in humanistic psychology circles think the corporation people are cold and insensitive and inhuman. To me, they are both psychotic realities, and I'm not sure which one is crazier. And if you think about *shared* realities, the corporation people are in the *majority*[1]

Where you really have a choice is when you can go from one reality to the other, *and* you can have a perspective on what's going on. One of the craziest things is when a humanistic psychologist goes to teach a seminar at a corporation and doesn't alter his behavior. That inability to adjust to a different shared reality is a demonstration of psychosis as far as I'm concerned.

Therapists feel letters. I don't think that's any more peculiar than drinking cups of blood. Everywhere I go, people tell me they feel O and K. That's pretty weird. Or you ask people "How do you feel?" and they say "*Not* bad." Think about that for a moment. That's a very profound statement. "I feel *not* bad." That's not a feeling. Neither is "OK."

One of the most powerful tools that I think is useful for you to have as professional communicators is to make the distinction between perception and hallucination. If you can clearly distinguish what portion of your ongoing experience you are creating internally and putting out there, as opposed to what you are actually receiving through your sensory apparatus, you will not hallucinate when it's not useful. Actually there is nothing that you *need* to hallucinate about. There is no outcome in therapy for which hallucinations are necessary. You can stay strictly with sensory experience and be very powerful, effective, efficient, and creative.

You need only three things to be an absolutely exquisite communicator. We have found that there are three major patterns in the behavior of every therapeutic wizard we've talked to—and executives, and salespeople. The first one is to know what outcome you want. The second is that you need flexibility in your behavior. You need to be able to generate lots and lots of different behaviors to find out what responses you get. The third is you need to have enough sensory experience to notice when you get the responses that you want. If you have those three abilities, then you can just alter your behavior until you get the responses that you want.

That's what we're doing here. We know what outcomes we want, and we put ourselves into what we call "uptime," in which we're completely in sensory experience and have no consciousness at all. We aren't aware of our internal feelings, pictures, voices, or anything else internal. We are in sensory experience in relationship to you and noticing how you respond to us. We keep changing our behavior until you respond the way we want you to.

Right now I know what I'm saying because I'm listening to myself externally. I know how much sense you're making of what I'm saying by your responses to it, both conscious and unconscious. I am seeing those. I'm not commenting on them internally, simply noticing them and adjusting my behavior. I have no idea what I feel like internally. I have tactile kinesthetic awareness. I can feel my hand on my jacket, for instance. It's a particular altered state. It's one trance out of many, and a useful one for leading groups.

Woman: How do you adjust yourself in uptime? You said you keep adjusting until you get the response you want. What adjustments are you making? Do you explain more? Or talk more? Or. . .

Well, I adjust all the possible parameters. The most obvious one to me is voice tone. You can adjust your facial expression, too. Sometimes you can say the same words and lift your eyebrows and people will suddenly understand. Sometimes you can begin to move your hands. With some people, you can draw a picture. Sometimes I can just explain the same thing *over* again with a different set of words. Those are some of the logical possibilities that are available. There are lots and lots of possibilities.

Woman: Well, as you're changing your behavior, don't you have to be somewhat aware of what's going on inside you?

No. I think most people try to do it reflexively, with conscious self-awareness, and most of the strategies of reflexive consciousness don't work. That's why most people have such crummy personal relationships. If I want you to act a certain way, and I make *you* the reference for what I'm doing, then all I have to do is keep acting differently until *you* look and sound and behave the way I want you to. If I have to check with myself to find out, then I'm going to be paying attention to my feelings and my internal voices, which isn't going to tell me whether I'm getting what I want. Most therapists succeed with their clients a dozen times before they notice it.

Woman: OK. I can see how that would work in therapy, being a therapist. But in an intimate relationship it seems like being in uptime wouldn't be as intimate.

Oh, I disagree. I think it would be much *more* intimate that way. I don't think intimacy is built on talking to yourself and making pictures internally. I think intimacy is built on eliciting responses. If I'm in uptime when I'm interacting with somebody, then I'm going to be able to elicit responses from them which are pleasurable, and intimate, and anything else I want.

Woman: If I'm talking to someone about something that I'm feeling and thinking is important to me, then I wouldn't be in uptime, would I?

If that is your definition of intimacy, then we have different definitions of intimacy!

Woman: I'm saying that it's part of being intimate; that's one way of being intimate.

OK. I disagree with that.

Woman: How can you do that if you're in uptime?

You can't do that when you're in uptime. You can talk about things that you *have* thought and felt at *other times* but then you wouldn't be in uptime. I agree that uptime would be a poor strategy for talking about internal states, but I don't happen to consider that intimacy. For your description, uptime is not a good strategy. Uptime is the only one I know which is a generally effective strategy to interact with people in terms of getting responses.

For what you're talking about, I would design a completely different strategy, because you're going to have to know what you're thinking and feeling in order to talk about it. But I don't think that will produce connectedness with another human being. Because if you do that you're not paying attention to *them,* you're only paying attention to *yourself.* I'm not saying that it's bad, I'm just saying that it's not going to make you feel more connected with someone else. You're not going to have more contact with the woman sitting next to you if you're inside making pictures and talking to yourself and having feelings, and then telling her about them. That's not going to put *you* in contact with *her.* All that's going to do is tell her conscious mind a lot about what's going on inside you when you're *not* paying attention to her.

I have an attorney who has a great strategy for solving legal problems. He first has a visual construction in his head of what problem has to be solved. Next, in outline, he goes auditory internal A and checks with a visual eidetic A, auditory internal B and checks with visual eidetic B, and so on, until all of his auditory and visual eidetics add up to that visual construction. Then he knows that he's got that problem solved. It's a super strategy for legal problems, but it's a *terrible* strategy for personal relationships, and he uses it for that, too. He will make a picture of how he wants to interact with somebody, and then try to find pictures of when he's done it before. He can never do anything new with anyone unless he's already done all the component pieces before. It's just not a terribly good strategy for that task. And while he's using that strategy, he's gone—he isn't there at all!

Recently on TV, a psychologist was instructing people about how to have better communication. In essence, she was saying "Make a picture of the way you want to be, and then behave that way." But there was nothing in it about noticing feedback from other people. She had all these cardboard people standing next to her who were her students, going "Yes! We are very happy and we can communicate. And it is so nice to meet you, yes!" They didn't even know whether they shook hands or not. They had no contact at all, because they were inside making pictures. They all had smiles on their faces, so maybe they were happy, but it's not a very good strategy to communicate.

We once ate lunch with a retired army colonel who decided that he was going to become a communicator. He has two strategies. One is to give commands, and the other is designed to get agreement. Neither strategy has anything to do with gathering information; his entire strategy just simply ends when there is agreement. So no matter what he says, if you say "I agree with you," he can't function anymore. He's the kind of person whom you would never naturally agree with about anything, no matter what he said, because he's got a voice tone that gets you to respond negatively.

When we sat down, everyone went crazy, because they kept saying "Well, I wouldn't put it quite that way," and getting into arguments with him. Finally I stopped them all, and Leslie and I said in unison "We agree with you." Whatever he said, we'd say "We agree with you." When we did that, he couldn't generate any behavior! He ceased to function. He would sit there quietly for ten or fifteen minutes, until he would take issue with something that the rest of us were talking about.

We would simply say "We agree with you" and he was gone again. His strategy to decide what he wanted on the menu was to get *everyone* to have *anything* off the menu. His strategy was not designed to get food that would please his palate; it was designed to get other people to have the same thing that he had. I guess that's a good strategy for a colonel in the Army. But it's a lousy strategy to get something good in a restaurant, or to pick a restaurant, or to have friends, which is something he didn't have.

Having total sensory experience is a life-long project, and there isn't any limitation to it as far as I know. I now see things, hear things and get information tactually that two years ago would have seemed like ESP to me. That's a statement about my willingness to commit some time and energy to training myself to refine the distinctions I make between internal and external realities, the refinements I can make in every sensory channel, and in every internal representational system.

A lot of our training in our ability to make visual distinctions we got from Milton Erickson. He is one of the most exquisite visual detectors in the world. He can see things that really are "extra-sensory" for other people, but they *are* there, and they are coming in through the same senses. In the exercise we did, many of you called me over for assistance, saying "Well, this person doesn't make any eye movements." And you finally admitted "Well, there's some slight movement of the eyes." When you say something is *slight,* that is a statement about your ability to detect it, not about what's going on with the other person.

It's like "resistance." If therapists would take "resistance" as a comment about *themselves* instead of their clients, I think the field of psychotherapy would develop at a faster rate. Whenever a client "resists," it's a statement about what *you* are doing, not about what *they* are doing. Out of all the ways that you've attempted to make contact and establish rapport, you have not yet found one that works. You need to be more flexible in the way you are presenting yourself, until you get the rapport response you want.

What we would like to do next is to offer you an exercise to increase your sensory experience, and to distinguish between sensory experience and hallucination. This exercise has four parts:

Experience vs. Hallucination Exercise: Part I

We want you to sit in groups of three. One of you we'll call A, one B, and one C. A, your job is detection. B, your job is to practice experiencing different kinds of experience. C is simply an observer, and can also help A and B keep track of what to do next. B, you select, without mentioning anything verbally, three *different* experiences that you had which were very intense experiences. They can be from any part of your life, but make them distinctive, one from the other; don't take three similar occasions. You can just identify them by dropping inside and finding representative examples, and simply number them one, two, and three.

Then hold hands with A and announce "one." Then go internal, drop out of sensory experience, go back to that time and place, and have that experience again without any overt verbalization. Take a minute or two or three to relive that experience fully.... Then announce "two" and relive it.... Then announce "three" and relive that....

Now there is one incredibly important factor. For those of you who are very visual, it will be imperative that you do not see yourself there, but *see what you saw when you were there.*

For example, close your eyes and *see yourself* from above or the side somewhere, riding on a roller coaster, just about to go down that first big drop.... Now step into that image of yourself inside the roller coaster and see what you would see if you were actually there riding it. Those are very different experiences. The kinesthetics come in profoundly once you break the dissociation of seeing yourself over there, and put your perceptual position inside your body on the roller coaster.

As you go back and find these three experiences and re-experience them, it is important that you do *not* do it dissociated. You may begin by seeing yourself; then get *inside* the picture. When you are inside the picture and you feel the experience in your body again as you did before, you begin to squeeze A's hand, thereby cuing them tactually that you are now having that experience.

A, your job is simply to observe the changes in B, as s/he goes through the three experiences. I want you to watch skin color changes, size of lower lip, breathing, posture, muscle tonus, etc. There will be many profound changes in B that you can see visually as B goes through this experience.

Part 2

B will do exactly the same thing as in Part 1: s/he will announce "one" and re-experience it, then "two" and "three." But this time A will not only watch the changes but describe them out loud. C's job is to make sure that all the descriptions that A offers are *sensory-based* descriptions: "The corners of your mouth are rising. Your skin color is deepening. Your breathing is high and shallow and increasing in rate. There's more tension in your right cheek than your left." Those are descriptions that allow C—who is watching as well as listening to your description—to verify, or not, what in fact you are claiming. If A says "You're looking happy; now you're looking worried," those are *not* sensory-based descriptions. "Happy" and "worried" are judgements. C's job is to make sure that A's descriptions are sensory-based, and to challenge any utterance that is not sensory-based.

Part 3

This time B goes into one of the three experiences without identifying it by number. You just pick one of the three and go into it. A sits there, again observing B, saying nothing until s/he finishes that experience. And then A, you tell B which experience it was: "one," "two," or "three." B continues to run through those three experiences in any order other than the original order, until A is capable of correctly naming which experience you are having. If A can't do it the first time through, simply start over again. Don't tell them which one was which, or that what they thought was number one was really number three; just tell them to back up and start over again. It's a way of training your senses to be acute.

Part 4

This time B goes into any one of the three experiences again and A hallucinates and guesses, as specifically as s/he can, what the *content* of that experience is. And believe me, you can get *very* specific and *very* accurate.

In parts 1, 2, and 3 we ask you to stay in sensory experience. In part 4 we're asking you to hallucinate. This is to make a clean distinction between sensory-based experience and hallucination. Hallucination can be a very powerful, positive thing. Anybody who has ever done a workshop with Virginia Satir knows that she uses hallucination in very powerful and creative ways, for instance in her family sculpting. At some point after she has gathered information she'll pause and sort through all the visual images that she has, preparatory to sculpting or making a family stress ballet. She will change the images around until it *feels* right to her. That's "see-feel," the same strategy as spelling or jealousy. Then she takes the images that satisfy her kinesthetically, and she puts them on the family by sculpting them. That's a case where hallucination is an integral part of a very creative and effective process. Hallucination isn't good or bad; it's just another choice. But it's important to know what you are doing. OK. Go ahead.

* * * * *

All right. Are there any comments or questions about this last exercise we did? Some of you surprised yourselves by the guesses you made, right? And others of you scored zero.

Whether you did well or not is really irrelevant. Either way, you got important information about what you are able to perceive, and whether or not what you hallucinate has any relationship to what you perceive.

You can take the training we're giving you and you can notice as you are communicating with a client or a loved one that the responses that you are getting are not the ones that you want. If you take that as an indication that *what you are doing is not working* and change your behavior, something else will happen. If you leave your behavior the same, you will get more of what you are already getting. Now, that sounds utterly simple. But if you can put that into practice, you will have gotten more out of this seminar than people ever get. For some reason, that seems to be the hardest thing in the world to put into practice. *The meaning of your communication is the response that you get.* If you can notice that you are not getting what you want, *change what you're doing.* But in order to notice that, you have to clearly distinguish between what you are getting from the outside, and how you are interpreting that material in a complex manner at the unconscious level, contributing to it by your own internal state.

The exercise you just did was essentially limited to one sensory channel. It was a way of assisting you in going through an exercise in which you clean up your visual input channel. You also get some kinesthetic information through holding hands. You can do it auditorily as well, and also kinesthetically. You can generalize that same exercise to the other two systems. If you are going to do it auditorily, A would close his eyes. B would then describe the experience without words, just using sounds. The tonal and tempo patterns will be distinctive and since A's eyes will be closed, all he has is the auditory input.

Or you could just think about the experience and talk about cooking lunch. That's the way couples often do it with one another. He makes a picture of his wife having an affair and then they talk about going camping, right? And he goes (angrily) "Yeah, I'd really like to go with you. I think we'd have a good time. I'm going to bring the ax so I can chop up some *firewood.*"

Another thing couples do is fight in *quotes.* Do you know about quotes? Quotes is a wonderful pattern. If any of you have clients who work at jobs and have resentment for their bosses or fellow employees, but who can't really express it because it's inappropriate, or they might get fired or something, teach them the pattern of quotes in language. It's marvelous because they can walk up to their employer and say "I was just out on the street and this man walked up to me and said '*You're a stupid jerk.*' And I didn't know what to say to him. What would you do if somebody walked up to you and said '*You're a jerk.*'? Just right out on the street, you know."

People have almost no consciousness of any meta-levels if you distract them with content. Once at a conference I talked to a large group of psychologists who were pretty stuffy and asked a lot of dumb questions. I told them about quotes as a pattern. Then I said *for example*—I even told them what I was doing—Milton Erickson once told me a story about a time he stayed at a turkey farm, and the turkeys made a lot of noise and kept him awake at night. He didn't know what to do. So finally one night he walked outside—and I faced all those psychologists out there—and he realized he was surrounded by turkeys, hundreds of turkeys everywhere. Turkeys here, and turkeys there, and turkeys all over the place. And he looked at them and he said "*You turkeys!*"

There were a couple of people there who knew what I was doing and they absolutely cracked up. I stood on the stage in front of these people who were paying me a fortune and I went "*You turkeys!*" They didn't know what I was doing. They all sat there nodding seriously. If you are congruent, they will *never* know. If you feed people interesting content, you can experiment with any pattern. As soon as I said "I'm going to tell you a story about Milton" everybody went "content time" and that was all it took.

In the middle of telling the story, I even turned around and laughed at the top of my lungs. And then I turned back and finished it. They just thought it was a weird behavior, because I laugh a lot. Or I could have made the laughing part of the story. "Milton turned around and laughed." At the end of the day all these people came up to me and said "And I want to tell you how important this has been to me" and I said "Thank you. Did you hear the story about Milton? I don't want you to think that *it's about you!*"

You can try *any* new behavior in quotes and it won't seem to be you doing it. Quotes gives you a lot of freedom to experiement with gaining flexibility, because it means that you can do anything. I can go into a restaurant and walk up to a waitress and say "I just went in the bathroom and this guy walked up to me and said 'Blink,'" and find out what happens. She'll blink, and I'll go "Isn't that weird?" and walk away. It wasn't *me,* so I didn't have to worry about it. It's a big piece of personal freedom; you are no longer responsible for your own behavior because it's "someone else's behavior."

When I was going to psychiatric meetings and stuff, I would walk up to someone and say "I was just in a conference with Dr. X, and he did this thing I've never seen anyone do before. He walked up to this person, lifted up his hand like this, and said 'Look at that hand.'" Then I'd do a fifteen or twenty minute trance induction and put the person into a trance. Then I'd slap him in the stomach so he came out, and say "Isn't that a weird thing for him to do?" He would go "Yeah, that's a really weird thing for him to do. He shouldn't do things like that." And I'd go "*I* would never do anything like that. Would you?" And he'd say "No!"

Quotes also works great if you're doing therapy with a family that fights and argues and won't listen, because you can lean forward and you can say "I'm *so* glad you're such a responsive family, because with the *last* family that was here I had to look at each and every person and say '*Shut your mouth.*' That's what I had to tell *them.*" It reminds me of a group we did in San Diego; there were about a hundred and fifty people and we told them "The next thing that we'd like to tell you is how couples often fight in quotes."

"Well, if you were to tell me that, you know what I would say to you?"

"Well, if you told me to do that, I'd just tell you to go to hell!"

"Well, listen, if you ever said that to me I'd reach right over and . . ."

The trouble is they usually *lose* quotes, and actually get into a fight.

64

Most of you have heard quotes in family therapy. You ask "How did it go?" If they stumble on reporting an argument, they'll start in quotes and then they'll be into it again! All their non-verbal analogues will support it. Quotes is a dissociative pattern, and when the dissociation collapses, the quotes go.

Grief is usually a similar pattern. What's going on in the grief-stricken person is this: they make a *constructed* visual image of being with the lost person. They are seeing themselves with the loved one who is now dead or gone, unavailable somehow. Their response called "grief" or "sense of loss" is a complex response to being dissociated from those memories. They see their loved one and themselves having a good time, and they feel empty *because they are not there* in the picture. If they were to step inside the very same picture that stimulates the grief response, they would recover the positive kinesthetic feelings of the good experiences they shared with that person they cared very much about. That would then serve as a resource for them going on and constructing something new for themselves in their lives, instead of a trigger for a grief response.

Guilt's a little different. There are a couple of ways to feel guilty. One of the best ways to feel guilty is to make a picture of the response on someone's face when you did something that they didn't like. In this case you are making a visual eidetic picture. You can feel guilty about anything that way. However, if you step *outside* the picture, in other words reverse the procedure that we use with grief, what happens is that you will no longer feel guilty, because then you literally get a new perspective.

It sounds too easy, doesn't it? It *is* too easy. Ninety-nine out of a hundred depressed clients that I have seen have exactly the same pattern. They will be visualizing and/or talking to themselves about some experience that is depressing to them. But all they will have in awareness are the kinesthetic feelings. And they will use words which are appropriate: "weighed down, burdened, heavy, crushing." However, if you ask them any questions about their feelings, they will give you an elegant, non-verbal description of *how* they create their depression. "How do you know you're depressed? Have you felt this way a long time? What started this syndrome?" The exact questions are wholly irrelevant; they are just ways of accessing that process.

Depressed people usually make a series of visual images, usually constructed and outside of awareness. Usually they have no idea that they are making any images. Some of you had that experience with your partners today. You told them that they were accessing in a system, and they went "Oh, I don't know about that" and they didn't, because that wasn't in their awareness. Depressed people are running profoundly effective hypnotic inductions by seeing images and talking about them outside of awareness and responding in consciousness with only the feelings. They are going to be bewildered about where their feelings come from, since where they come from is totally outside of their awareness.

Many, many people who have weight problems are doing the same thing. They will have a hypnotic voice that goes "Don't eat that cake in the refrigerator." "Don't think about all the candy in the living room." "Don't feel hungry." Most people have no idea that commands like that are actually commands to *do* the behavior. In order to understand the sentence "Don't think of blue" you have to access the meaning of the words and think of blue.

If a child is in a dangerous situation and you say "Don't fall down," in order for him to understand what you have said, he has to access some representation of "falling down." That internal representation, especially if it is kinesthetic, will usually result in the behavior that the parent is trying to prevent. However, if you give positive instructions like "Be careful; pay attention to your balance and move slowly," then the child will access representations that will help him cope with the situation.

Man: Can you say more about guilt?

Guilt is like everything else. It's just a *word,* and the question is "What *experience* does the word refer to?" For years now people have walked into psychiatric offices of all kinds and said "I have guilt." Therapists have heard the word "guilt" and said "Yeah, I know what you mean." If that same person had walked in and said "I have some X," those therapists wouldn't have made the jump to thinking that they understood what the person meant.

The point we are trying to make about guilt and depression and jealousy and all those other words is that the important thing is to find out *how it works*—find out what the process is. How does someone know when it's time to be guilty as opposed to when it's not time to be guilty? And we said that an example—and this is ONLY ONE example—of how to feel guilty is to make eidetic images of people looking disappointed, and then feel bad about it. There are other ways you can feel guilty. You can make constructed images or you can talk yourself into feeling guilty. There are lots and lots of ways to go about it. It's important with each individual that you find out *how* they do it, if you want to change that process to something else. If the way they make themselves feel guilty is with eidetic images, you can have them change the eidetic image into a constructed image. If they do it with constructed images, you can have them change it into an eidetic one. If they talk to themselves, you can have them sing to themselves.

If you have the sensory refinements to be able to discover the specific steps in the process that the person goes through to create any response which they don't find useful and which they want to change, it gives you multiple points of intervention. The intervention can be as simple as substituting one system for another, because that will break up the pattern.

One woman had a phobia of heights. Our office was on the third story, which was kind of convenient. So I asked her to go over and look out the window and describe to me what happened. The first time she went over, she just choked. I told her that wasn't an adequate description. I had to know how she got to the point of choking and being very upset. By asking a lot of questions, I discovered that what happened is that she would make a constructed picture of herself falling out, have the feeling of falling, and then feel nauseous. She did that very quickly, and the picture was outside of consciousness.

So I asked her to walk over to the window while she sang the National Anthem inside her head. Now that sounds kind of silly, except that she walked over to the window and she didn't have the phobic response! None whatsoever. She'd had the phobia for years and years and years.

A man who was a Cree Indian medicine man, a shaman, came to a workshop and we were discussing different mechanisms that worked cross-culturally as far as inducing change in a rapid and effective way. If a person has a headache, an old semi-gestalt thing to do is to sit them in a chair, have them look at an empty chair, have them intensify the feeling of the pain, and have the intensified pain they are feeling develop into a cloud of smoke in the other chair. Slowly the smoke forms itself into an image of someone they have unfinished business with, and then you do whatever you do. And it works; the headache goes away.

The counterpart for this shaman was that he always carries a blank piece of paper. Whenever anybody comes to him and says "I have a headache, will you assist me?" he says "Yes, of course, but before I begin I want you to spend five minutes studying this piece of paper in absolute detail, because it contains something of great interest for you." The thing in common about those two interventions is that they both involve switching representational systems. You break up the process by which the person is having the experience they don't want to have, by having their attention riveted in some *other* representational system than the one in which they are presently receiving messages of pain. The result is absolutely identical in both cases. By studying the blank piece of paper intently, or by intensifying the feeling and making it change into a picture in the chair, you are doing the same thing. You are switching representational systems, and that is a really profound intervention for any presenting problem. Anything that changes the pattern or sequence of events a person goes through internally—in responding to either internal or external stimuli—will make the response that they are stuck in no longer possible.

We had a man in Marin, California, and every time he saw a snake— no matter how far away it was, no matter where he was in respect to it or who was around it—his pupils would immediately dilate. You had to be close enough to see it. He would make an image of a snake flying through the air. This was outside of awareness until we uncovered it. When he was six years old somebody threw a snake at him un- expectedly and it scared him badly. He then responded kines- thetically as a six-year-old to the internal image of a snake flying through the air toward him. One thing we could have done was to simply change the content of that picture. We could have had him make a picture of someone throwing kisses. What we actually *did* was simply switch the *order* in which the systems occurred. We had him have the kinesthetic response first and then make the picture internally. That made it impossible for him to be phobic.

You can treat every limitation that is presented to you as a unique accomplishment by a human being, and discover what the steps are. Once you understand what the steps are, you can reverse the order in which the steps occur, you can change the content, you can insert some new piece or delete a step. There are all kinds of interesting things you can do. If you believe that the important aspect of change is "understanding the roots of the problem and the deep hidden inner meaning" and that you really have to deal with the content as an issue, then probably it will take you years to change people.

If you change the form, you change the outcome at least as well as if you work with content. The tools that it takes to change form are easier to work with. It's a lot easier to change form, and the change is more pervasive.

Man: What are some questions that you ask to elicit the steps in the process that people go through?

Ask them to have the experience. Ask them about the last time they had the experience, or what would happen if they were to have it right here, or if they remember the last time it happened. Any of those questions will elicit the same unconscious responses we've been showing you here. Whenever I ask a question or make a statement about something to someone here in the group, if you are alert the response will already be made non-verbally much earlier and more completely than the person will consciously be able to verbalize the answer explicitly.

"How do you know when you are being phobic, as opposed to when you are not being phobic?" "How do you know?" questions usually will take you to just about everything. People have a tendency to demonstrate it, rather than bring it into consciousness.

Our book *The Structure of Magic, I* is devoted to what we call the "meta-model." It's a verbal model, a way of listening to the *form* of verbalization as opposed to content. One of the distinctions is called "unspecified verb." If I'm your client and I say to you "My father scares me," do you have an understanding of what I'm talking about? No, of course not. "My father X's me" would be as meaningful. Because for one person "Father scares me" may mean that his father put a loaded .38 to his head. And for someone else it may simply mean that his father walked through the living room and didn't say anything! So the sentence "My father scares me" has very little content. It simply describes that there is some process—at this point unspecified. The pattern, of course, is to be able to listen to language and know when a person has adequately specified some experience with a verbal description.

One of the things we teach with the meta-model is that when you get a sentence like "My father scares me" to ask for a specification of the process that the person is referring to called "scare." "How specifically does your father scare you?" "How specifically do you know you are depressed, or guilty, or phobic?" "Know" is another word like scare.

It doesn't specify the process. So if I say to you "Well, I *think* that I have a problem" that doesn't tell you anything about the process. If you say "*How* do you think it?" initially people will go "*What?!*" But after they get over the initial shock of being asked such a peculiar question, they will begin to demonstrate the process to you, at first non-verbally. They'll go "Well, I just think it." (eyes and head moving up and to his left) Or they'll go "Ah, I don't know. I just, you know, it's just a thought I have." (eyes and head moving down and to his left) The combination of the unspecified verbs that the person is using and the quite elegant non-verbal specification by eye movements and body shifts will give you the answer to the question, whether they ever become conscious of it or not.

If you keep asking questions, usually people will become conscious of their process and explain it to you. Usually people do it with disdain, because they assume that everybody thinks the same way they do, with the same kind of processes. One well-known therapist told us seriously one day "Every intelligent, adult human being always thinks in pictures." Now, that's a statement about *him*. That's the way he organizes a great deal of his conscious activity. It has very little to do with about half the population we have encountered in this country.

Quite often at seminars like this, people ask questions in the following way. They go "What do you do with someone who's depressed?" (pointing at himself) The word "someone" isn't specified, verbally. We say it's a word with no referential index. It doesn't refer to something specific in the world of experience. However, the nonverbal communication was very specific in that case, and people do the same thing with other non-verbal processes. If you are able to identify things like accessing cues and other non-verbal cues, you can be pretty clear about how something works. People will come in and say "Well, I have a problem" and their non-verbal behavior has already given you the sequence that produces it.

So a "How specifically?" question or a "How do you know?" question will usually give you a complete non-verbal specification of the process that the person goes through. *Magic I* has a very complete specification of how to ask appropriate questions using the meta-model.

One of our students taught the meta-model to a hospital nursing staff. So if a patient said "I'm sure I'm going to get worse" or "I can't get up yet," the nurse would ask "How do you know that?" The nurse would then follow that up with other meta-model questions, to help the patient realize the limitations of his world model. The result was that the average hospital stay was reduced from 14 days to 12.2 days.

The whole idea of the meta-model is to give you systematic control over language. When we first took the time to teach it to our students, the result was the following: first there was a period where they went around and meta-modeled each other for a week. Then they began to hear what they said on the outside. They would sometimes stop in midsentence because they would begin to *hear* themselves. That's something else the meta-model does: it teaches you how to listen not only to other people but to yourself. The next thing that happened is that they turned inside and began to meta-model their own internal dialogue. That changed their internal language from being something that terrorized them to being something that was useful.

The meta-model is really simplistic, but it's still the foundation of everything we do. Without it, and without systematic control over it, you will do everything that we teach you sloppily. The difference between the people who do the things that we teach *well* and those that don't, are people who have control over the meta-model. It is *literally* the foundation of everything we do. You can be bright and witty and sharp and make the most complex metaphor in the world, but if you can't gather information well, both internally and externally, you won't know what to do. The meta-model questions are the ones that really give you the appropriate information immediately. It's a great tool for that, both on the outside and the inside. It will turn your internal dialogue into something useful.

When you use language with people, they assume that all the stuff they are accessing on the inside is the same as what you said. There's *so much* going on inside that they have no consciousness of the external form of your communication. You can utter sentences of syntax which have *no* meaning and people will respond to you as if what you said is completely meaningful. I'm surprised that anyone ever noticed that some schizophrenics speak "word salad." I have gone into places and spoken word salad and people have responded to me as if I had uttered perfect English. And of course you can embed crazy commands in word salad.

Once we were having a party at our house and we wanted to buy some champagne. We live in an area where there are no stores, so we went into a restaurant and said "Look, we want to buy a couple of bottles of champagne to take home." And the guy said "Oh, we can't do that. It's against the law." We said "Well, we're having a party and we come here and eat a lot and isn't there anything you can *do something!*" He stopped for a moment, and he said "Wait a second. I think I can do something." So he took the bottles and gave them to himself, and then he went outside behind the restaurant and gave them to us and we tipped him. Our behavior was totally bizarre, but he *had* to respond, because the only thing that was evident in his consciousness was this odd sequence. It's really important to understand that most people are very chaotically organized on the inside.

Man: Does the intellectual level of the client make a difference, say retarded versus genius?

No. I don't know of any. Unconscious minds operate amazingly the same no matter what the educational level or intelligence level is. "IQ" is also a function of the kinds of structures we've been talking about.

Woman: When you ask the person to go through whatever the experience is that troubles them and you watch them, you become aware of what the process is that they go through?

Yes, in a special sense of the word "awareness." There is nothing that I have done here at any point today that I am conscious of, in the normal sense of being reflexively conscious of what I am doing. The first time I know what I'm going to do or say is when I find myself doing it or hear myself saying it. This is an important point. I really believe that the face-to-face task of communicating with another human being, let alone a group of people, is far too complex to try to do consciously. You can't do it consciously. If you do, you break up the natural flow of communication.

Are there any of you who play music? How many people in here can play an instrument? OK. How many of you, when you play something well, play it consciously? ... Exactly. None of you. You are aware of the result, the sounds you are making, but not of the process of making them. And what happens when you become conscious of what you're doing in the middle of playing something? Boom! You mess it up. Yet in order to *learn* to play that very same piece of music, you went through some conscious steps.

As we are communicating to you here, I am aware in the sense that I respond directly. But I have no reflexive consciousness of what I am doing. If I did, I'd do a crummy job.

Let's say you go back into your office Monday morning and a new client walks in and says "I have a phobia of gum chewing." A little voice goes off inside your head and says "Ah! This is an unprecedented opportunity for me to try to do something new." And then you look up and ask the person "Well, when was the last time that you had a *very intense* phobic response?" Then they begin to go through certain eye movements and stuff. If you begin visualizing the blackboard up here, and the list of the accessing cues, and talking to yourself about the things you heard us say, and having feelings about whether you are going to be able to do this or not, you will have no sensory information on which to base what you do. That's the sense in which reflexive consciousness in face-to-face communication is not going to be useful. If you have to tell yourself things, and make pictures, and have feelings while you are doing therapy, probably you will end up doing therapy on yourself. I think that's what happens much of the time. Often therapists are not doing therapy with the other human being in the room. They are doing therapy with themselves. And many clients who change, change by metaphor.

Most people in the field of therapy go to school, but they don't learn anything about people that is relevant to therapy in any way. They learn about statistics: "Three and a half percent of clients are..." But you very rarely have a hundred people walk into your office so that you can work with three and a half of them. So you go to workshops to learn how to do therapy. There are a lot of people who are very good therapists who do workshops but who don't know how they do what they do. They will tell you what they *think* they are doing, thereby distracting you from paying attention to the client they are working with. If you are lucky you will pick up the kinds of cues we're talking about subliminally, and be able to respond out of yourself in some systematic way. However, that doesn't work with a large number of people. There are a large number of people doing therapy unsuccessfully. What you need to begin to do is to restructure your own behavior in terms of paying attention to your clients.

As professional communicators, it seems to me to make a lot of sense for you to spend some time consciously practicing specific kinds of communication patterns so that they become as unconscious and as systematic in your behavior as riding a bicycle or driving a car. You need to train yourselves to be systematic in your behavior, which requires some conscious intervening practice time. So that when you see visual accessing cues and hear visual predicates, you can automatically have the choice of responding by matching, or responding by mismatching, or any combination that you can think of.

In other words, you need a good unconscious systematic repertoire of patterns for each choice point that you have that's going to come up repetitively in your work: How do I establish rapport with this other human being? How do I respond in a situation in which they don't have information consciously and verbally to respond to my question? How do I respond to incongruity? Those are all choice points. Identify what choice points are repetitive in your experience of doing your work, and for each of those choice points, have a half a dozen different responses—at least three, each one of which is unconscious and systematic in your behavior. If you don't have three choices about how to respond to things that occur in the therapeutic situation, then I don't think you are operating out of a position of choice. If you only have one way, then you are a robot. If you have two, you'll be in a dilemma.

You need a solid foundation from which to generate choices. One way to get that solid foundation is to consider the structure of your behavior and your activity in therapy. Pick out points that are repetitive, make sure you have lots of responses to each of those points, then forget about the whole thing. And add one ingredient, a meta-rule which says *"If what you are doing is not working, change it. Do anything else."*

Since consciousness is limited, respect that and don't go "Good, I'm going to do *all* those things that happened in this workshop." You can't. What you *can* do is for the first five minutes of every third interview every day begin by saying "Look, before we begin today there are a couple of things I need to know about your general cognitive functioning. Would you tell me which color is at the top of a stoplight?" Ask questions that access representational systems, and tune yourself for five minutes to that person's responses so that you will know what's happening later in the session under stress. Every Thursday you can try matching predicates with the first client that comes in, and mismatching with the second. That is a way of systematically discovering what the outcome of your behavior is. If you don't organize it that way, it will stay random. If you organize it and feel free to limit yourself to specific patterns and notice the outcome, and then change to new patterns, you will build up an incredible repertoire of responses at the unconscious level. This is the only way that we know of to learn to become more flexible *systematically*. There are probably other ways. This just happens to be the only one we know about now.

Man: It sounds to me as if you are telling us to experiment with our clients. I think I have a professional obligation to—

I disagree. I think you have an obligation to experiment with *every* client to make yourself more skilled, because in the long run you are going to be able to help more people more expediently. If, under the guise of professionalism, you *don't* try to expand your skills and experiment, basically I think you are missing the point and professionalism becomes just one way to limit yourself. Think about "professionalism." If professionalism is a name for a set of things that you *can't* do, then you are restricting your behavior.

In cybernetics there's a law called the Law of Requisite Variety. It says that in any system of human beings or machines, the element in that system with the widest range of variability will be the controlling element. And if you restrict your behavior, you lose on requisite variety.

The prime examples of that are mental hospitals. I don't know about your mental hospitals here, but in California we've got some real whackos in ours, and we have a lot of patients, too. It's easy to distinguish the staff, because the staff has a professional ethic. They have a group hallucination and this group hallucination is more dangerous to *them* than to anyone else, because they believe that they must restrict their behavior in certain ways. Those ways make them act consistently, and the patients don't have to play by those rules. The widest range of flexibility is going to allow you to elicit responses and control the situation. Who's going to be able to elicit the most responses—the psychiatrist who is acting "normal" or the patient who is acting weird? I'd like to give you my favorite example.

We're walking down a corridor in Napa State Mental Hospital in California with a group of resident psychiatrists. We approach a large day room and we are talking in normal tones. As we reach the door and open it and walk in, all of the psychiatrists begin to whisper. So of course we began to whisper too. Then finally we looked at each other and said "Why are we whispering?" And one of the psychiatrists turned to us and whispered "Oh, there's a catatonic in the room. We don't want to disturb him." Now when a catatonic can have requisite variety over a professional, then I join the catatonics.

When you go to California, most therapists have a *different* professional ethic. For example, in order to be a good communicator, you must dress like a farm worker. That's the first rule. The second rule is that you must hug everyone *too* hard. Those people are always laughing at the psychiatrists because they have to wear ties! To me, their behavior is just as restricted and one-dimensional and limited. The trouble with many professional ethical codes, whether they are humanistic, analytic or anything else, is that they limit your behavior. And whenever you accept any "I won't do it," there are people you are not going to be able to work with. We went into that same ward at Napa and I walked over and stomped on the catatonic's foot as hard as I could and got an immediate response. He came right out of "catatonia," jumped up, and said *"Don't do that!"*

Frank Farrelly, who wrote *Provocative Therapy,* is a really exquisite example of requisite variety. He is willing to do anything to get contact and rapport. Once he was doing a demonstration with a woman who had been catatonic for three or four years. He sits down and looks at her and warns her fairly: "I'm going to get you." She just sits there catatonically, of course. It's a hospital, and she's wearing a hospital gown. He reaches over and he pulls a hair out of her leg just above the ankle. And there's no response, right? So he moves up an inch and a half, and pulls out another hair. No response. He moves up another inch and a half, and pulls out another hair. *"Get your hands off me!"* Most people would not consider that "professional." But the interesting thing about some things that are not professional is that they *work!* Frank says that he's never yet had to go above the knee.

I gave a lecture at an analytic institute in Texas once. Before we began, for three hours, they read research to me demonstrating basically that crazy people couldn't be helped. And at the end I said "I'm beginning to get a picture here. Let me find out if I'm right. Is what you are trying to tell me that you don't believe that therapy, the way it's done presently, works?" And they said "No, what we're trying to tell you is that we don't believe that *any* form of therapy could *ever* work for schizophrenics." And I said "Good. You guys are really in the right profession; we should all be psychiatrists and believe that you can't help people." And they said "Well, let's talk about psychotics. People who live in psychotic realities and blah blah blah," and all this stuff about relapses. I said "Well, what kinds of things do you *do* with these people?" So they told me about their research and the kind of therapy they had done. They never did anything that elicited a response from these people.

Frank Farrelly had a young woman in a mental hospital who believed that she was Jesus' lover. You must admit that is a slightly unusual belief. People would come in and she would go "I'm Jesus' lover." And of course they would go "Unnhhh!" and say "Well, you're not. This is only a delusion you're having ... *isn't it?*" If you go into mental hospitals, most mental patients are *very* good at acting weird and eliciting responses from people. Frank trained a young social worker to behave consistently in a certain way and sent her in. The patient went "Well, I'm Jesus' lover," and the social worker looked back and said wryly "I know, he talks about you." Forty-five minutes later the patient is going "Look, I don't want to hear any more of this Jesus stuff!"

There's a man named John Rosen whom some of you have heard of. Rosen has two things he does consistently, and he does them very powerfully and gets a lot of good results. One of the things Rosen does really well, as described by Schefflin, is that he joins the schizophrenic's reality *so well* that he ruins it. That's the same thing that Frank taught his social worker to do.

The psychiatrists in Texas had never tried anything like that before. And when I suggested it to them, they all made faces because it was outside of their professional ethic. They had been trained in a belief system that said "Limit your behavior. Don't join your client's world; insist that they come to yours." It's much harder for somebody who's crazy to come to a professional model of the world, than it is for a professional communicator to go to theirs. At least it's less apt to happen.

Man: You guys are stereotyping a lot of people here!

Of course we are. Words do that; that's what words are for. Words generalize experience. But you *only* need to be offended if *they apply to you directly.*

One of the main places that communicators get stuck is on a linguistic pattern that we call "modal operator." A client says "I can't talk about that again today. That's not possible in this particular group. And I don't think that you're able to understand that, either." When you listen to content, you get wiped out. You will probably say "What happened?"

The pattern is that a client says "I can't X" or "I shouldn't X." If somebody comes in and goes "I shouldn't get angry" what you do if you're a gestalt therapist, is "Say 'I won't.'" Fritz Perls was German, and perhaps those words make a difference in German. But they don't make any difference in English. "Won't" and "shouldn't" and "can't" in English are all the same. It makes no difference whether you shouldn't or you couldn't or you won't, you still *haven't*. It makes no difference whatsoever. So the person says "I won't get angry."

Then if you ask "Why not?" they are going to give you reasons and that's a great way to get stuck. If you ask them "What would happen if you did?" or "What stops you?" you'll go somewhere else more useful.

We published all this in *The Structure of Magic* some years ago, and we ask a lot of people "Have you read *Magic I*?" And they go "Well, laboriously, yes." And we ask "Did you learn what was in it? Did you learn Chapter Four?" That's the only meaningful part of the book as far as I can tell. And they say "Oh, yes. I knew all that." And I say "OK, good. I'll play your client, and you respond to me with questions." I say "I can't get angry." And they say "Ah, well, what seems to be the problem?" instead of "What prevents you?" or "What would happen if you did?" By not having the meta-model responses systematically wired in, people get stuck. One of the things that we noticed about Sal Minuchin, Virginia Satir, Milton Erickson and Fritz Perls is that they intuitively had many of those twelve questions in the meta-model wired in.

You need to go through some kind of program to wire in your choices so that you don't have to think about what to do. Otherwise, while you are thinking about what to do, you will be missing what's going on. We're talking right now about how you organize your own consciousness to be effective in a complex task of communication.

As far as the conscious understanding of the client goes, it's really irrelevant. If the client wants to know what's going on, the easiest way to respond is "Do you have a car? Do you ever have it repaired? Does the mechanic describe in detail what he is going to do before he does anything?" Or "Have you ever had surgery? Did the surgeon describe in detail which muscles were going to be cut, and how he was going to clamp the arteries?" I think those are analogies which are pertinent to respond to that kind of inquiry.

The people who can give you the most detailed and refined diagnosis of their own problems are the people I've met on the back wards of many of the mental institutions in this country and in Europe. They can tell you why they are the way they are, where it came from, and how they perpetuate the maladaptive or destructive pattern. However, that explicit conscious verbal understanding does them no good whatsoever in changing their behavior and their experience.

Now what we would like to do is to make a suggestion. And of course we are only hypnotists, so this is only a suggestion. And what we'd like to do is to suggest to the unconscious portion of each of both of you, whose communication we have been delighted to receive the entire day today, that since it has represented for you at the unconscious level all the experiences which have occurred, both consciously and otherwise, that it make use of the natural process of dreaming and sleep, which will occur tonight as a natural course in your life, as an opportunity to sort through the experiences of today. And represent even more usefully than up to this point the material which you have learned here today without fully realizing it, so that in the days and the weeks and the months ahead you will be able to discover to your delight that you are doing new things. You had learned new things without even knowing it, and you will be delightfully surprised to find them in your behavior. So if you should happen to remember, or not, your dreams, which we hope will be bizarre this evening, allowing you to rest peacefully, so that you can arise and meet us again here alert and refreshed, ready to learn new and exciting things.

See you tomorrow.

II

Changing Personal History and Organization

Yesterday we described a number of ways that you can get rapport with another person and join their model of the world, as a prelude to helping them find new choices in behavior. Those are all examples of what we call *pacing* or *mirroring*. To the extent that you can match another person's behavior, both verbally and non-verbally, you will be pacing their experience. Mirroring is the essence of what most people call rapport, and there are as many dimensions to it as your sensory experience can discriminate. You can mirror the other person's predicates and syntax, body posture, breathing, voice tone and tempo, facial expression, eye blinks, etc.

There are two kinds of non-verbal pacing. One is direct mirroring. An example is when I breathe at the same rate and depth that you breathe. Even though you're not conscious of that, it will have a profound impact upon you.

Another way to do non-verbal pacing is to substitute one non-verbal channel for another. We call that "cross-over mirroring." There are two kinds of cross-over mirroring. One is to cross over in the same channel. I can use my hand movement to pace your breathing movement—the rise and fall of your chest. Even though the movement of my hand is very subtle, it still has the same effect. It's not as dramatic as direct mirroring, but it's very powerful. That is using a different aspect of the same channel: kinesthetic movement.

In the other kind of cross-over mirroring, you switch channels. For example, as I speak to you ... I watch ... your breathing ... and I

79

gauge the ... tempo ... of my voice ... to the rise ... and the fall ... of your chest. That's a different kind of cross-over. I match the tempo of my speech to the rate of your breathing.

Once you have *paced* well, you can *lead* the other person into new behavior by changing what you are doing. The overlap pattern we mentioned yesterday is an example of that. You join the client in their representation of the world and then overlap into a different representation.

Pacing and leading is a pattern that is evident in almost everything we do. If it is done gracefully and smoothly it will work with anyone, including catatonics. Once I was in Napa State Mental Hospital in California, and a guy had been sitting there for several years on the couch in the day room. The only communication he was offering me were his body position and his breathing rate. His eyes were open, pupils dilated. So I sat facing away from him at about a forty-five degree angle in a chair nearby, and I put myself in exactly the same body position. I didn't even bother to be smooth. I put myself in the same body position, and I sat there for forty minutes breathing with him. At the end of forty minutes I had tried little variations in my breathing, and he would follow, so I knew I had rapport at that point. I could have changed my breathing slowly over a period of time and brought him out that way. Instead I interrupted it and shocked him. I shouted "Hey! Do you have a cigarette?" He jumped up off the couch and said "God! Don't do that!"

I have a friend who is a college president. He is living in a delusional reality that he's intelligent and that he has a lot of prestige and all those things. He walks around stiffly, looks gruff and smokes a pipe; he does this whole number. It's a completely delusional reality. The last time I was in a mental hospital, there was a guy there who thought he was a CIA agent, and that he was being held there by the communists. The only difference between them is that the rest of the people in the world are more apt to believe the college president than the psychotic. The college president gets paid for his delusions. In order to pace either of them I'm going to accept their reality. With the college president I'm going to say that "*Since* he's so intelligent and prestigious he will be able to"—and then I'll say whatever I want him to do. If I go to an academic conference and I'm there with all the people who live in the psychotic reality of academia, I am going to pace that reality. I'll present a *paper,* because raw experience wouldn't pace their reality. If there was any experience there, it would just go right by them.

With the psychotic who believes he's a CIA agent I'll open the door, look back, slip in and close the door quickly, and whisper "At last we got through to you! Whew! I almost got caught coming in here! Now, quick, I only have a few minutes to give you these instructions. Are you ready? We have gotten you a cover as a college professor, and we want you to apply for this job and wait until you hear from us. You can do that because you've been trained to do it as an agent, right? Do it well, so that you're not discovered and sent back here. Got it?"

When you join someone else's reality by pacing them, that gives you rapport and trust, and puts you in a position to utilize their reality in ways that change it.

Non-verbal mirroring is a powerful unconscious mechanism that every human being uses to communicate effectively. You can predict by looking at people communicating with each other in a restaurant whether they are communicating well or not by observing their postures and movements.

Most of the therapists I know who mirror do it compulsively. We did a seminar in which there was a woman who was an exquisitely good communicator who mirrored very compulsively. As she was talking with me, I began sliding off my chair, and she literally fell on the floor. If you believe that you have to have empathy, that means that you have to have the same feelings that your client does in order to function well as a therapist. Someone comes in and says "Well, I have this kind of phobic response every time I walk down the street and begin to talk to somebody; I feel like I'm going to throw up, you know. I just feel real nauseous and light-headed and I feel like I'm going to sway...." If you *have* to mirror, you're going to get sick.

How many of you have ever finished a day of doing therapy or educational work and gone home and felt like you took some of the residue home with you? You know that experience. The statistics show about eight years shorter life span for people in therapy than almost any other profession.

If you work with people who are diseased or dying, you don't want to mirror that directly, unless you want a very short career. People in therapy are always talking about pain, sadness, emptiness, suffering, and enduring the tribulations of human existence. If you have to understand their experience by experiencing it, then my guess is you're going to have a really unpleasant time. The important thing is to have a *choice* between direct mirroring or cross-over mirroring. With some-one who breathes normally, pace with your own breathing. With someone who is asthmatic, pace with your hand movement or something else.

Now let's do something with this, and all the things we talked about yesterday. Is there someone here who has a past experience that they think about from time to time, and it makes them have a feeling that they don't want? ...

OK. Linda, this is secret therapy. Your task is always to keep the content of what goes on from the people here. Because if you tell them the content, they will become involved. And if they become involved, it will be harder for them to learn.

Whenever we ask a person to come and make a change here as a demonstration, we will *insist* that they keep the content to themselves. Usually we'll say "I want you to pick a code word, a color, a number, a letter for what you want to change." So the person will say "I want to be able to M" or "I don't want to have to three." That has a couple of positive dimensions. If the outcome we're after is to *teach people how to do what we do,* then we will demand that it be content-free pure process therapy. Then the only things you have available to pay attention to are the pieces of the process. You cannot hallucinate effectively on "number three"—at least not *as* effectively as you can on "assertiveness" or "love" or "trust" or any of those other nominalizations.

In addition it has an extra advantage. If you are in any context in which people know each other, many people are reluctant to work on material which they think might change their relationship with the people who are there. By doing secret therapy you avoid that difficulty because nobody knows what they are working on.

Linda, what do you recall that gives you the unpleasant feeling? Is it a set of images or a voice? OK. She already answered the question nonverbally. If you were watching her eyes, you saw them move up to her left and then down to her right. So she makes an eidetic visual image and then has a feeling about it.

Linda, when you see this image you have certain feelings which are unpleasant to you. Now I'd like you to look at the image and find out if you still get the unpleasant feeling when you look at it now. And I'd like you to do a good job of that. You can close your eyes and really take a good look at it. (Pause. As she experiences the feelings, he touches her right shoulder.) And as you can all see by her responses, Linda is telling the truth: when she sees that picture she feels bad. So there is some past experience that occurred, and things didn't turn out quite the way you would have liked them to. That's an understatement if I've heard right.

Linda: Right. That's exactly right.

So from time to time an image comes into your mind, and when you think about it, you get the same kind of feelings that you had as a result of that experience. Now, I would like you to think what resource you would have needed back then to have made a different response to that situation, a response which would have given you a much more acceptable outcome if you had made it. Wait a minute, because I want to tell you what I mean by "resource." By resource I don't mean some outside help or anything like that. What I mean by a resource is more confidence, more assertiveness, more trust, more caring—any *internal* resource. At this point in time, some time has elapsed; I don't know how much, but during that interval you have gained resources as a human being that you didn't have access to then. I want you to select a resource that would have enabled you to have had a wholly different experience back then. I don't want you to tell me what it is. I just want you to think of what it would be. (Pause. As she thinks of the resource, he touches her left shoulder.)

Did those of you watching notice some changes? Let's call the response she gets from the picture Y, and the new resource that she needed back there we'll call X. Now, let's demonstrate. Which of those two responses is this? (He touches her right shoulder.) ... Now, you should be able to see the color changes, lip size changes, breathing changes, actual trembling in her body, that we have called Y.

Now which response is this? (He touches her left shoulder.) ... Now, when I say that she needs this resource X, I have given you as much information verbally as you ever get from your clients when they tell you what they want. If a client says "I want to be more assertive; I want to be more trusting; I want to be more caring, more respectful of other people," they have given you exactly the same amount of information as saying "I need X." In a way they have given you *less*. Because if they say "I want to be more assertive," you're going to take *your* meaning of assertive and assign it to their behavior. If they say "Well, what I need is some X," you won't run the risk of misunderstanding them. Sometimes I think it would be easier to do therapy in a foreign language that you didn't speak. That way you would not have the illusion that the words you heard had the same meaning for the person who utters them as they have for you. And believe me, that's an illusion.

Now why does response Y occur when I touch her right shoulder? ...

Have you noticed that that occurs? Has anyone in here noticed that? What's going on here? It's really spooko time! Linda, do you believe in free will?

Linda: Yeah.

(He touches her right shoulder.) Now who tightened the muscles around your mouth? *Whose* free will do you believe in? Free will is a funny phrase. It's also a nominalization. When you came up here in response to my request, you made a statement about your own free will. I said "I want somebody up here who makes pictures that they don't want to make." That is a statement that someone is making those pictures and it isn't you. It's your unconscious or your "mother," one or the other.

Now, what's going on? Did anybody make sense out of that?

Woman: When you were asking her to go deep inside of her and see that image, you put your hand on her right shoulder as she was feeling the bad feelings, so she had an association with the touch.

Do you mean to tell me that now every time I touch her on the shoulder like that, she'll have that response? (He touches her right shoulder again, and response Y occurs.)

Man: It sure looks that way. I agree with you.

How could something that powerful be overlooked by modern psychology? Here you are, adult human beings. Most of you have been to college, and most of you are professional communicators. You've learned about human beings and how human beings work. How do you make sense out of this? ...

Does the name Pavlov ring a bell? This is straight stimulus-response conditioning. Linda had a certain experience which was her response to an accessing question that I asked her—namely about this experience that she wants to change. As she fully recovered that experience—and I knew when she had fully recovered it by observing her responses—all I had to do was touch her. That touch is now associated with the entire experience that she recalled. It's the same process as the thing that she wants to change. How is it that when she makes that picture she has a set of feelings automatically? She sees a picture, bam!—she has the unpleasant feeling. It's the same process.

When a person is in a certain state of consciousness such as the experience Y for Linda, you can introduce a new dimension in any sensory system, such as a touch. We call this an "anchor," in this case, a kinesthetic anchor. As long as I repeat that touch with the same pressure at the same point on Linda's body, *and* she has no stronger competing states of consciousness when I begin, it will always re-access that experience. It's straight conditioning. It constitutes, in my opinion, one of the most powerful covert tools that you can use as a therapist or as a communicator. It will get you almost everything. About ninety percent of what goes on in therapy is changing the kinesthetic responses that people have to auditory and visual stimuli. "My husband makes me feel bad." "My wife always makes me angry."

Now let's demonstrate one—and this is only *one* way—to use it. What I'd like you to do, Linda, is to go back to this experience. Close your eyes, and go back to that experience. This time I want you to take this resource with you (He touches her left shoulder.) and I want you to see yourself respond in a whole new way. Go all the way through it until you're satisfied.

What she's doing now is reliving it *with* the new resource available—which wasn't available the first time this happened—until she is satisfied with her response in that situation. We call this process "changing personal history." You go back into your personal history with resources you did not have *then,* taking them with you this time. We don't know what the content of this is, and there's no need for us to. She is reliving the experience now. After this she will have *two* histories, the "real" one in which she didn't have the resource, and the new one in which she *did* have the resource. As long as these are full experiences—and we're guaranteeing that by anchoring—both will serve equally well as guides for future behavior.

Linda: (She opens her eyes and smiles broadly.) I love it!

OK, now, Linda, I would like you to go back and make the old picture again, the one that made you feel bad, and tell me what happens. Observers, what do you see, X or Y? And this is where the sensory experience really counts. You can *do* the therapy but knowing whether or not it worked is the most essential piece.

Man: I see a mixture of X and Y.

What happens in your experience, Linda? When you see that picture, do you feel the same way you did before?

Linda: No, I do not.

Don't reveal any content; just tell us how it's different.

Linda: Uh, my fear is gone.

Now, there's another way to check your work. Anchoring can be used in a number of ways. Now, watch this. (He touches her right shoulder.) Is that the same response that touch elicited before?

Woman: Partially.

Partially. Now, if it were to be entirely reversed, I would consider that doing the client a disservice. If you are in the business of choice, you are in the business of *adding* choices—not subtracting them, and not substituting one rigid stimulus-response circuit for another. If you have a client who feels helpless and small each time he goes to work, and you change that so each time he goes to work he feels assertive, happy, and confident, he is no better off, in my opinion. He still has only one choice about how to respond. And if you have one choice, you're a robot. We think therapy is the business of turning robots into people. That's not an easy task. We all get robotized. Part of your job is to change that situation unconsciously, so that people actually exercise choice in their behavior, whether it's conscious or not.

What is choice? Choice, to me, is having multiple responses to the same stimulus. Do you realize that each time you read a book there are probably no new words in that book? It's the same old words in a new order? Just new sequences of the same words? No matter where you go, you're going to hear the same old words, or just new sequences of the same old words. And each time I read a fiction book, it's the same thing. Practically every word we've used today has been an old word. How can you learn anything new?

Now, we need to do one more thing that's very important. Linda has the choice sitting here in this room. You've all seen that. We want her to also have this choice in other contexts. All of you have had the following experience. You work with a client and you and the client both know that they have new choices. They leave the office and you're happy and they're happy and congruent, and two weeks later when they come back they go "Well, it didn't quite ... I don't know what happened. I knew it ... and I uh ..." Or worse yet they come back and present you with the exact same problem, with very little memory that you even worked on it two weeks ago!

Linda was in an altered state up here. She radically altered her consciousness to go after old experiences, to integrate them with new kinds of resources. The point is—and this was a primary insight of family therapy twenty years ago—if you simply induce changes in an altered state of consciousness known as an institution, or a therapist's office, or a group setting, it's very unlikely that most of your work will transfer the first time. You'll have to do it several times. You have to be sure that the new understandings and learnings, the new behavior, the new choices, transfer out of that altered state of consciousness into the appropriate context in the real world.

There's a very easy process that we call "bridging" or "future-pacing" that connects the new response with the appropriate context. It's another use of anchoring. You know what the new response is, and you know that the person wants it to occur in some context, so you simply ask them the following question: "What is the first thing that you would see, hear, or feel, that would allow you to know you are in the context where you want to make this new choice?"

Linda, there are other situations in your present life that are similar to the one that you saw in those pictures, right?—situations in which you respond the same way you responded to that picture, instead of the way you would like to respond. Now, what I need to know is what allows you to know that a context is similar to that one. Is it something about what you see? Is it the tone of someone's voice, the way someone sounds, the way someone is touching you? ...

Linda: It's the way someone looks.

OK, I want you to *see* what that looks like. And as you see that, each time you see anything similar, you will feel *this*. (He touches the resource anchor.) I want you to remember that you have this particular resource....

That's bridging. It takes a minute and a half or two minutes, and it guarantees that your work will transfer out into the real world. The same stimulus that in the past elicited the maladaptive stereotyped behavior, the feeling that she wants to change, now serves as a stimulus for which the resource is a response. Now she will automatically have access to the new choice in the contexts where she needs it—not just in the office, the group, the institution. This is stimulus-stimulus conditioning.

You're not going to be there to squeeze her shoulder, so you need to make some part of the actual context the trigger for her new behavior. The best thing to use as the trigger is whatever was the trigger for the unwanted behavior. If her boss' tone of voice makes her feel helpless, then make that tone of voice the trigger to access the resources of creativity, confidence, or whatever. Otherwise, if the old anchors that exist are stronger than the new ones that you've created, the old ones will override the new ones.

That is what prompted the development of family therapy. They take a schizophrenic kid and they put him in a hospital and they give him M&M's in the right order and the kid gets better and he's well and normal, happy, learning. Then they put him back in the family and he's schizophrenic again in a matter of weeks. And so they said "Ah!

88

Something in the family keeps the kid the same, so therefore we will treat the whole family." You don't *have* to treat the whole family. That's one way to do it: it's a choice. If you bring the family in, the anchors are there, and you can use them. In fact, I'll demonstrate. You can sit down now, Linda. Thank you.

I'd like two people to come up here and role-play a husband and wife....

Thank you. Larry and Susie. Now as a wife, would you give me some complaints. What does he do or not do?

Susie: He drinks too much beer. He'll never watch football with me.

He'll never watch football with you? And how does that make you feel?

Susie: Mad. Deserted.

Deserted, so what you want is some attention from him.

Susie: Right.

And when you try to get attention from him, what—look at that, he went right up into a visual access. Boom! That's what typically happens. The wife says "I feel I want him to touch me," and the husband goes (looking up) "Well, I don't see how that's useful." Right? And then he comes into the house and says "Look, this place is a mess. I can't stand to see a cluttered house." And she says "But it feels cozy this way."

Now what I'm going to do here is use anchoring. I say "Well, I find that hard to believe, but let me check it out." So I come over here and ask the husband a few rhetorical questions, simply for the purpose of eliciting responses. I say "Larry, let me ask you a question. Are there some times when you feel like you really want to be close to her, give her some attention and some good feelings and really get close to her? Are there times like that?"

Larry: Sure, there are times. (He touches Larry's wrist.)

"Now, I know, based on my past experience as a therapist, that couples usually get in trouble with words, because people are not very good with words. They don't train adults to use words; they don't even train children. So what I'm going to recommend to you, Susie, is that you try the following: I'm going to give you a non-verbal signal to try with Larry for the next two weeks just as a way to find out whether or not he really is open to paying attention to you. What I would like you to do is this: Any time you want five or ten minutes of his undivided attention and some affection, walk up to him and hold him on the wrist like this. OK, and would you do that right now? I want to check and make sure you know what I mean."

"Now, Susie, when you do this, look at him and he will nod or shake his head depending upon whether or not he feels this is an appropriate time to spend some time with you. This way he gets a message from you which is unambiguous, because if you come up to him and say (harsh voice, punching his arm) 'Want to watch football?' he might misinterpret that." I can send this couple off and let them try it. I'll tell her "Now, you're only to use this twice a day." Of course she'll be curious and she will try it. And what's underneath the "non-verbal signal?" *An anchor.* So what will happen? Will he nod "yes" or shake his head "no"?

Now, the first few times when she does this, she'll complete the whole pattern. But pretty soon it will streamline. She'll walk in and just start to reach for him and that will be enough. Pretty soon she'll be able to walk in and just look at him and that will elicit the same response.

Couples get into trouble because they don't know how to elicit responses from one another. The response they *intend* to get is completely different from the one they *actually* get. For instance, say I have a guy here who really wants her to come and comfort him sometimes. So he sits on the end of the bed and stares at the floor. She, of course, assumes that this means that he wants space for himself, so what does she do? She leaves the room. They end up in therapy *seventeen years* later and he says to me "She doesn't support me when I need support." And she says "*I do, too!*" He says "You've never done it in seventeen years when I really needed it." I say "How do you let her know you need it?" He says "Well, when I sit on the end of the bed, I show her." And she says "*Huh!* Oh, I though you wanted to be alone." That's why we say "The response that you get is the meaning of your communication." This is a way that you can get the responses that people want connected with their own behavior. Now when Susie here wants affection, she has a direct way of eliciting that part of him. After you give a couple a few anchors, they begin to do it on their own without ever knowing what happened. They suddenly start getting what they want "mysteriously." That's one way of using anchoring with couples.

Most couples have simply habituated to each other's behavior, and they cease to do anything new with each other. It's not that they are not capable of it, it's that they are so anchored into rigid patterns of interacting that they don't do anything new. Very rarely do I find any serious dysfunction between couples other than having habituated into rigid patterns.

Whenever there are rigid and repetitive patterns or responses that you want to interrupt, you can begin by anchoring something unpleasant or attention-getting, and fire that anchor whenever the pattern or response occurs.

With a couple I saw once, his whole experience in life was making constructed images of possibilities, and her function in life was responding to anything he said by making an eidetic image of something that was similar and talking about how it didn't work. So he would go "I want to make a skylight in the bedroom" and she would say "We were over at so and so's house and their skylight leaked." They never had any other kind of communication. There was nothing else!

I did therapy with these two in my living room. When I came in, I sat down and said "You know, I'm kind of a city kid and living out here in the country I've had some real surprises. Did you know that a rattlesnake came right through my living room, right here, yesterday? Right across the floor. It was the damndest thing." As I said that, I looked down at the floor just behind their chairs and slowly followed an imaginary snake with my eyes as it went across the floor.

Then the couple began to speak. Whenever they would start to argue, I would look down at the floor again and they would stop. I began to anchor their terror of snakes to having that conversation. After about an hour of doing that, they didn't have that conversation any more. It was too unpleasant, because after a while their feelings about snakes became associated with arguing. If you're going to talk to somebody and you know that there's even a possibility that you might need to interrupt them, you can set them up like that before you begin the session.

You can interrupt behaviorally like that, or you can interrupt with words "Oh wait a second! What—" Or you can look at their ankle and say "Are you allergic to bee stings?" That'll get their attention. "Stop! I just thought of something I have to remember to write down."

Anchoring is an amazing thing. You can anchor air and people will respond to it. Any good mime anchors air by his movements, defining objects and concepts in empty space. Recently I was teaching a sales course and somebody said "You always tell us to be flexible. What happens if you try a whole bunch of stuff, and someone responds to you really negatively?" I said "Well the first thing to do is move, and then point to where you were, and talk about how terrible that is."

That's called dissociation. You can go in and try the "hard sell." When you see that they are responding negatively, you can step aside and say "Now, *that* kind of talk puts people off," and try something else.

Those of you who are interested in really becoming more generative, when you get tired of touching people's knees and forearms, understand that anchoring is one of the most universal and generalizable of all the things that we have ever done.

Once I was lecturing to two hundred and fifty fairly austere psychologists, being academic, talking about representational systems and books, and drawing equations. In the middle of my academic lecture I just walked up to the edge of the stage, looked up for a moment, and said "That's weird" and then continued. A little later I looked up and did it again: "Well, that's really weird." I did that a couple more times during my talk, and most of the people in the first four or five rows became fixated, staring at this spot on the ceiling. Then I moved over to the side, and talked right through to them. I could get arm levitation and other unconscious responses.

If people would notice that what they are doing is not working and do something new, then being in a couple would be a really interesting experience. Actually they need to do something even before that. They need to realize what outcome they want, and *then* notice whether or not they are getting it.

One thing that we have done with couples is to take away their ability to talk to each other. "You can't talk to each other any more until I tell you to. If I catch you talking to each other, I'll give you warts." They have to generate new behavior, and they begin to become interesting to each other, if nothing else. Even if they keep the same patterns of behavior, at least they generate some new content. They have to learn new ways to elicit the responses that they want. He wants her to iron a shirt for him, so he comes in and walks up to her and gestures with his hands. So she goes out and gets a piece of bread and butters it for him and brings it back in, right? Now, in the past, when he'd say "Will you iron my shirt?" and she did something else, he would criticize her. "You never do what I want," and so on. Now when he gets the piece of bread, he can't criticize because he can't talk. In order for him to get what he wants, he's got to change *his own* behavior. So he tries again. He hands her the shirt . . . and she puts it on. He's got to keep coming up with new behaviors until he finds one that works. Then I can use that as an example. I can say "Look, even if you do it with words, if what you do doesn't work, try altering *your own* behavior.

As they learn to vary their behavior, they will be establishing new anchors. Only about half of them will be useful, but that still gives them a *lot* of new possibilities in their relationship.

The nice thing about family therapy is that people bring their anchors with them. If you have a child who is responding in a troublesome way, you can observe what he is responding to, because all the primary hypnotic relationships are there. When children have symptomatic behavior, their symptomatic behavior is always a response to something. Anyone's symptomatic behavior is a response to something, and the question is, *what*? If you can change what they are responding to, it's often *much* easier than changing their behavior. You don't always have to know what it is, but it's often very easy to tell. You have a "hyperactive" kid with his parents and for the first five minutes of the session he's not hyperactive. Then the father looks at the mother and says "What are you going to do about this kid?" When the kid immediately starts jumping around, it gives you a mild indication of what he's responding to. But you won't notice that if you're inside making pictures and talking to yourself about which drugs you are going to give him.

Man: What if you have a suicidal kid? How do you look for the stimulus for that? Always depressed, always sitting there—

Well, ninety-nine times out of a hundred, depression will fall into the pattern we already talked about. I wouldn't try family therapy, not until I'd taken care of the suicide part of it. I would try a question like "What resource would you need as a human being to know that you could go on living and have lots of happiness?" and then do what we did with Linda, the "change history" pattern.

Our presupposition is that any human being who comes and says "Help! I need help" has already tried with all their conscious resources, and failed utterly. However, we also presuppose that *somewhere* in their personal history they have had some set of experiences which can serve as a resource for helping them get exactly what they want in this particular situation. We believe that people have the resources that they need, but they have them unconsciously, and they are not organized in the appropriate context. It's not that a guy *can't* be confident and assertive at work, it's that he *isn't*. He may be perfectly confident and assertive on the golf course. All we need to do is to take that resource and put it where he needs it. He has the resource that he needs to be confident and assertive in his business on the golf course, but he has never made that transfer, that connection. Those are dissociated parts of himself. Anchoring, and the integration that occurs with anchoring, will give you a tool to collapse dissociations, so that the person has access to the resource in the context that they need it.

Man: Are there situations where that's not true and the therapist needs to give the person a—

No, I don't know of any.

I'd like to mention something that is relevant for your own learning. There's a phenomenon in the field of psychotherapy which does not seem to occur in some of the other fields that I have worked in. When I teach somebody how to do something and demonstrate that it works, they usually ask me where it *won't* work or what you do about something else. So when I demonstrate how you can work with people who are bothered by images from their past, you ask "When won't it work?"

Now, the interesting thing about that pattern of behavior is that if what I've demonstrated is something that you'd like to be able to do, you might as well spend your time learning it. There are lots and lots of things that we cannot do. If you can program yourself to look for things that will be *useful* for you and learn those, instead of trying to find out where what we are presenting to you falls apart, you'll find out where it falls apart, I guarantee you. If you use it congruently you will find lots of places that it won't work. And when it doesn't work, I suggest you do something else.

Now to answer your question. The limiting case is a person who has had very, very little real world experience. We had a client who had been locked up for twelve years in his parents' house and had only left the house to see a psychiatrist three times a week, and had been on tranquilizers from age twelve to twenty-two. He didn't have much personal history. However, he had twelve years of television experience, and that constituted enough of a resource that we were able to begin to generate what he needed.

Let me reinterpret the question. If you ask a client "How would you like to be?" and they congruently say "I don't know what I want. I really don't. I don't know what resource I would have needed back then," what do you do? You can ask them to guess. Or you can say "Well, if you knew, what would it be?" "Well, if you don't know, lie to me. Make it up." "Do you know anyone who knows how to do this?" "How would you feel if you did know? What would you look like? What would your voice sound like?" As soon as you get a response, you can *anchor* it. You can literally construct personal resources.

For most of the people who come to you, and for all of you sitting here, your personal history is a set of limitations on your experience and behavior in the present. Anchoring, and the construction of new possibilities using anchoring, can literally convert your personal history from a set of limitations to a set of resources.

Another way to answer the question is that if a person hasn't had the direct experience they need as a resource, they have some representation of what it could be, even though it may be other people's behavior. That is, there is a representation within them which they label "other people's behavior" that they don't allow themselves to have. However, it is a representation that's in them. If you can access it fully, you can anchor it. You can do it directly or covertly. "Well, I can't see the images that you are looking at right now, your representation of this friend of yours who knows how to do this, so would you pretend to be that friend to give me an idea of what we are working toward?" "Display that behavior for me so that I can get an idea about how Joe would act." "Show me how you *wouldn't* act." Then anchor it as they do it. That's now a piece of behavior that is as real as any other behavior.

Or you can make them do it. When people tell you "Well, gee, I could never be like that," it's not necessarily true. We had a woman that came in and told us that it was impossible for her to say what she wanted and to assert herself. She couldn't get people's attention. And she was an assertiveness trainer, too, which is interesting. She couldn't go to a regular therapist because it would ruin her reputation. So we told her to wait a second, we were going to go discuss it, and we went out in the living room and read magazines for about two and a half hours until she came flying angrily out of the office "If you don't get back in here, blah blah blah." If you are flexible enough in your behavior, you can elicit what you want right there on the spot. We made the assumption, the presupposition, that this woman knew how to get somebody's attention if a proper context were supplied. We supplied the proper context; she made the move. We just anchored it, and then transferred it to other contexts where she wanted it.

There's a huge advantage to doing it this way. We don't have to decide before we start working with somebody how many parts they have and what the parts do. I think the Michigan TA model is up to nine specific parts: critical parent, natural child, adult, little professor, etc. At theoretical conventions they argue about how many parts a person should have. That's how the TA trainers and therapists instruct themselves about how to organize another person's experience. None of my clients have a "parent," "child" and "adult," *except* the ones that come from a TA therapist. And then they actually have them.

With anchoring, you don't have to decide before you begin the session what the legitimate categories of human experience or communication are going to be. You can simply accept whatever comes up without understanding the meaning of any of it. I don't know what X and Y were for Linda, but I know that I can operate at the process level, without ever knowing the content, and assist her in changing. You don't have to decide beforehand how many parts you are going to allow that person to have. You don't have to demand that your clients be flexible enough to reorganize their experience into *your* categories. You simply accept whatever is offered, anchor it, and utilize it.

Woman: Do you always anchor the negative feeling? Because that's already in her repertoire.

We don't *always* do *anything*. It's often useful to anchor the response a person doesn't want, and there are several ways to use it. You've all had the experience of beginning to work with a client on a particular problem—especially children, because children are so fluid in their consciousness—and suddenly you discover you are doing something else. The initial anchor that I established stabilized the thing we were going to work on, so we can always go back to it. If I had wanted to go back and find out where it came from in Linda's personal history, that anchor would have given me an excellent way to do it.

In gestalt therapy if a client is troubled by a feeling, the therapist will say "Intensify the feeling, stay with the feeling, exaggerate it! Go back through time ... and what do you see now?" The therapist is stabilizing one part of the person's experience, namely the kinesthetic component, the feelings that person has. And they are saying "Keep those constant, and then let them lead you back in your own personal history to a full, all-system representation of what we are working on." By using an anchor you can always get back to the same set of kinesthetic responses that you began with, and thereby easily stabilize what you are working on. That's one use.

Another use that I demonstrated is testing. After we had done the integration work, after she had the resource and relived the experience with the resource so that she changed her personal history, I gave her a few moments, and then I reached over and triggered the original anchor. The response I got was an integrated response, thereby informing me non-verbally that the process had worked. I recommend that you never let the client know you are checking your work that way. It gives you a covert, non-verbal way of checking to make sure that your integrations have worked before the person leaves your office. Given our historical development in humanistic psychology, most of you want verbal, explicit, conscious kinds of feedback. That is the *least* useful kind of feedback you can get from your client.

Now I'd like you to realize that there is *nothing* that your client will do that you won't anchor. As long as you are going to anchor it, you might as well know what the anchor is. If the client comes in and says "I'm really depressed" and you just go "umhm," that's as adequate an anchor as touching them on the arm. And since you will be doing that, you might as well know which anchor is which. We recommend to people in the beginning that they practice using kinesthetic anchors for a period of a month. As they do that, they will discover that they are anchoring anyway, constantly, in all representational systems. Most of the time people use anchors in a way that slows down the process of change, because they don't know what they are anchoring or how they are anchoring.

There is another important point. When you say "Do you always anchor the *negative* thing?" there was nothing "negative" about it. "Negative" is a judgement about experience. It is not experience itself; it's a judgement specifically made by the person's conscious mind. The experience that Linda had which was unpleasant now serves for her, as well as for everyone else in this room, as a foundation for your learning in the future if you use it that way. If you grew up for the first twenty years of your life without a single unpleasant experience, you would be dull and unable to cope with anything. It's important that you understand that all experiences can serve as a foundation for learning, and it's not that they are positive or negative, wanted or unwanted, good or bad.

As a matter of fact, it's not even that they *are*. Pick any experience that you believe happened to you, and I will guarantee you that on close examination it didn't. The original personal history that Linda relived, re-experienced today as she went through the experience, is as much a myth as the new experience she went through with the resource. The one we made up is as real as the one she "actually had." Neither one of them actually occurred. If you want a demonstration of this, wait two or three months, remember about having been here for three days and then look at that videotape that they are making now. You will discover there is very little relationship between it and your memories of "what happened here." Since your personal history is a myth anyway, *use it as a resource* instead of a set of limitations. One way to do that is with anchoring.

Those of you who have done TA "redecision" work as a client: remember all those vivid scenes and experiences that you so well recollected from when you were two years and eight months old?

Woman: Well, mine really happened.

Nothing ever *really* happened. The only thing that happened is that you made a set of perceptions about events. The relationship between your experience and what *actually* occurred is tenuous at best. But they really are your perceptions. Doing a redecision about an experience that never occurred is just as valuable as—perhaps *more* valuable than—doing a redecision about one that did occur, especially if it's less painful, and especially if it opens more choices. I could very easily install memories in you that related to real world experiences that *never* occurred and could *not* be documented in any way—that were just bizarre hallucinations out of my fantasy. Made-up memories can change you just as well as the arbitrary perceptions that you made up at the time about "real world events." That happens a lot in therapy.

You can also convince your parents. You can go back and check up with your parents and convince them of things that never actually occurred. I tried that, and it worked. My mother now believes she did things to me when I was a child that never happened. And I *know* they never happened. But I convinced her of it. I told her I went to a therapy group and I made these changes which were really important to me, and it was all based on this experience when I was little. As I named the experience, she had to search through her history and find something that approximated it. And of course we had enough experience together that she could find something that was close enough that it fit that category.

It's the same as if I sit here and say "Right now, as you sit there, you may not be fully aware of it, but soon you will become aware of a sensation in one of your hands." Now, if you don't, you are probably *dead.* You are bound to have *some* sensation in one of your hands, and since I called your attention to it, you'll have to become aware of any sensation. Most of the things that people do as therapies are so general that people can go through their history and find the appropriate experiences.

You can do marvelous "psychic" reading that way. You take an object that belongs to someone and hold it in your hand. That allows you to see them really well with your peripheral vision. You speak in the first person so that they will identify directly and respond more, and say something like "Well, I'm a person who ... who is having some kind of trouble that has to do with an inheritance." And then you watch the person whose object it is and that person goes "An inheritance!" Right? And then he goes "Ummmmmmmm" through all his memories, right? And somewhere in his life there was something that had to do with some inheritance and he goes "You're right! Uncle George! I remember now!"

Peripheral vision is the source of most of the visual information I find useful. The periphery of your eye is physiologically built to detect movement far better than the foveal portion of your eye. It's just the way it's constructed. Right now I'm looking in your direction: if there were a trajectory, my eyes would be on you. That just happens to put everyone else in my peripheral vision, which is a situation that is effective for me. As I'm talking, I'm watching the people in the room with my peripheral vision to detect large responses, sudden movements, changes in breathing, etc.

For those of you who would like to learn to do this, there is a little exercise that is quite easy. If I were helping Jane here to learn to have confidence in her peripheral vision, the first thing I would have her do is to walk up to me and stand looking away from me at about a forty-five degree angle. Now without changing the focus of your eyes, Jane, either form a mental image of where you think my hands are, or put your hands in a position that closely corresponds. Now look to verify whether you are correct or not. And now look back over there again, and do it again. Once she can do this at forty-five degrees, then I'll move to ninety. You are already getting all the information you need in your peripheral vision. But nobody has ever told you to trust that information and use it as a basis for your responses. Essentially what you are doing with this exercise is teaching yourself to have confidence in the judgements that you're probably *already* making by getting information through your peripheral vision. This exercise is a stabilized situation. That's the most difficult. Movements are *much* easier to detect. If you can get position information, the movement stuff will be easy.

This is particularly important in conference work, or in family therapy. I don't pay attention to the person who is actively communicating verbally; I'll watch anyone *else*. Anyone else will give me more information than that person, because I'm interested in what *responses* s/he is eliciting from other members of the family or the conference. That gives me lots of choices, for instance, about knowing when they are about to be interrupted. I can either reinforce the interruption, make it myself, or interrupt the interruptor to allow the person to finish. Peripheral vision gives you much more information, and that's a basis for choices.

Your personal history serves as a foundation for all your capabilities and all your limitations. Since you only have one personal history, you have only one set of possibilities and one set of limitations. And we really believe that each of you deserves more than one personal history to draw upon. The more personal histories you have, the more choices you'll have available to you.

A long time ago we had been trying to find expedient ways of helping people to lose weight. Most of the vehicles that were available at that time didn't seem to work, and we discovered that there were some real differences between the way people have weight problems. One of the major things we discovered is there were a lot of people who had *always* been fat. There were other people who had *gotten* fat, but there were a lot of them who had *always* been fat. When they got skinny, they freaked out because they didn't know how to interact with the world as a skinny person. If you've always been fat, you were never chosen first to be on a sports team. You were never asked to dance in high school. You never ran fast. You have no experience of certain kinds of athletic and physical movements.

So instead of trying to get people to adjust, we would simply go back and create a whole new childhood and have them grow up being a skinny person. We learned this from Milton Erickson. Erickson had a client whose mother had died when she was twelve years old, and who had been raised by a series of governesses. She wanted to get married and have children, but she knew herself well enough to know that she did not have the requisite background to respond to children in the ways that she wanted to be able to respond to them. Erickson hypnotized her and age-regressed her into her past and appeared periodically as the "February Man." The February Man appeared repeatedly throughout her personal history, and presented her with all the experiences that she needed. We simply extended this further. We decided that there was no need to just appear as the February Man. Why not March, April and May? We started creating entire personal histories for people, in which they would have experiences which would serve as the resources for the kinds of behaviors that they wanted to have. And then we extended it from weight problems to all kinds of other behaviors.

We did it once with a woman who had grown up being asthmatic. At this time, she had three or four children who wanted to have pets. She had gone to a very fine allergist who insisted that she wasn't allergic to animals as far as he could tell. If he tested her without telling her what the skin patches were, she didn't come out being allergic to animals. However, if you put an animal in her presence, or told her that one had been in the room recently, she had a very strong allergic reaction. So we simply gave her a childhood of growing up without being asthmatic. And an amazing thing happened: not only did she lose her allergic response to animals, but also to the things she had been found to be allergic to by the skin-patch testing.

Woman: How long does that take, ordinarily, and do you use hypnosis for that?

Richard: *Everything* is hypnosis.

John: There's a profound disagreement between us. There is no such thing as hypnosis. I would really prefer that you didn't use such terms, since they don't refer to anything.

We believe that *all* communication is hypnosis. That's the function of every conversation. Let's say I sit down for dinner with you and begin to communicate about some experience. If I tell you about some time when I took a vacation, my intent is to induce in you the state of having some experience about that vacation. Whenever *anyone* communicates, they're trying to induce states in one another by using sound sequences called "words."

Do we have any official hypnotists here? How many of the rest of you know that you are unofficial hypnotists? We've got one. And the rest of you don't know it yet. I think that it is important to study official hypnosis if you are going to be a professional communicator. It has some of the most interesting phenomena about people available in it. One of the most fascinating things you will discover once you are fully competent in using the ritualistic notions of traditional hypnosis, is that you'll never have to do it again. A training program in hypnosis is not for your clients. It's for *you,* because you will discover that somnambulistic trance is the rule rather than the exception in people's everyday "waking activity." You will also discover that most of the techniques in different types of psychotherapy are nothing more than nypnotic phenomena. When you look at an empty chair and start talking to your mother, that's a "deep trance phenomenon" called "positive auditory and visual hallucination." It's one of the deep trance phenomena that defines somnambulism. Amnesia is another pattern you see everywhere.... What were we talking about?

I remember one time about two months after I entered the field and started studying it, I was sitting in a room full of adults in suits and ties. And a man there was having them talk to empty chairs. One of them said "I feel foolish" and I burst into laughter. They all looked at me as if *I* was crazy. They were talking to people who *weren't there,* and telling me that *hypnosis is bad*!

One of the things that will help people to learn about being good therapists is to be able to look at what they do and listen to it and realize how absurd most of what is going on in therapy is. That doesn't mean it doesn't work, but it still is definitely the major theater of the absurd at this time. And when I say absurd, I want you to separate the notion of absurdity from the notion of usefulness, because they are two entirely different issues. Given the particular cultural/economic situation in the United States, therapy happens to be an activity which I think is quite useful.

To answer the other half of your question, we don't ordinarily create new personal histories for people anymore. We have spent three hours doing it. And we have done it fifteen minutes a week for six weeks, and we trained somebody to do time distortion once, and did it in about four minutes. We programmed another person to do it each night as they dreamed. We literally installed, in a somnambulistic trance, a dream generator, that would generate the requisite personal history, and have her recall this in the waking state the next day, each day. As far as I know, she still has the ability to create daily a personal history for anything she wants. When we used to do change work with individuals, a session for us could last anywhere from thirty seconds to seven or eight hours.

We have a different situation than you do. We are modelers. Our job is to test all the patterns we have, so that when we do a workshop, we can offer you patterns that we have already verified are effective with all the presenting problems that we *guess* you are going to have to cope with.

We trained a group of people who work at a mental health clinic. The director took lots and lots of training with us and they do this kind of work in the clinic. They are supported by the state; they don't make their living from client money. They now average six visits per client and they have almost no returns. Their work lasts.

One of the interesting things is that the guy who directs the clinic also has a part-time private practice. In his private practice he is apt to see a client twelve or fifteen times instead of six times. And it never dawned on him what caused that. The same patterns that you can use to change somebody quickly and unconsciously can be used to hook them and keep them as patients. That's a strange thing about therapy: The more effective you are, the less money you make. Because your clients get what they want and leave and don't pay you anymore.

Woman: I have a patient who can't stand to be touched, because of a rape experience. How should I anchor her?

You can anchor in any system. But I would recommend that you *do* touch her, because that's a statement about her limitations. You can begin by accessing some really pleasant experience in her and anchoring that, and then expanding your anchor a little bit at a time until she can enjoy being touched. Otherwise she's going to respond like that for the rest of her life. If you respect her limitations, I think you are doing her a huge disservice. That's the very person that you want to be able to be touched without having to recall being raped. And of course your sequencing is important. You start with a positive frame. For example, you can start by talking with her, *before therapy begins,* about a vacation or something else pleasant, and when you get the response, anchor it. Or you can check to make sure that at least some time in her life she had a pleasant sexual experience, and anchor that.

Man: Do you have to anchor as obviously as you have been demonstrating?

We are being very obvious and exaggerated in our movements as we are anchoring here because we want you to observe the process and learn as the changes occur. If we had brought Linda up here and anchored her auditorily, with voice tonalities, you'd have *no* idea what we did. The more covert you are, the better off you will be in your private practice. You can be very covert in the way you touch. You can use tones of voice. You can use words like "parent," "child," and "adult," or postures, gestures, expressions. You can't *not* anchor, but most people aren't systematic.

Anchors are everywhere. Have you ever been in a classroom where there's a blackboard and somebody went up to the blackboard and went—(He pantomimes scraping his fingernails down the blackboard. Most people wince or groan.) What are you doing? You're crazy!

There's no blackboard. How's that for an anchor?

We first noticed anchoring as we watched other people do therapy. The client comes in and says "Yeah, man, I've been just down in the dumps for seven years, and ..." The therapist leans over and puts his hand on the client's shoulder and says "I'm going to put the full force of my skills behind the changes that we will work toward together in this session." And then the therapist does some really good work. The client changes, and feels really good. Then the therapist says "That really pleases me" and as he does he leans forward and puts his hand on the client's shoulder again. Whammo, that anchor accesses the depression again.

I've seen a therapist take away a phobia and give it back *nine* times in a single session, without having the faintest idea what she was doing. At the end of the session she said "Well, we'll have to work more on this next time."

Do yourself a favor. Hide yourself where you can see your clients make the transition from the street to your office. What happens is a miracle. They are walking down the street, smiling, feeling good. As they enter the building, they start accessing all the garbage that they are going to talk about, because the building is an anchor. You can't *not* anchor. It's only a question of whether you do it in a *useful* way or not.

We know an old Transylvanian therapist who solved the problem by having two offices. He has one office in which you come in and you tell him all your troubles. And then he says nothing to you; he just stands up and takes you into the next room and does change work. And then pretty soon he just takes you into the other room and you change; you don't have to go through the personal history which has all the pain and suffering.

When couples have been together for a while they usually end up not touching each other much. Do you know how they do that? Let me show you. Come up here, Char. This is a good way to alienate your loved ones. You're in a really bad mood, really depressed. And I'm your loving husband, so I come up and I go "Hey, it's going to be all right," and put my arm around your shoulders. Then all I have to do is wait until you're in a good mood and really happy, and come up and say "Hey, you want to go out?" and put my arm around you again. Boom! Instead of touching each other when they are happy and making all kinds of great anchors, couples usually anchor each other into unpleasant states.

All of you who have done work with couples or families know you can be sitting there and everything is going along nicely and suddenly one of them explodes. If you didn't happen to notice the little sound, or the movement, or the body sway away from the other person, it's baffling. What happened? Nobody knows. The anchors that people are responding to in "maladaptive behavior" are usually outside of their awareness.

There's a great exercise you can do. Get together with a family or a couple, wait until one of those explosions happens, and detect what you think was the cue that initiated the explosion. Then adopt it in *your* behavior, and find out if you can get them to explode again. If you can get them to explode, you know you've identified exactly the key point in their interaction. Let's say it's a raised eyebrow. Then all you have to do is anchor a pleasant response kinesthetically, and then fire off that anchor and raise your eyebrow at the same time. In the future when someone raises their eyebrow, it won't have that effect any more.

You can also use anchoring in the context of an organization or a corporation. They are just like families, basically. If you know ahead of time that a group of people is going to get together and they've been meeting for years, they're going to disagree in patterned ways. One of the things you can do is to meet with each of them individually beforehand, and establish a covert non-verbal anchor to change the most salient irritating parts of their non-verbal communication.

Some people have voice tones that when you hear them you just feel bad and disagreeable, no matter what they say. Nobody could continue to talk that way if they had auditory feedback loops. If they could hear themselves, they would talk differently. I guess it's a protective device.

Bullfrogs do that. A bullfrog makes such a huge sound, it would deafen itself if it heard itself, because its ear is so close to the source of that loud noise. The nerve impulses for the sound, and the nerve impulses from the muscles that make the sound, arrive at the brain 180 degrees out of phase and cancel each other. So the bullfrog never hears itself. And it seems like a lot of people I meet operate the same way.

Another thing that often happens in a corporate situation is this: Somebody becomes *so* excited about a point they want to make that he begins to really push and gesture. Suddenly the person on the other side sees the pointing finger and the intense look on his face and that triggers an anchored response in them. Away they go. Their response is partially to this human being in this time and place, and a whole lot to other times and places—anchored by the excited face and the pointing finger. Human beings operate in what we call a "mixed state" most of the time. If I ask you to look around and find someone in this group who reminds you of someone else, I will guarantee that your responses to that person will be a mixture of responses to them here and now, and old responses to whoever it is they remind you of—unless you are very, very careful and clean in your responses to that person. You are all sensitive to that process; it's called a "contaminated" response in TA, and it's a common way that people respond.

Woman: Does it make any difference whether you touch the right or left side of the body when you anchor kinesthetically?

There are fine distinctions—there's a lot of artistry. But for the purposes of doing therapy, you don't need to know about them. If you want to be a magician, it's a different game. If you want to create artificial credit cards that aren't there, and things like that, there are certain useful kinds of distinctions. But for the purpose of doing therapy, kinesthetic anchors are adequate, and either side of the body will be as good.

Sometimes it helps to be able to anchor tonally. Virginia Satir anchors tonally. She has a certain tone of voice she uses whenever she does change work. She talks in a regular tonality for six hours, and then suddenly she changes her tonality. When she uses that tonality, boom! that's it. The people change. Erickson has a special tonality he uses when he wants people to go into trance.

A lot of people in trance have their eyes closed. What does Erickson do for anchoring at that point, since he's in a wheel chair and he can't reach around and do kinesthetics? Close your eyes for a moment. I'm going to talk, and as I talk I'm going to move my head back and forth. I want you to notice whether you can detect the spatial dislocation of my voice, even from this distance. If you can, fine. If you can't, you detected it unconsciously I'll guarantee you, because that's one of the major anchoring systems that Erickson uses with people who have their eyes closed in trance.

All of those will work. The choice you make about what system you anchor in will determine the kind of response you get. If you want to involve the person's consciousness, anchor in all systems. If you want to be covert and go around a resistant conscious mind, anchor in any system that is *not* represented in consciousness. If the person's predicates and their eye movement patterns give you the information that they are primarily kinesthetic, don't anchor in that system unless you want their conscious resources involved. If you anchor that same person tonally, they will have no conscious representation of it.

106

Anchoring Exercise

We are going to ask you to begin with kinesthetic anchors. They seem to be the easiest to learn, and the most useful. You'll generalize naturally from those. You can anchor in any system. Pair up again, A and B. You are both going to operate in both positions.

A, your job is to do the following: Face B, and place your right hand lightly on B's left knee. Then ask an accessing question: "Do you remember the last time that you had a really good sexual experience?" Wait for an appropriate response. You've got to be able to detect a response before you can anchor it. As you begin to see changes, you begin to apply pressure with your hand. You observe the changes in the parameters of muscle tone, skin color, breathing, lip size, etc. As you detect them, let those actually drive the pressure in your hand. When the changes level out, then you just lift your hand off. Then you will have a perfectly timed anchor. Don't anchor initially until you can see a difference in your partner's response.

Your ability to see a difference depends on how forceful you are in amplifying what you are getting. If you do things like this: (low, slow voice) "Have you ever been really excited?" or (high, quick voice) "Have you ever been really sad?" that won't work as well as if you congruently say excitedly "Look, have you ever been really excited?" The more expressively you access, the more expressively they will respond.

Then you place your left hand on their right knee, and ask them "What in your experience is the *opposite* of that?" They will access whatever is the opposite, for them. As the changes occur, again you increase the pressure as you see the changes until they plateau, and then lift your hand off.

Then you have two anchors. What we want you to do is to use one, and notice the changes. Pause, and then use the other one, and notice the changes. It works even better if you distract your partner's consciousness with something neutral, like "Do you remember seeing the lights as we came into the building?" as you use that anchor. See if you can regularly get the same response when you use your anchors.

When you are satisfied that you have two anchors that work, and you can see the difference between them, then we want you to hold both at the same time, for about 30–60 seconds, and watch an amazing event, called "integration." Watch your partner's face. You will first see half of the face with one of those responses and the other half with the other, and then they will integrate. Anchors are not buttons; you have to hold them until you see the full response. Once the integration begins, you don't have to hold any more.

The purpose of this exercise is not to do therapy with your partner. The purpose is simply for you to verify with your own sensory apparatus that anchors exist, and that you are capable of anchoring. All you are doing is learning to anchor. This afternoon we'll teach you how to use it to do therapy. Go ahead.

* * * * *

There was one question that came up repeatedly during the exercise. Bill said "Well, I was imagining a time with my wife that was extremely sensually pleasurable there on the one knee. And on the other knee, I was remembering a time when she didn't seem to be willing to be with me, or the demands of keeping the house, etc. didn't allow us time to sit down together, and I got angry." Bill's partner was able to get the two distinctly, and to go back and reaccess them; the anchoring worked fine. He collapsed the two anchors and the integration occurred. And their question is "What will happen now when he sees his wife?" The answer to this is really important insofar as our understanding of our work goes. What will happen now is that when he sees his wife, he will have the *choice* of those purely sensual, pleasant feelings in the past, *or* the feelings of anger from the past, *or*—and this is very important— *any combination of the two.*

Those were two antagonistic, dissociated feeling states in the past. When you anchor each one, you also anchor the antagonistic physiology, muscle patterns, breathing, etc. Then when you stimulate both at the same time, the physiological patterns which are antagonistic literally interrupt each other—you could see that in the person's face, in their breathing, and so on. In the process they become integrated so that the person can come up with *any* combination of those feelings which were previously dissociated, and respond appropriately in context. The presupposition behind our behavior in this area is that given a set of choices, a person will always make the best choice that they have *available* in the context. I think it's entirely appropriate for anyone to have the ability both to be fully sensual with another person as well as to be angry, *and* all the mixes in between. By integrating in this way, using anchoring as an integrative device to break down the dissociations, we make sure that you have a full range of response in that area.

One of the lies we told you was that the anchoring exercise you did is not therapy. "You are just going to anchor this here and that there and then you are going to collapse the two and integrate them." I want you to think about that. What you did with the knee anchors and the integration is formally identical to gestalt two-chair work. Gestalt people use chairs as anchors and when you switch from one chair to the other, your feelings actually change. If you were on the outside as the therapist, you would actually see facial, postural and color changes as the person moved from one chair to the other. Those chairs are anchors. The problem is that it's hard to get integration. How do you push the chairs together? So you have to make people go back and forth really fast.

Now we'd like you all to pair up again and do the "changing personal history" pattern that we did this morning with Linda. I'll review it briefly:

First, what response does your partner have now that s/he wants to change? Anchor that to stabilize the situation, and to give you access to it.

Now, how would you like to behave, or what resource would you need, to behave in a way that's more congruent with your present resources? When you originally went through this experience, you didn't have all the resources you now have. Which resource would you take back to change your personal history? When have you had an experience of that resource? Anchor the response.

Then put the two together. Hold both anchors as your partner goes back and relives the past with the new resource, changing and creating new old history, until s/he is satisfied. Here your sensory experience is important. Check for congruency. Did you like the way it turned out? If not, do it again. What *other* resource do you need? Sometimes you have to give people a couple of resources. Or sometimes people think that all they needed is a certain resource and they take it and go back and it turns out to be a dud. The conscious mind has a limited understanding of what's needed back there. The only way you're going to find out is by having them go back to re-experience parts of their personal history.

After they are satisfied that they have a new resource that worked back there, you need to bridge, or future-pace. What experiences in your present life are sufficiently similar to that old one to trigger the unwanted response? What is the first thing you see, hear, or feel that lets you identify this kind of situation? Then anchor the new resource to those contextual cues. OK. Go ahead.

* * * * *

There are many, many useful ways of organizing the whole process called psychotherapy. One of the ways that is quite simple, and therefore elegant, is to treat every psychological limitation like a phobia. A phobia can be thought of as the paradigm case of psychological limitation. A person who has a phobia made a decision, unconsciously, under stress, sometime earlier in their life in the face of overwhelming stimuli. They succeeded in doing something that humans often have a hard time doing. They succeeded in one-trial learning. Every time that set of stimuli comes up again later in their life, they make *exactly* the same response. It's a remarkable achievement. You change over the years, and despite external contextual changes, you are still able to maintain that stimulus-response arc.

The thing that makes phobias sort of interesting is the fact that the responses are so consistent. If a person says "I can't be assertive around my boss," they are essentially saying "Somewhere in my personal history I have an experience or a set of experiences of being assertive. I cannot get to that resource in the context of my boss." When a person responds with a phobic response to a snake, that's a similar situation. I know that at other times in their experience, in their personal history, they have been able to be quite calm and courageous. However, in the context of a snake, they can't get to that resource.

Up to this time in the development of psychology and psychiatry and counseling, people haven't tried to organize information to go directly after things. Freud set up a rule "You must go into history," so we've decided if you can understand how something developed historically, you can work with it. I think you only need to do that once or twice, though. Given that you understand, historically, how people are capable of creating phobias, you don't need a historical understanding of each and every phobia, as long as you understand that there are similar processes at work. The way in which people get phobias is fascinating. However, once you understand something about the structure you can go ahead and change it, because all phobias are going to work in the same way. People have strategies which produce phobic responses. Who here has a phobia?

Woman: I've got one about driving a car across a bridge and falling in the car into the water.

If you were observing her, everything that you need to know about changing her has already happened. Would you like to get rid of it? Is it something that restricts your behavior?

Woman: Oh, I'd love to get rid of it!

Are you sure?

Woman: Of course. Yeah, I'm sure. I just wasn't sure I wanted to share it, but I've already shared it!

But you didn't need to share it! You could have kept it a secret. We don't need any content. In fact, we prefer not to have any. Is there someone else here with a phobia who would be *un*willing to talk about it? Any time we ask for volunteers, you keep the content to yourself. None of you knew what Linda was thinking about this morning. That's the format we'll always use for demonstrations, so feel free to demonstrate. One way for us to respect your integrity as human beings, whether it's in private practice or in a group demonstration like this, is for you to keep the content to yourself. We don't need it. We operate with process anyway. Content is irrelevant, and besides that, it's often depressing. We don't want to hear it. And when you tell people the content of your problem, you look like a fool. It's a good thing we interrupted you before you told them what the content was, right? OK. What's your name?

Woman: Tammy.

Tammy. Very good. (He contorts his body and several different intense expressions pass across his face.) Any weird non-verbal analogue is good, especially if you get clients who have been in therapy before. You need to do something to throw them off balance— anything to break up their patterns. Because otherwise they will come in and tell you the same thing they told everyone else. They will come in and tell you a prerecorded message. We once heard a tape recording of a client with the therapist before us, and in the whole first session with us she said exactly the same thing; the same words in the same order. We were fascinated to find out how much she could reproduce. It was almost identical until we intervened in the process. I jumped up and started roaring about God. "God said '*You will change!*'" The easiest way to do therapy is to enter the client's reality. This woman was extremely religious, and the easiest way to assist her in making a change was to make myself an intermediary between God and her. That's what all priests do, isn't it? It was acceptable to her. All I did was feed back information that she had given to me from her unconscious—which were the instructions she needed.

Now, Tammy, let's pretend that we don't know that this is about bridges. Would you give me a code word for the phobic response that you have had for some years?

Tammy: Pink.

Pink. She's phobic of pink. Now you have as much information as when she says "I'm afraid of driving across bridges." You still have no idea what the response is, where it came from, or what the dimensions are internally and externally. Secret therapy and code words vividly point out the illusion of understanding another person when they use words that do not refer to sensory-based descriptions.

Now, before we begin, let me ask you something, Tammy. Would you think of a situation in which you expressed yourself with what you regard as a fine representation of your full capabilities as an adult human being, as a mature woman. Sometime in the past few years—it may have been a stressful situation or maybe just a happy occasion— you behaved in a way that you found particularly satisfying. I want you to take your time and find such a situation, and let me know when you have it. Do you understand the request? (She nods.) ...

OK. First of all, I hope you all noticed a distinct change in her face, in her breathing, etc. Those of you who were watching her could see that Tammy constructed a visual image. She searched visually and she went up and to her right. She is a normally organized right-hander, cerebrally. She didn't see the situation from *inside* of it. She saw herself in the situation. As such, her kinesthetic response was not as strong as it would be if she did the following.

Would you make that image of yourself again, and when you see it clearly, I want you to step *inside* the image so that you are actually back in that situation that represents for you an example of your full capacity as a woman. When you can actually feel in your body again the feelings of competence and strength that you associate with that situation, just reach over with your left hand and hold my hand....

OK. I have no idea what her specific experience is. I *do* know, however, from the remarkable, dramatic change that Tammy just offered me non-verbally, that she succeeded in carrying out my instructions. And I agree with her. That looks really good. That fits my hallucinations about what competence, etc. is. Tammy, do you happen to know what the original experience was that this phobia is connected to?

Tammy: No, I don't.

OK, that's typical. It's typical that the person only knows that in certain kinds of situations they have a very powerful kinesthetic response—in fact in your case I would describe it as an overwhelming response. That response is so overwhelming that in the past when you have been in these situations you literally exercise no choice. You have found it to restrict your behavior in the past, right?

Tammy: Oh, yes—in my dream world, too.

Most phobic people do not know what their original trauma was, and, indeed, it is not even necessary to know that. I'm going to do it as if it were necessary, but it's just part of the mythology.

Tammy has succeeded for years in making the same response over and over and over again. She has demonstrated adequately that she knows how to do *that*. A phobia can be thought of as nothing more than a one-trial learning that was never updated. And it worked, by the way. I will often turn right to the person and say this: I want to reassure the part of you that has been making you phobic all these years that I respect what it has done, and I regard that as a valid response. You're here. You survived. If there hadn't been a part to make that effective response to keep you out of certain situations, you might not be here. My desire is not to take away the choice of being phobic but to update it so that you can also make other responses which are more congruent with your full resources as a fully grown woman. We're going to use that same capacity to do one-trial learning to help you learn to do something else.

In a moment I'm going to ask you to do some time-traveling. As you go back I want you to increase pressure here on my hand at any point that you need to be reminded of your competence as a fully grown, mature woman. This is your connection with the present time and all the powerful adult resources that you have as a fully grown person. Do you know what the feelings of the phobia are?

Tammy: Umhm. (He touches her arm.)

That's all you need to do to anchor the phobic response. Or you can ask a different question: What is the last time that you had an intense response like that?

Tammy: Umhm. (He touches her arm again.)

I got the same response that she gave a moment ago when I said "Do you know what the feelings of the phobia are?"—the same facial expression, the same breathing. That's now anchored on her arm. This anchor constitutes a stabilizing factor to help us go back and sort through her personal experience to find the original experience. It's not *necessary* to do it this way; this is *one* way to do phobias.

Your holding hands with me constitutes your connection to all the strength and resources you have as an adult woman. There were experiences in your past, namely those connected with this phobia, which we're going to go back and relive, but in a way that involves no discomfort at all, a way that involves total comfort. And I call to your mind the notion of dissociation that we talked about yesterday. We told you during the exercise you did yesterday afternoon to be sure you step inside the picture so that you recover the full kinesthetics. The opposite holds true here. For years Tammy has been exposed to certain kinds of real life situations and responded with a lot of emotion, a lot of kinesthetic feelings over and over again. To have her go back and relive that experience again and have those feelings again will simply reinforce it. That's ridiculous. And most people's unconscious minds say "Bullshit! We aren't going back there; that hurts!" and they are called "resistant clients," right? Respect that resistance as a statement that says "Look, make some new arrangements so we don't have to go through the pain again."

The specific arrangements *might* go like this: I'd like you to close your eyes, Tammy. You can vary the pressure in your hand any time you need more strength. You can draw it directly from here, and that's also a way for me to know where you are. In a moment I'm going to reach over and touch you here on your arm. That's going to help you remember a little bit of the feelings of pinking. I don't want you to go through the feelings again. I want you to take these feelings—*only* as much of them as you need—and drift back until there comes before your eyes a scene in which *you see yourself over there* at a younger age in a situation which has some connection with how you first learned to respond that way.

At some point while you see those images which are connected intimately with these feelings of pinking, I'm going to say "What do you see now?" I would like you to stabilize the image at that point. Likely it will be an image of yourself at a younger age, dressed in some particular way, in some colors, in some context. I don't know what any of that will be and at the moment you don't either, because you don't know where this came from. As soon as I ask you to stop the image, I want you to form a snapshot and just hold it stable. I don't want you to run any movies yet, because we need to make one more arrangement to make you even more comfortable before you run the movie

Remember that you can modulate how much of *these* feelings (He touches the phobia anchor on her arm.) you are going to use to drift back until you see a clear focused visual image connected with these feelings, that represents where this original learning took place. That's right, you draw on all the strength you need here, as you drift back through time, even further, take your time ... even more. There's no rush. Be perfectly comfortable. Now look at that image. And simply nod your head when you clearly see an image of yourself at a younger age. . . .

Tammy: I see myself at a younger age but I'm not in any situation. I'm just—

That's fine. Can you see what color shoes you are wearing?

Tammy: Black.

OK. Now I want you slowly to look at the surface that's right under the shoes. From there let your eyes slowly notice what is around you as you stand there in those little black shoes. Remembering to breathe, remembering to use these feelings of strength and competence. You've demonstrated adequately that you know about those old feelings. Now I want you to demonstrate that you can have *these* feelings of strength as you watch that image. Remembering to breathe; oxygen is essential for this whole process. That's right. When you have the still image, just nod. . . .

OK. Now, I would like you to hold that image constant, just a snapshot. Relax your right hand—not your left. Your left can be as tight as you need it to be in order to get access to these feelings of strength that you need. And you are breathing nicely now. Continue your breathing.

Now, I would like you slowly to float up and out of your body so that you can actually see yourself sitting here holding hands with me, ridiculous as that may sound. Take all the time you need. And when you have succeeded in floating out of your body so that you can see yourself from above or the side or the front or the back, just nod that you have succeeded. Excellent.

Now, *staying in that third position,* I want you to look past yourself sitting here holding my hand and feeling the feelings of strength and adult resourcefulness. *This* time, with feelings of strength and comfort, I want you to watch and listen carefully to everything that happened to young Tammy way back there, so that you can make new under-standings and learnings about what occurred, and therefore have new choices. You are to do this, watching from the third position, having the feelings of resourcefulness and strength connected with my hand here. Knowing that you did live through that and you won't have to again, let that younger part of you feel the old feelings *over there* as she goes through that old experience for the last time. When you've seen and heard it all, adequate for your making new understandings, simply nod your head and stay there. You can begin the movie now. . . . (She nods.)

All right, now very, very slowly I want you to float down from the third position and step back in and reunite with your body, sitting here with feelings of resourcefulness and strength. . . .

And now I want you to do something very powerful and important for yourself. Younger Tammy did something very powerful for you; she went through those feelings again for you, and she let you watch and listen with comfort and strength to stimuli which in the past have triggered overwhelming responses. This time you were able to see and hear those without pinking. I want you to walk over to young Tammy in your mind's eye. I want you to reach out and use all of the adult female resources you have, to comfort her and reassure her that she will never have to go through that again. Thank her for living through the old feelings for the last time for you. Explain to her that you can guarantee that she lived through it because you are from her future.

And when you *see* on her face and in her posture and in her breathing that she is reassured that you will be there to take care of her from now on, I want you to really reach out, take her by the shoulders and pull her close and actually feel her enter your body. Pull her inside. She is a part of you, and she's a very energetic part. That energy is freed now from that phobic response. I would like your unconscious mind to select some particular pleasurable activity that some of that energy can now be used for, for yourself here in the present and in the future. Because energy is energy and you deserve it. Just sit there and relax and enjoy those feelings. Let them spread through your whole body. Take your time. You've got plenty going on inside. I'm going to talk to the group.

Do you understand the anchors? First, she holds hands with me. This is a "bail-out" anchor, a resource anchor that will always get her out of trouble and says "Here, you're grounded right here." It's also a really exquisite biofeedback mechanism. By temperature and pressure and moisture changes in her hand, I get an incredible amount of information about her complex internal experience. An anchor here on her arm stabilizes the phobic feelings to use as a lead to go back and find some visual experience that will serve as a metaphor for her entire set of experiences called "the phobic response."

Once she sees herself at an earlier age over there, using the feelings to lead her back to something she had never known about consciously before, then I dissociate her a second step—I ask her to float up out of her body. You could see the changes in posture and color and breathing and so forth which indicated which position she was operating from.

Once the two-step dissociation has been established, I have her watch and listen with comfort to the old experience. She saw and heard things today which have never been available to her before.

Tammy: That's true.

She was so overwhelmed in the past by the kinesthetic phobic response that she couldn't see and hear what was going on. Consciousness is limited. As she watches and listens to herself at a younger age, the competent feelings of comfort and resourcefulness are being associated with the auditory and visual stimuli from the past.

And when she's gone through the whole thing, then we reintegrate. Every model of therapy, every psychotheology, is built on dissociation and sorting to help people reorganize. Whether you call it "parent-child-adult," "topdog-underdog," using chairs or words doesn't matter as long as you label and sort a person's behavior, dissociating parts of them, one from the other. You have the responsibility as a professional communicator to *put your clients back together* before the session is over. One easy way to make sure the dissociations that you create are re-integrated before the end of the session is to simply reverse the process by which you create the dissociation.

In this particular case, the dissociation is (1) see yourself over there at a younger age, (2) float up and out of your body. For the integration, (1) float back down and rejoin yourself here—and you could see the tremendous change in her that indicated that she had succeeded in doing that, (2) then walk over in your mind's eye, reach out, comfort and reassure the younger Tammy, thank her for going through this so that you could learn, pull her into you, re-integrate her and feel the feelings of energy.

What we're doing here is *structured* regression. Primal Therapy claims to get complete regression back to infancy. If that were true, then Primal Therapy would achieve change only insofar as it doesn't work! If Primal Therapy really got complete regression, it would be doing exactly what Tammy has been doing with the phobic response up until today. Complete regression simply means that you relive the experience in all systems. If you do that, you reinforce it.

A partial, structured, regression of the type Tammy and I were working with here allows you the freedom to go back and connect new kinds of resources with the auditory and visual stimuli which in the past have elicited old, uncomfortable, kinesthetic responses. It's impossible for her to go through this experience and still maintain that old response because she's done one-trial learning again. Now she doesn't *have* to be phobic. I haven't taken that choice away. There may be some context in which being phobic in response to something may be useful. I'm not playing God. I presuppose that people make the best choice in context. My job is to make sure that resources which have been dissociated from a certain context become available in that context. I leave it to the unique human being, with all the various needs they have that I don't even know anything about, to make an adequate selection somewhere along the continuum between resourcefulness and terror. And she will. Those resources have been dissociated in the past, but they are now integrated and they are now both responses to the same stimuli.

Man: You are making certain assumptions about integration and a lot of things that have happened.

Right. Is there any particular assumption you'd like to challenge?

Man: Um, all of them.

Good. Pick one.

Man: That she feels any different now than she did before.

OK. Let me give you a way of testing. (He turns to Tammy.) Let me ask you a question. (He touches the phobia anchor. She turns to him and smiles: "Umhm?") That's fine; you answered it. Does that make sense to you, sir? Do you remember that the last time I touched her there she had a phobic response? I had anchored the phobic reaction there, and then I demonstrated that I had control of her phobia. When I reached over and touched her arm she became phobic. Now I reach over and touch her and what does she do? She looks at me as if to say "What do you want?" That is a far more elegant demonstration than any verbal feedback I could get. I'm not saying don't use verbal conscious feedback, but understand that when you ask for that, you are tapping into the *least* informative part of the person: their conscious mind.

Let me give you another way of testing. Tammy, I'd like you to try something for me. This is just a scientific experiment. Are there any bridges here in town? I would like you to close your eyes and fantasize driving across a bridge, and I want you to do it in a special way. I want you to do it from the point of view of *being in a car*—not watching yourself—so that you see what you would see if you were actually driving across the bridge. What happens when you do that? ...

Tammy: (She raises her eyebrows, looks slightly puzzled.) I drove across the bridge.

"I drove across the bridge." What could be a more elegant response? If she had told me "I was *so happy* driving across the bridge," I'd say "What? Wait, it's just an ordinary bridge."

Tammy: But always before when I drove across a bridge, I immediately began to program myself "What am I going to do when the car goes off the side?"

And what did she say this time? "I just drove across the bridge." When you associate the strength and confidence with those auditory and visual stimuli, driving across a bridge becomes *just* another human activity, the same as the experience that the rest of you have had driving across bridges your whole life. This is also a way of testing our work to find out if it is adequately future-paced. We know what she looked like when she had a phobic response. If the same phobic response comes up, we know somehow the integration didn't happen. We'll find out what happened and re-do it. Her response was "Oh, driving across the bridge." Earlier, with Linda, we were talking about achoring the new response to a cue from the environment. Here we're testing and we're bridging or future-pacing at the same time.

Woman: Can you do this with yourself?

Yes, with two qualifications. Tomorrow we're going to teach a pattern called "reframing" which teaches you how to establish an internal communication system with some sophistication and subtlety. If you have such an internal communication system, you can always check internally to make sure that all parts of you are congruent. If you get a "go-ahead," of course you can do it by yourself. If there's some hesitation, reframing gives you a way of getting congruence, internal agreement.

Another precaution is that you get a really good anchor for a powerful, positive "blast-out" experience, so that if you begin to collapse back into the old unpleasant feelings, you can bring yourself out. Feeling more unpleasantness will not help you in this at all. I had a powerful anchor. Make sure you have one for yourself. I would recommend that you do it with somebody else if you have a very intense phobic response. It isn't that difficult, and it obviously doesn't take that long. Find somebody else, if only to operate the bail-out anchor if you begin to go back into the unpleasantness. You can go slightly into the phobic response and say to your friend "Look at what I look like now, and what I'm breathing like now. If you see that again, squeeze my hand." That would be adequate. You can run the rest of it yourself.

Woman: Can you do this with children?

Children don't seem to have that many phobias. For those who do, this will work fine. Whatever you do with kids, I recommend that you sneak up on it. A friend of mine had a nine-year-old kid who was a lousy speller. I said "Look at this list of ten spelling words." The kid looked at it, and I said "Now close your eyes and tell me what they are—not how to spell them." He had some difficulty doing that; he didn't have well-developed visualization. However, I said "Remember the Wookie in *Star Wars*? Do you remember when the Wookie opened his mouth and showed his teeth like this?" And he went "Oh, yeah!" and then he was visualizing immediately. I had him print the words out in the Wookie's mouth. There's always *some* experience somewhere in a person's personal history that has the requisite qualities you need. If you combine that experience with the task that you are trying to do— and especially with children, make a game out of it—there is no problem. "What do you think the Wookie would see if he were watching you go through that thing with your dad?" That's another way of getting the dissociation.

Children are really fast. As an adult you are a lot slower than a child. You are less fluid in your states of consciousness. The primary tool that we offer people who work with children is to use anchoring as a way of stabilizing what you are trying to work on, to slow the kid down enough so that you can cope. Because kids are really fast.

Woman: Why two steps of dissociation?

You don't *need* it. That's just a guarantee; it's insurance that she doesn't collapse back into the old feelings. If we had only dissociated her one step, if she collapsed she would collapse right back into the old experience, and it would be very difficult to get her back out. By doing it in two steps, if she begins to collapse, she will collapse into the first step and it's easier to get back out. You can tell whether she is up above or back down here by the changes in posture and skin color and breathing, etc. Knowing that, if I see her collapse from two to one, I give a squeeze here, or I say "Now let *her* feel the old feelings over *there.*

You watch from *up here.*" Those are ways of insuring that she doesn't just re-experience the bad feelings.

Woman: You asked Tammy to take the feeling and find a picture of herself at a younger age. What if she can't find one?

That's a statement about the *therapist,* not the client. It should be taken as a comment about what the therapist is doing, indicating that the therapist should change his behavior and do it differently.

Let me answer your question in this way. I don't believe that Tammy actually had the experience that she watched herself go through. She may or may not have; I don't know. But it is irrelevant. Once a very well-known therapist was visiting with us, and we received an emergency referral, a suicidal woman. The psychiatrist had given up, saying "Here, would you please take this woman over? I'm out of choices." Since this famous therapist was staying with us, we thought it would be an unprecedented opportunity to demonstrate some of the uses of hypnosis Erickson had taught us. Because for that therapist, at that point in his evolution, hypnosis was a dirty word. He thought it was "manipulative." And we told him "There are ways in which Ericksonian hypnosis is far less manipulative than any insight, conscious-mind therapy we have ever run across. Let us demonstrate with this woman."

So we began to work with this woman. The visiting therapist was sitting there watching and listening. About ten minutes into the session, he got a revelation. It was obvious. I said "Do you have something you want us to do?" I had never had a chance to watch this therapist work live before. He took over and started going *"Blood ... stairway ... childhood, younger brother ... mother cries ... screams."* He developed this incredible fantasy, which he then essentially "sold" to this woman. At first the woman would go "Gee, I don't remember anything like that." Finally the woman went "Uuuuhhhh! That's it! I must have done it!" very much like a family reconstruction, if you've ever been through one of those with Virginia Satir. Suddenly the woman made all these internal connections, and the visiting therapist did all this therapy about this past experience and the woman changed dramatically. Her behavior changed dramatically, and she *stayed* changed, too. She was a continuing client of ours.

Now, when she came back in two weeks, we couldn't resist. We induced a somnambulistic trance, and established an anchor for amnesia so that we could erase anything we did during that session— because she was doing fine and we didn't want to interfere. We just wanted to check and find out what had happened. We asked her unconscious mind if in fact the experience described by the therapist during the session—or anything approximating it—had ever occurred. The answer was unequivocally "No." However, that is no different than what just happened here. If the experience that Tammy generated has all the elements of whatever the original experience or set of experiences was, it will serve as a metaphor *which will be as effective as an actual, factual, historical representation.* And from my sensory experience I can guarantee that it was effective.

Woman: What I still don't understand is what you do if the client is stuck because she has an expectation of getting a picture of a childhood incident, and now she's sitting there doing this and she can't get a picture.

OK, that's the same choice point as the congruent "I don't know" that we talked about earlier. Ask her to guess, make it up, lie, fantasize; it doesn't matter.

Actually, age regression is a very easy phenomenon. We said "Go back through time." She had very little conscious idea what we meant by that, but she responded quite easily to it.

Man: What specifically were you seeing on her face?

The same response that she originally demonstrated when we asked her about the feelings of the phobia. I watched her age regress until I saw a *very* intense example of it. There was a patch of yellow on her cheek. There was whiteness around the eyes and the side of the face. There was some kind of scrunching of her chin. There was an increase in moisture on her skin, especially on the bridge of her nose. When that became intensified, I said "Now look at an image, that image there."

If you tell people to go back through time and they frown, that's also a cue. And you might try something tricky like saying "Well, go forward in time." "Go through time, jump back in time." "Go around time." Anything. It doesn't matter. The specific words you use are wholly irrelevant as long as you get the response you want.

Another way to think about it is that everybody with a phobia knows the *feelings* of the phobia. They have a fragment of the experience, so they can get the rest by *overlap.* How do you find your car keys when you want to go to the store and you don't know where they are?

Woman: I start feeling around through my pockets.

Man: I go through the house and look.

Man: I search my mind, going back to try to visualize where they are.

Woman: I shake my purse so I can hear them.

OK. If all else fails, you can go back to the front door and walk in again. Now, if you think about the responses we just got, those include the three main representational systems. If you have any fragment of any experience, you can have it all by overlap. She had the feelings here. The feelings, once anchored, stabilized her state of consciousness. Everything that she accessed as she closed her eyes and went back in her personal history had that set of feelings in common, guaranteeing that whatever picture she selected would be in the class called phobic experiences.

I used the same principle to help her have a complete focused visual image of herself at a younger age. At first she had only a picture of herself, but no context. I ask her what color shoes she is wearing. I presuppose that she can see her feet and her shoes, and that she can see colors. She accepts the presupposition; she says "Black." Since she can see the shoes, then obviously, "logically," she can see what they are on top of, the surface she's standing on. I request that. When she gets the surface, it blends into walls and into trees, or whatever the rest of the image was. It's a very easy overlap, or intersection, technique that allows me to assist her in recovering the image by constructing portions of it, a little at a time.

Man: What's the difference between this technique and systematic desensitization?

About six months. That's the major difference, which is a very *expensive* difference. My understanding is that it's straight conditioning. We have simply associated a new set of feelings, namely competence and strength, with the auditory and visual stimuli.

There is another very important difference. We are picking a specific set of feelings and associating it, instead of just trying to wipe out the set that is there. The people that I've observed do desensitization are usually trying to *eliminate* a certain kind of behavior rather than replacing it with something which is a positive response. They are the kind of people who answer "Not bad" when you ask "How are you feeling?"

We claim that every piece of behavior has a positive function. It's the best choice a person has in context. It was far better for Tammy to be phobic about bridges than it was to have no program at all. If you do systematic desensitization, and you don't replace the "negative" behavioral pattern with something positive, it takes a long time because the person will fight. It's their only defense. That's why it takes six months, because a person has to randomly put something else in its place.

Man: There is a replacement, though, with relaxation.

Sometimes it's done that way, but relaxation is not the resource that everyone is going to need in a phobic situation. If you're driving across a bridge, you don't want to become relaxed suddenly. If somebody is in a situation in which they need to cope and you give them feelings of relaxation, they may not cope! There may be real, genuine dangers in that situation, so one of two things will happen: either the symptom will come back later because it's protective, or the person will get hurt. We got a very strong anchor for confidence and for the resources that she has as an adult woman. We used *that;* we did not use relaxation. She was *very* alert during this process. Desensitization was an important step, in that people were able to cure phobias with it. I think that it just needs to be dressed up a little bit. Instead of using relaxation and associating it with *everything,* try associating other things besides relaxation. There are much more powerful resources in people.

There is nothing that we have offered you so far, nor is there anything we will offer you during the rest of this seminar or in an advanced workshop, that isn't already in someone's behavior somewhere. What we've done as modelers is to figure out what the essential elements are, and what is unnecessary. Every therapy has dissociation. Every therapy has the kinds of sorting techniques we're using here, whether it's chairs or knee anchors or words. What is useful to have in every therapy is *some* way of doing all that: *some* way of sorting, *some* way of dissociating, *some* way of integrating. The names you use are wholly irrelevant, and most psychotheologies are also irrelevant. There's really nothing *that* different between what we did and what gestalt people do by taking people back through time. TA people do a process called "redecision." They are all very, very similar.

We looked at all those different processes and tried to find out what the essential elements were, and what was extra and unnecessary. Then we streamlined it to try to find something that works systematically. I don't think there's anything wrong with desensitization, except that sometimes it doesn't work. That's because there are a lot of things that are extra, and some things that are essential are not always there. Some people who do desensitization also add the necessary resources unconsciously. But when they teach somebody else to do it, they don't teach that, because it's not in their consciousness. Our function as modelers is to sort those things out.

The other thing is that I don't know what kind of desensitization you are referring to specifically. Some use meters and machines. I am a far more sophisticated biofeedback mechanism than any set of machines. I use really sophisticated sensory apparatus and internal responses as a way of amplifying or diminishing certain parts of the response that I am receiving. That's part of what makes one-trial learning possible in the kind of work we've been doing here with anchoring.

Man: What if a client is unable to use visual imagery?

It is not essential that people visualize to be able to do the phobia process, because the same formal pattern can be done auditorily or kinesthetically. The pattern of this technique does not require visualization. We wanted to use all systems as a demonstration. We don't need to do it with all systems. You could also first take a little time to teach the person how to visualize, using overlap.

Woman: Could you do this process without touching?

Sure, you can use a tonal anchor or a visual anchor. You can do it without touching. However, I would recommend that you do it with touching. Kinesthetics is an irresistible anchoring system. When somebody is touched, they feel it. When you make a visual sign at someone, they may look away or close their eyes.

Man: So the bail-out anchor could be a certain tone of voice?

Yes. Tonal anchors in this society are the most powerful because most Americans do not hear consciously. The number of people in this country who hear is almost nil, slightly more than the number of card-carrying musicians.

In England it's considered important to make class distinctions. In order to make class distinctions, you have to be able to hear different accents and tonalities. So English people are more acute at hearing tonal changes. Anyone who is bilingual or polyglot, and who has learned a tonal language, will have a good sensitivity to those kinds of changes.

Most people in the U.S. do not actually hear the sequence of words and the intonation pattern of what they, or other people, say. They are only aware of the pictures, feelings and internal dialogue that they have in *response* to what they hear. Very few people are able to repeat back, in the same intonation, what you say to them. We hear people *literally*. We do not add anything or subtract anything from what they say. That is a rare human experience, and for a long time we didn't realize that; we thought everybody heard words.

The real beginning of all this work started when we began taking people's words as a *literal* description of their experience, not just a metaphor. We started communicating back as if they were literally the way they had described themselves, and we found out that was the case. When someone says "When I focus on those ideas they feel right, but I tell myself it wouldn't work," that is a literal description of their internal experience.

Now we would like you to pick a partner, preferably somebody you have not had much contact with. It's easier to operate at the process level with strangers because their behavior is less apt to be an anchor for some behavior in you. We assume that you are all going to get changes with one another, given your usual patterns of communication. Try something new. The whole point of going through the exercise is to be exposed to new material and to do it, to discover how well it fits with your own personal style as a communicator. Until you engage all your sensory channels in playing with this material, you won't have it. Understanding fully is to be able to comprehend it in all representational systems, including behavior.

We'd like you to practice the two-step visual/kinesthetic dissociation process that we did with Tammy here. You don't need a full-blown phobia. You can use this process with any unpleasant response, to become familiar with the pattern. This, or the "change history" process will work for nearly any presenting problem that I know of. Anchoring will get you almost everything. When you're done, use bridging or future-pacing to be sure that the new response will be triggered by the context where it's needed. Go ahead.

*   *   *   *   *

OK. How did it go? What questions do you have?

Woman: I noticed I was getting distracted because my partner was using many words that didn't match the experience I had internally.

What you need is a very subtle maneuver: You say "Shut up!" or you kick your partner!

One of the things that all of you can learn from this is that it's very easy to learn to talk in a way that matches your client's experience. The way to do that is described in our book, *Patterns I*. It describes the patterns of language that *sound* specific, but are actually simply process instructions with zero content.

For example, here's an exercise you can all do. Get comfortable and close your eyes. Take a couple of deep breaths and relax.

Sometime within the last five years, each of you has had a very strong experience in which you learned something of great value for yourself as a human being. You may or may not have a conscious appreciation of exactly which episode in your life history this is. I would like you to allow that experience to come up into your consciousness. Sit there for a moment, with feelings of comfort and strength, knowing you're actually *here,* now. With those feelings of comfort and strength, let yourself see and hear again what it was that happened to you back there. There are additional things to be learned from that experience. I would like you to allow yourself the treat of seeing and hearing yourself go through that again so as to make new understandings and learnings which are embedded in that experience in your past history....

And when you've seen and heard something that you believe to be of value for yourself, I would like you to pick a specific situation that you know will occur within the next couple of weeks. Notice—again by watching and listening with feelings of strength and comfort—how you can apply that new learning and that new understanding to this new situation that is going to arise in the next couple of weeks. In so doing you are making elegant use of your own personal history, and you are transferring understandings and learnings from one part of your personal history, so as to increase your choices as a creative human being in the present. Take all the time you need, and when you finish, drift back and rejoin us....

Some of you may have a clear, solid, resonant understanding of what you've succeeded in doing; some of you may simply have a sense of well-being, a feeling of having done something without actually understanding in detail explicitly what it was that you were able to do by making use of a particularly powerful experience from your past in a new way....

Now I'd like you to begin to drift back slowly, understanding that if you've completed the process to the best of your conscious understanding, fine.... If you haven't yet finished, you've set into motion a process which can be completed comfortably outside of your awareness as you return your attention slowly here to this room....

Now, what did I actually say? I didn't say *anything*! Zero. There was *no content* to that verbalization. "To do something of importance for yourself ... certain learnings ... unconscious understanding from that specific experience in your past." None of those have any content. Those are pure *process* instructions. And if you have the sensory experience, you can see the process happening as you do it. That is where your timing is *very* important.

Let me give you a very different experience. I'd like you to close your eyes and visualize a rope ... which is *green.* How many of you already had a different colored rope? If I give you instructions that have any content whatsoever, as I just did, I am very, very apt to violate your internal experience. I will no longer be pacing you adequately.

A skill that all communicators need is the ability to give *process* instructions: instructions that have no content whatsoever. That's the sense in which I mentioned earlier that Ericksonian hypnosis is the *least* manipulative of all the forms of psychotherapy I've ever been exposed to. In any communication with content there's no way for you to *not* introduce your own beliefs and value systems by presupposition. However, if you restrict yourself to process work, to content-free verbalizations with your clients, you are guaranteeing that you are respecting their integrity. If you do secret therapy there's no way that you can interfere with their beliefs or value system because you don't know what they are. You don't have any idea what they are doing, and there's no need for you to, either.

Woman: Why do you have to integrate the negative anchor, instead of just ignoring it altogether?

Lots of people go to hypnotists to stop smoking. The hypnotist hypnotizes them and says "From this point on, cigarettes will taste terrible." And he wakes them up and sends them away, right? They don't smoke any more because it tastes terrible. *However,* that leaves them with a whole set of dissociated motor patterns. It's the same with alcoholics. Alcoholics Anonymous says "Once an alcoholic, always an alcoholic." That's a statement to me that their program fails to integrate motor programs which can still be triggered at a later date by the presence of alcohol. So all it takes is one drink and they have to continue—binge drinking—or one cigarette later on and boom! that person is a smoker again.

Dissociated motor patterns can always be triggered unless you integrate them. If you dissociate and sort someone, make sure you put them back together. Don't leave those dissociated motor patterns lying around. That's one of your professional responsibilities. People have enough dissociations on their own already. They don't need more.

Man: Have you ever worked with multiple personalities?

Multiple personality is a little bit complicated, because it depends upon who messed the person up in the first place. You really need to know the model of the therapist that wrecked the person to begin with. I have never personally met a multiple personality that wasn't *made by a therapist.* That doesn't mean they don't exist, it's just that I've never met one. My guess is that there might be a few out there somewhere, but I'll tell you there aren't as many as therapists keep creating and bringing to me.

We became interested in multiple personalities years ago, and wrote to a man who had written a big paper about it. He invited us to come and meet one named Helen. She had about twenty personalities, but the cover name for everyone was Helen. And the fascinating thing was that all of her multiple personalities were more interesting than she was.

Her therapist had a very elaborate model of her personalities. She had an organization part: a part that was very organized and did secretarial work and all kinds of stuff like that. So I said "Well, get that one for me." The therapist had this great non-verbal analogue: he stood up and shouted "JOYCE! COME OUT, JOYCE!" and he hit her on the forehead, Bwamm! and she went through all these changes. Brrnnnggnhhh! It was right out of the movies; it was really spooky. This guy does exorcisms on the helicopter pad at a Catholic college, and he's considered to be a respectable psychiatrist by people who think *we are weird!* In some ways he's very effective because he is so expressive, but I don't think he understands the full ramifications of what he is doing. He has anywhere from sixteen to twenty-two multiple personalities in his practice at any time, and he can't understand why the rest of the therapeutic community doesn't recognize the epidemic of multiple personalities that he has discovered!

So the organization part of this woman came out, and I introduced myself. Then I said "Most of these parts have amnesia for what goes on in this person's life. Being the organization part, I figure you would have kept pretty good track of it all." "Oh, yes, of course I kept good track of it." I said "Well, how did you end up with so many personalities?" And she said to me "It's as if there were a whole bunch of different parts and there was a round peg that went through the middle. And when I met Dr. So-and-so, he took the peg and pulled it out." That is almost verbatim what she said to me, and this is a woman who does not have a high school education.

She didn't think that this was bad, by the way. Her description was that he pulled the peg out so that they all became more apparent as separate personalities, and now they were going to go back through and make them all into one again. The tragic thing is that when he succeeded in integrating her, she had total amnesia for her entire life, and was a drip as far as I could tell. She had these *great* parts. She had a sexy part that was just *rrrnnnhhh*! Another part told jokes and was really corny. Another part was very shy and coy. But when he "cured" her, she had amnesia for her entire life and she had none of the resources of any of those parts. She was just dull.

Now I don't think that you can wipe out parts. So I kept mentioning the names of the parts that I liked, and I got really *great* unconscious responses from her. They were still there, but they weren't fully available to her.

To do a good job with a multiple personality, I think you need to know the model of the therapist that created it. Some therapists' model of multiple personality is that you have all these parts and an unconscious that runs the program. That's one model, a very common one. The way you'd integrate that one is totally different than you would some other model. This guy's model was that there were three parts here and they had their own unconscious, and then there were two parts over here and they had an unconscious, and then there was an unconscious for these two unconsciouses, and so on. It was really stacked in levels. When you integrated, you would always have to integrate at the same logical level. My guess is that he didn't do that, and that is how he got so much amnesia.

You can use what we call the "visual squash" with multiple per-sonalities. The visual squash is a visual method of integration using visual anchors. You hold out your hands and see yourself as one part here on your left, and as another part here on your right, and you watch them and listen to them. Then you slowly pull the two images together, and visually watch them merge together and then notice how that image is different. If you like it, then you do the same thing again kinesthetically, and squash the two images together with your hands. Then you pull the integrated image into your body.

We just stumbled across this. At first it sounded kind of weird, until we studied a little bit about neurology. It's a good metaphor for what goes on in the metaphor called "neurology." And if you don't think neurology is a metaphor, you are naive, I want to tell you! But anyway, their metaphor and our metaphor were very similar. And if you try it, it's very dramatic. It's a very powerful method.

I once cured a multiple personality with *only* that. I went through all the levels one by one and squashed all the personalities together.

I once had a therapist call me on the telephone from the Midwest. He said he'd read my book and there was nothing in it about multiple personalities, and he didn't even believe in them, but one had just come into his office and what should he do? I went through the instructions on the phone with him for forty minutes and cured his patient over the telephone. "OK, now tell her to hold out both hands. Tell her to visualize Jane in her right hand and visualize Mary in her left hand. Just take two of them and collapse them together into one image. And then tell her to pull it into her body and integrate it. Then tell her to get the integrated image that she just had, and put it together with another one." So you do them one at a time.

Most people don't really ask multiple personalities any questions. But I really questioned the ones that I've been around, to find out how they functioned. The experience of being multiple for one may be very different than it is for another.

One of the women that I worked with described every single one of her parts as part of the same process. She was really, really visual; she had a picture of them all. There was a couch backstage, in the back of her mind, and all these women sat back there on the couch doing their nails and chatting. Every once in a while, one of them would hop up and walk through the curtains. When it walked through, it would step into her body. Some of them knew about what the other ones did, because they would go and peek out through the curtains. I hypnotized her and went backstage with her and did the visual squash technique and put them all together.

That visual squash method is a very powerful way of integrating sequential incongruities by making them simultaneous in a dissociated state. If you have a sequential incongruity, you can never represent both parts simultaneously in any system other than the visual, as far as I can tell. It takes a very complex auditory representation to have two voices going on at the same time—as opposed to alternating—and people can't pull it off kinesthetically. But you can take sequential incongruities and make them simultaneous by visual/kinesthetic dissociation, and then integrate them by pulling the hands together, and then get the integration in the other two systems.

I don't understand the significance of moving the arms when you do the visual squash, but if you do it without the arms it doesn't work. And I have *no* idea why. I've tried it both ways; if people don't actually hold out their hands in front of them like this and pull the images together, it doesn't work. People don't have to hold out their hands to get cured of phobias, but apparently with multiple personalities they have to. That doesn't make any sense to me logically, but it happens to be the case. If I were to make a generalization, I would make the reverse one. But I have found out that's the case in experience.

We are a lot more willing to experiment against our intuitions than most people. When most people have a strong intuition, they'll follow it. A lot of times when we have a strong intuition, we'll violate it to find out what will happen—especially when we have clients that we have ongoing contact with, and can be sure of being able to deal with the consequences. That kind of experimentation has resulted in many useful patterns and discoveries.

One woman had been a homosexual for years, and had fallen in love with a man. She was really stuck in this dilemma. A very strong part of her now wanted to become heterosexual. There was another part of her that was afraid it was going to have to die. She was going through the visual squash with these two parts. She was trying to pull her hands together, and she was wailing "I can't do it! I can't do it! I can't do it like that!" Richard and I were standing on either side of her. We looked at each other, and then we each grabbed one hand and pushed them together suddenly. The changes that occurred in that woman were fantastic!

You can create change without being elegant; I think people do it all the time. However, the ramifications of doing something like that are not predictable, and predictability is something that we have always tried to develop. We just went blammo, pow! and rammed it in. She did change; she got what she wanted, and it's lasted a long time; I'm sure of that because I still know that woman. However, I don't know what the side effects were. She isn't totally wonderful in many areas of her life, and I don't know how much of that is a consequence of what we did. She's certainly better off than she was. And at the time we really wanted to know what would happen.

When you start including more sophisticated ingredients in your work and tinkering with them carefully, then you get better, more elegant changes. You can also predict what will happen much more precisely. Sometimes you get much more pervasive change, too, which I think is very important. If you can do just one little tiny thing and get the outcome that you want, it will also generalize and get all the other outcomes that are really needed but haven't been mentioned. The less you do in the more appropriate place, the more generalization to other contents and contexts will occur naturally. That's one reason why we stress elegance so much: "Be precise, if you're doing therapy."

If you're just doing utilization skills it's a very different game. Business people are usually only interested in *utilizing* strategies. If you are doing sales training, then all you need to know is what strategies you want your salespeople to have, and how to install them. If the trainer for an organization is a Neuro Linguistic Programmer, then he says "OK, we're going to have this person be a salesperson and they're going to do this, and in order to do that, you have to have these three strategies." Then he can stick them in and block them off so that nothing else gets in their way. Those strategies don't have to generalize anywhere else in the person's life. It's not necessary for that business outcome. It might be desirable, but it's not necessary.

If somebody's personal life is really interrupting their business functioning, you can put a barrier around it to keep those strategies separate. There are a lot of different kinds of outcomes you're going to have as a business person, but they're fairly limited.

As a lawyer, for example, you're mostly just *utilizing* strategies; you're not concerned with installing anything. You're only concerned with using a strategy to get a specific outcome: to make a witness look like a jerk, or to get your client to trust you, or something like that.

I once did some work with a lawyer who is a trustworthy person, but nobody trusts him. His non-verbal analogues are terrible; they make everyone suspicious. His problem was that he couldn't get clients to confide in him so that he could represent them well. And half the time he was court-appointed, which made it even worse. What he really needed was a complete overhaul in his analogue system. Rather than do that, I taught him a little ritual. He sits down with his client and says "Look, if I'm going to be your lawyer, it's essential that you trust me. And so the question that's really important is how do you decide if you trust somebody?" He asks "Have you ever really trusted anybody in your life?" and he sets up an anchor when the client accesses that feeling of trust. Then he asks "How did you make that decision?" Then all he has to do is to listen to a general description of their strategy: "Well, I saw this, and I heard him say this, and I felt this." Then he presents information back in that format: "Well, as I sit here, I want you to see blah blah blah, and then I say to yourself blahdeblah blah, and I don't know if you can feel this," and fires off the anchor that he made when the person had the trusting feelings. I taught him that ritual and it was good enough.

But there is a real difference between that outcome and the outcome that you're working toward as a therapist. Therapy is a much more technical business in the sense of changing things. As a therapist you don't need to be nearly as flexible in terms of utilization as somebody who's a lawyer. A lawyer must be a master of the art of utilization. You need to be able to do many different things in terms of eliciting responses. You have to get twelve people to respond the same way. Think about *that*. Imagine that you had twelve clients, and you had to get them all to agree when you weren't in the room! That's going to take skill.

One thing you can do is to identify the one or two individuals, or several, on the jury who might, by virtue of their own strategies, persuade the others to go along. And of course that is what family therapy is all about. Everything is going to interact in a system. I don't care who you put together for what length of time, the systems are going to start clicking. I try to figure out who in the family elicits responses the most often. Because if I can get that one person to do my work for me, it will be really easy. Very often it's someone who doesn't speak much. Son here says something. He has external behavior. And when he does, you get an intense internal response from the mother. Although her external behavior is subtle, some little cue, *everybody* responds to it. When the father does something with external behavior, this kid responds, but not much else happens. And if the daughter does something, maybe we get a response here and maybe there.

I want to know who *everybody* else in the family responds to a lot. I also want to know if any one single person in that family can always get *that* person to respond. Let's say every single time the son does anything with external behavior, the mother responds. If I can predict something about how that happens, I can make one little change in the son, and then the mother will respond and get everybody else in the family to respond for me. I always spend fifty percent or more of whatever time is allotted to me gathering information, and testing it to make sure that I'm right. I'll feed in an innocuous thing here, and predict what will happen over there. I keep running the system over and over and over again until I'm absolutely sure that if I make a change with this kid, it's going to change the mother's behavior in a way that will change all the other people in the family. That will set up a new stable system. Otherwise you usually get an unbalanced system, or they change in the office but they go home and go back to normal. I want something that's really going to carry over and be very, very permanent.

If I can set up a stable system by making only one change, it will be very pervasive with a family system. I think the main mistake of all family therapists is that they do too much in a session. If you're working with an individual, you can do a thousand things and get away with it, unless they go home to a family. One of the first things I always ask people when they come in is "What is your living situation?" because I want to know how many anchors I have to deal with at home. If they live with one other person, it's not so bad. You've just got to be careful that there's no secondary gain: that they don't get rewarded for whatever behavior it is they want to change.

Man: How much dependency on you is created by your methods?

One of the things we strive for in our work is to make sure that we use transference and countertransference powerfully to *get* rapport, and then to make sure that we *don't* use it after that. We don't need it after that. And since they don't get to sit there and tell us their problems, we don't become their best companion. There are real risks in doing content therapy because you may become someone's closest friend. Then they end up paying money to hang out with you because no one else is willing to sit around and listen to them drivel about unpleasant things in their life. We don't get much dependency. For one thing, we have a tool that we teach our clients to use with themselves, called reframing, which we are going to teach you tomorrow.

If you ask the people who were up here for demonstration purposes, my guess is they would assign very little responsibility to us for the changes that occurred in them—much less than they would in traditional content-oriented therapy. That's one of the advantages of secret therapy. It doesn't create that kind of dependency relationship.

At the same time, people who work with us usually have a sense of trust; they know that we know what we are doing. Or they may be totally infuriated with us, but they are still getting the changes they want. And of course we work very quickly, and that reduces the possibility of dependency.

In our actual private practice, which is severely reduced now because we're moving into other areas of modeling, we tell stories. A person will come in and I don't want them to tell me anything. I just tell them stories. The use of metaphor is a whole set of advanced patterns which is associated with what we've done so far. You can learn about those in David Gordon's excellent book, *Therapeutic Metaphors*. I prefer metaphor artistically. I don't have to listen to client's woes, and I get to tell very entertaining stories. Clients are usually bewildered or infuriated by paying me money to listen to stories. But the changes they want occur anyway—no thanks to me, of course, which is fine. That's another way to make sure there is no dependency. You do things so covertly that they don't have the faintest idea what you are doing, and the changes they want occur anyway.

Is there anybody here who has been to see Milton Erickson? He told you stories, right? Did you find that six months, eight months, or a year later you were going through changes that were somehow associated with those stories that he was telling?

Man: Yes.

That's the typical report. Six months later people suddenly notice they've changed and they don't have any idea how that happened, and then they get a memory of Milton talking about the farm up in Wisconsin or something. When you were with Erickson did you have the experience of being slightly disoriented, fascinated and entranced by the man's language?

Man: I was bored.

Milton uses boredom as one of his major weapons. If Milton were here, one thing he might do is bore you to tears. So you'd all drift off into daydreams and then he has you. I get bored too quickly myself to use that as a tactic. Milton, sitting in a wheelchair and being seventy-six years old, doesn't mind spending a lot of time doing that. And he does it exquisitely.

We have, during these days together, succeeded brilliantly in completely overwhelming your conscious resources. This was a deliberate move on our part, understanding as we do that most learning and change takes place at the unconscious level. We have appealed explicitly to each of both of you, that your unconscious minds would make a useful representation necessary for your education, so that in the weeks and days and months ahead you can be delightfully surprised by new patterns occurring in your behavior.

And we suggest to your unconscious mind that you make use of the natural processes of sleep and dreaming, to review any experiences that have occurred during these two days, and sort out those things that your unconscious believes will be useful for you to know, making a useful representation at the unconscious level, meanwhile allowing you to sleep deeply and soundly, so that in the days and weeks and months to come, you can discover yourself doing things that you didn't know you learned about here, so as to constantly increase, at the unconscious level, your repertoire in responding to people who come to you for

136

assistance.... And you didn't even know they were there. Not at all.

The last time that I went to see Milton Erickson, he said something to me. And as I was sitting there in front of him, it didn't make sense. Most of his covert metaphors have made ... *eons* of sense to me. But he said something to me which would have taken me a while to figure out. Milton said to me "You don't consider yourself a therapist, but you are a therapist." And I said "Well, not really." He said "Well, let's pretend ... that you're a therapist who works with people. The most important thing ... when you're pretending this ... is to understand ... that you are *really* not.... You are just pretending.... And if you pretend really well, the people that you work with will pretend to make changes. And they will forget that they are pretending ... for the rest of their lives. But don't you be fooled by it." And then he looked at me and he said:

"Goodbye."

III

Finding New Ways

There are several organizing assumptions that we use to put ourselves in a state which we find useful to operate in as we do therapeutic kinds of work. One is that it's better to have choice than no choice, and another is the notion of unconscious choice. Another is that people already have the resources they need in order to change, if they can be helped to have the appropriate resources in the appropriate context. A fourth one is that each and every single piece of behavior has a positive function in *some* context. It would be wanton and irresponsible of us simply to change people's behavior without taking into account a very important notion called "secondary gain." We assume that the pattern of behavior somebody is displaying is the most appropriate response they have in the context—no matter how bizarre or inappropriate it *seems* to be.

The context that your clients are responding to is usually composed of about nine parts of internal experience and about one part of external. So when a piece of behavior looks or sounds bizarre or inappropriate to you, that's a good signal that a large portion of the context that the person is responding to is something that is not available to you in your immediate sensory experience. They are responding to someone or something else internally represented: mother, father, historical events, etc. And often that internal representation is out of consciousness. Linda and Tammy can verify that the responses that they changed when they came and worked with us here, were responses to events that occurred sometime in the past.

137

That shouldn't surprise any of you. I'm sure that you all have been through experiences that support that statement. Our specific response to that understanding is to realize that all of us are complex and balanced organisms. One way to take that complexity into account when you go about assisting someone in making some change, is by using a pattern that we call *reframing*. Reframing is a specific way of contacting the portion or part—for lack of a better word—of the person that is causing a certain behavior to occur, or that is preventing a certain other behavior from occurring. We do this so that we can find out what the secondary gain of the behavior is, and take care of that as an integral part of the process of inducing a change in that area of behavior.

This is best illustrated by an example. A woman came to us referred by a psychiatrist. She wanted to lose 45 pounds. She had lost this weight in the past, but every time she lost it, she regained it. She could *get* it off, but she couldn't *keep* it off. We discovered through reframing that there was no part of her that had any objection to her losing weight. However, the part of her that caused her to overeat was doing that in order to protect her marriage. Can you make that connection? If you can't, let me explain a little further. In the opinion of this part of the woman who was overweight, if she were to lose the weight and weigh what she wanted to weigh, she would be physically attractive to men. If she were physically attractive to men, she would be approached and propositioned. In the opinion of this part she did not have adequate resources to make good decisions for herself in response to those propositions. She wasn't able to say "No." There was no part of her that wanted her to be overweight. There was, however, a part of her that *used* her being overweight to institutionalize the choice of not having to cope with a situation that it believed she couldn't cope with effectively, and that might lead to the end of her marriage. This is known as "secondary gain."

The heart of reframing is to make the distinction between the *intention*—in this case to protect her marriage, and the *behavior*—in this case overeating. Then you can find new, more acceptable, behaviors that satisfy the same intention.

One thing that people rarely understand is that people's symptoms *work*. As long as being fat worked and accomplished the intention, that part was going to keep her fat. When it had better ways of protecting her marriage, then it could allow her to lose the weight, which in fact she did without dieting.

Let's demonstrate now. Who wants to change?—*secretly*. . . .

OK, Dick, we want you to keep any content to yourself, leaving the people here free simply to observe the process that we go through. Either Dick is doing something now which he doesn't have a choice about, a sort of compulsive behavior which he would rather replace with something else, or there is something he would rather do but he isn't able to do. Those are the two verbal ways of coding the world of possibility.

Dick: It's the first.

OK. If it's all right with you, let's give the code name X to the pattern of behavior you presently have which you would rather replace with something else more appropriate. And I assume that pattern X, in your conscious judgement, is not a good representation of you as a total adult organism. We've just identified the pattern, the thing the person wants to change. That is step one.

The next step is to establish communication with the part of Dick responsible for this pattern X that he wants to change.

Embedded in this context is a notion that I will state directly to him and that I want to point out to the rest of you as well. Dick, I have respect for the part of you that is responsible for pattern X occurring over and over again in your behavior. You got here. You're sitting here and you are successful in doing a lot of the things that you do in your life. I am convinced that the part of you that runs pattern X—even though you consciously don't appreciate it—is attempting to do something positive in your behalf. I will induce no changes until the part of you that is responsible for running X is satisfied that the changes are more appropriate for *it,* as well as for you as a total organism.

This only makes sense if you have a belief system that says "Look. If he had conscious control over this behavior, it would have changed already." So some part of him which is *not* conscious is running this pattern of behavior.

I can guarantee you that ninety-nine times out of a hundred when a person wants to make a change and they come to you for assistance, there's going to be a dissociation, a conflict, between their conscious desires and some unconscious set of programs. The unconscious is far more powerful. It knows *far more* about his needs than his conscious mind, and *far more* than I could ever possibly know from the outside. I ally myself immediately with the unconscious, and that's what I just finished doing. That's *one* way to accomplish that, verbally and explicitly: "Look, I'm not talking to your conscious mind. I'm talking to the part of you responsible for this pattern of behavior. It's going to run the show. I'm going to serve as its consultant."

Now how do you communicate with that part? If you had to go to the Federal Building in San Francisco and get someone to sign a paper, you'd be faced with a very complex task. Because out of the 450 people in that building, there's only one of them whom you need to get to. If you were to adopt the strategy of searching for the one person whose signature you need by stopping at the door and talking to the guard and asking if he'll sign it, and then moving down the hallway, office after office, searching for the person who is authorized to sign, you'd waste a great deal of time. It would be an inefficient strategy for you to use to get what you want in that bureaucratic setting. That's a really close metaphor for a lot of the work that therapists do.

Therapists have been trained to pay a great deal of attention to the conscious requests of their clients. Typically the conscious mind is the one that knows the *least* about what's going on in their behavior. The fact that a person would come into my office and say to me "I'm X-ing and I no longer want to do that; help me make a change," is a statement to me that he's already tried to make the change with all the resources that he can get to consciously and he's failed miserably. It seems as absurd as beginning with the guard and working your way through every office, for me to engage his conscious mind in a discussion of these possibilities. I want to go directly to the office where the person who can sign that paper is residing. I want to go directly to the part of Dick which is controlling his behavior at the unconscious level in this context.

I also make the assumption that the part of you that makes you X— even though you don't like that consciously—is doing something on your behalf, something that benefits you in some way. I don't know what that is, and from your response you consciously don't know what it is, because you want to stop it.

So let's establish contact with that part officially. This is step two. It's already happened, but let's do it officially. Dick, do you know how to use words to talk to yourself on the inside? OK. What I'd like you to do is to go inside in a moment and ask a question. I'll tell you what the question is. Your job, after you've asked this question, is simply to attend to any changes you sense in your body sensations, any kinesthetic changes, any images, or any sounds that occur in response to the question. You don't have to try to influence this in any way. The part of you responsible for this pattern will make its needs known through one of those sensory channels. You just have to be sensitive to detect the response.

The question I would like you to ask is "Will the part of me responsible for pattern X communicate with me in consciousness?" And then simply notice what happens—any change of feelings, images, or sounds.

Your job out there, while Dick is doing this, is to observe him and always get the answer to the question I have him ask *before* he gives it to us. And you already have it. That's really typical. We talked the other day about meta-commenting as a choice in communication. This is one context in which I strongly recommend that you do *not* meta-comment, unless you simply want to shake somebody up. If you can always get the answer before your client does, you have a really powerful direct channel of communication to their unconscious, outside of their awareness, that allows you to do really powerful congruency checks. If the answer that *you* observe is different from the answer *they* get in their awareness, that's an important thing to know.

Dick, what was your experience after you asked the question?

Dick: Confusion.

OK. "Confusion" is a nominalization. It's not experience; it's a conscious judgement *about* experience. It's irrelevant to talk about his conscious judgements because he's already done the best he can with his conscious resources, and it hasn't worked. We need to work with experience. What was your experience that you labeled "confusion"? How did you know you were confused?

Dick: Flushing.

So you felt a flushing, a change in blood pressure. Was there a temperature change that went along with it, or a sense of pressure? Was it localized in some part of your body?

Dick: Some of both, mostly in my stomach.

In your stomach. OK, now that's a really elegant non-verbal response. In doing reframing we strongly recommend that you stay with primary representational systems: feelings, pictures, or sounds. Don't bother with words, because they are too subject to conscious interference. The beauty of a non-verbal kinesthetic signal such as this, is that it's considered involuntary. And you can test to be *sure* that it's involuntary. Dick, can you make that feeling of flushing happen consciously?

Dick: Maybe.

Try....

Dick: No.

That's also a really good way to subjectively convince someone that they are communicating with a part of them that normally is not available to them at the conscious level. And of course most hypnosis and biofeedback is based on the principle that you can alter consciousness and gain access to parts of your nervous system and physiology which you normally don't have access to. The question was a "yes-no" question; the response was a kinesthetic change, a feeling change. Now, so far all we have is a response; we don't know whether it means "yes" or "no" and neither does Dick, consciously.

One of the ways people really get into trouble is that they play psychiatrist with their own parts without being qualified. They interpret the messages they get from their own parts. So they begin to feel something and they name it "fear," when it may be some form of excitement, or some kind of aliveness, or anything. By naming it and then acting as if that is the case, they misinterpret their own internal communication as easily as they misinterpret communication externally. We don't want to run that risk, and there's an easy way to be sure what that signal means.

Dick, first I'd like you to go inside and thank the part for the communication it gave you, so that you validate that part for communicating with you. Next, say to it "I would like very much to understand your communication. So that I don't misunderstand what you mean, if you are saying 'Yes, you are willing to communicate with me in consciousness,' please intensify the same signal that you gave me before—the flushing in the stomach. If you are saying 'No, you're not willing to communicate with me in consciousness,' reverse it and diminish the response."

As Dick does this and you are watching to get the answer before he gives it to us, realize that if the signal had been a picture we would have simply varied the amplitude of the signal. We could make it brighter for "yes" and darker for "no." If it had been a sound we could have asked for an increase in volume for "yes" and a decrease for "no." In this way you avoid the risk of consciously misinterpreting the meaning of various internal kinesthetic, visual, or auditory signals. It gives you a very clean channel of communication with the part of Dick that is responsible for the pattern of behavior he wants to change. And of course that's *just* the part that knows how to make the change.

This process gives you an excellent opportunity to practice seeing what are traditionally called hypnotic responses. One of Milton Erickson's more useful definitions of deep trance is "a limited focus of attention inward." That's exactly what we asked Dick to do here—to limit his focus of attention to a signal which is internally generated. And the corresponding changes in the texture of his skin, breathing, skin color, lip size, etc., are all characteristic of what official hypnotists call trance phenomena.

Dick, rejoin us back here. What happened?

Dick: I had the feelings.

So the feelings intensified. You got a verification. We now have communication with the part; we have a "yes-no" signal. We can now ask that particular part *any* question and get an unambiguous "yes-no" answer. We have an internal channel of communication that Dick is running himself. We're not doing it. We're simply consulting with him about the next step. He now has established an internal channel of communication which allows him to communicate unambiguously with the part of him responsible for the pattern he wants to change. That's all you need. You can do anything at this point.

Step three is to distinguish between pattern X and the *intention* of the part that is responsible for the pattern. Dick, this part of you which is responding to you at the unconscious level has a certain intention it's trying to carry out for you. The *way* it's going about it is not acceptable to you at the conscious level. Now we're going to work with that part, through your channel of communication, to offer it better ways to accomplish what it's trying to do. When it has better ways than the way it goes about it now, you can have what you want consciously *and* this part can continue to take care of you in the way it wants to.

I want you to go inside again and ask a question. After the question, be sensitive to the signal system you have. Go inside and ask that part "Would you be willing to let me know in consciousness what you are trying to do for me by this pattern X?" Then you wait for a "yes-no" signal.... (Dick smiles broadly.)

I just said to ask "yes-no"; I didn't say "Give me the information." If you were attending, you noticed that something fairly dramatic happened. He asked for a "yes-no" answer. He got the "yes-no" signal *and* he also got information about the intention in consciousness.

Dick: Which pleased me.

Which pleased him and surprised him. Therapy is over at this point. There is now a conscious appreciation of what this part—that has been running pattern X—has been trying to do for him at the unconscious level. Dick, you didn't know what it was trying to do before, did you?

Dick: No, but I got a clue to it while you were talking, before I went down in. I got a feeling that it—

Part of our problem doing demonstrations is that after two days with you we have such good rapport with your unconscious there's a tendency for you to do it too fast.

So now he has a conscious understanding of the intention of this part of him that has been running X. Dick, is it true that you would like a part of you to have the responsibility of taking care of you in that way, even though the specific method it uses is not acceptable to you? You may not like the *way* that it goes about accomplishing pattern X, but do you agree that the *intention* is something you want to have a part do for you as a person?

Dick: Yes.

Now there is congruency between the intention of the unconscious part and the appreciation of the conscious.

That means it's time for step number four: to create some new alternatives to the pattern X that are *more* successful in accomplishing the intention, and that still allow consciousness to have exactly what it wants. What we're going to do is hold the intention—the outcome—constant, and vary the ways of achieving that outcome until we find some *better* ways of achieving it, ways that do not come into conflict with other parts of Dick.

Dick, do you have a part of yourself that you consider your creative part?

Dick: Humpf!

The creative part hops out! "Hi! Here I am. What do you want?" I hope you all appreciate the sense in which I said before that multiple personality is an evolutionary step. So you do have a part of yourself that you consider your creative part.

Dick: Oh, yes.

I want you to go inside and ask your creative part if it would be willing to undertake the following task. Let me explain it first before you do it. Ask it to go at the unconscious level to the part that runs pattern X, and find out what that part is trying to do for you. Then have it begin to create alternative ways by which this part of you can accomplish this intention. It will create 10, 20, or 1000 ways to get that outcome, and it's to be quite irresponsible in this. It simply is to generate a lot of possible ways for you to get the outcome, without trying to evaluate which ones would really work. Now, out of that multitude of things that it will offer, the part of you that's running pattern X will evaluate which of those ways it believes are more effective than pattern X in getting what it's been trying to get for you. It is to select at least three ways that it believes will work *at least* as effectively as, and hopefully *more* effectively than, the pattern of behavior it's been using up to now to accomplish that intention. Does that make sense to you?

Dick: I think so.

OK. Go inside and ask your creative part if it would be willing to do that. When it says "yes," tell it to go ahead. And the way I would like the part of you to notify you that it has accepted each one of the new choices is by giving you that feeling, that "yes" signal. You may or may not be conscious of what the new alternatives are. That's irrelevant for our purposes here.

Dick: It sounds like a big assignment.

Yes, it is, but thousands of people have done it all over the world. It's humanly possible and you are a human. You have to go inside and explain it to your creative part and to the other part, and if they both agree, tell them to go ahead. What you're going to do now is to use your own creative resources to begin to reorganize your behavior. . . . (long pause)

Did you get your three signals, Dick? (No.) How many have you gotten? (None.) None, you've gotten none. Would you go inside and ask that same part—again "yes" or "no"—if it has been presented with choices by your creative part. Ask if your creative part has been presenting it choices. . . . (He nods.) OK. Then it has been receiving?

Dick: Apparently.

So checking at the creative level, we find creativity is generating lots of possibilities. OK, would you go inside and ask if any of those choices that were presented were acceptable choices? Were any of them more effective than pattern X to accomplish what it wants?

Some of you like to offer advice to your clients. Any time you offer advice, that's going to be less effective than if you can throw them back, with appropriate explicit instructions, on their own resources to develop their own alternative ways. You are a unique human being and so are your clients. And there may or may not be overlap, as you found the first day during that afternoon exercise when we asked you to hallucinate. Some of you could guess the content of your partner's experiences in a way that was almost unbelievable. With other people, it doesn't work at all. If you have that incredible overlap, then you can offer useful advice. There's nothing wrong with it, as long as you are sensitive to the response you are getting as you offer it. But even then it will be more effective to throw a person back on their own resources. (Dick shakes his head.)

OK. You got a "no" signal. None of the new choices are acceptable. The creative part generated a lot of possible ways, none of which were as effective as the present pattern. Now, would you ask that part that runs pattern X if it would go to your creative part and become an advisor to your creative part so that it can come up with better choices about how to accomplish that intention? Ask it to explain what, specifically, about the choices the creative part has been presenting prevents them from being more effective ways of accomplishing the intention. Do you understand that instruction consciously, Dick? OK, would you go inside and explain it to that part and then ask it—"yes" or "no"—if it would be willing to do that? And if it says "yes," tell it to go ahead.

This particular process differs significantly from normal therapeutic and hypnotic techniques. We simply serve as consultants for the person's conscious mind. He does all the work himself. He is his own therapist; he is his own hypnotist at the moment. We're not doing any of those things. We communicate directly only with his consciousness and instruct it how to proceed. It's his responsibility to establish and maintain effective communication with the unconscious portions of him that he needs to access in order to change. Of course, once he learns to do that—using this as an example—he can do it without us. That's another advantage. This process has autonomy for your client built into it.

Dick, did you get three signals?

Dick: I'm not sure.

OK, would you go inside and ask that part if it now has at least three choices—whether or not you are conscious of what they are is irrelevant—which it finds more powerful than the old pattern X in accomplishing what it's trying to do. Again, use the same signal. It's important to continually refer back to the same signal, and it's important to get *three* new choices. If you have at least three choices, you begin to exercise variability in your behavior.

Dick: That was "yes."

OK, so now he got a positive; it said "Yes, I have at least three ways more effective than the old pattern X," even though he consciously doesn't know what those are.

Step five is to make sure those new choices actually occur in his behavior. Using the same signal system, Dick, we would like you to ask this part "Since you have three ways more effective than the old pattern X, would you take responsibility for actually making those things occur in my behavior in the appropriate context?" And you know that the "yes" is the intensification, and the "no" is the diminishment. Is that true?

Dick: I'm not sure that it is.

OK. Ask for that part to give you a "yes" signal before you begin, so that you know which is "yes" and which is "no." If you get them backwards, it's going to mess things up a little bit.

Dick: Yeah, I ... I ... I lost track.

Yes. I know. That's why I'm asking you to do this. Just go inside and ask the part to give you a "yes" signal, so that you know which one is "yes."

Dick: The "yes" signal is relaxing.

OK, fine. Let's back up a bit. Go back inside and ask the part if it agrees that these choices will work more effectively than X.

Dick: That was "yes."

Fine. Now ask that part if it would be willing to accept the responsibility for generating the three new choices—instead of pattern X—for a period of, say, six weeks to try them out.

Dick: "Yes."

Step six, in my opinion, is what makes this model for change really elegant. The ecological check is our explicit recognition that Dick here, and each one of us, is a really complex and balanced organism. For us to simply make a change in pattern X and not take into account all the repercussions in other parts of his experience and behavior would be foolhardy. This is a way of building in a protection against that.

We would like you to thank this part for all the work it has done. It's got what it needs; it's already satisfied with that. Now we want to find out if any other parts have input to this process. Ask "Is there any other part of me that has any objection to the new choices that are going to occur?" Then be sensitive to any response in any system: feelings, pictures, or sounds....

OK, you've got a response. And?

Dick: They have no objections.

How do you know that? This is important. I asked you to attend to all systems. You came back and said "No. There's no objection." How do you know there's no objection?

Dick: I felt no tension anywhere.

You felt no tension. Were there any changes you could detect either in your kinesthetics or visually or auditorily?

Dick: Well, the relaxation.

A relaxation. OK, that was an overall body relaxation. Just to be sure, just to check for congruency, thank whatever part made your body relax. And then ask "If this means no objection, relax me even further. If there is any objection, make some tension occur." Again, all we are doing is varying the signal for "yes" or "no." It's arbitrary whether you go "Yes for positive increase, No for diminish," or the reverse. It doesn't matter.

Dick: I'm getting some objection.

OK. What exactly was your experience? Were there changes in muscle tension?

Dick: Yes, around my eyes.

OK. Whenever you get a response to a general inquiry, it's important to check and be absolutely sure what that response means. Thank that part for the response of tension in the muscles around your eyes. Ask for an increase for "yes" and a decrease for "no" to the question: "Do you object to the new alternatives?" ...

Dick: There was a decrease.

It's slightly unusual to have the tension here. Typically at the ecological check almost everybody's heart speeds up. Most people associate a speeded-up heart rate with fear or anxiety. When I ask them to stop hallucinating and simply ask for an increase for "yes" and a decrease for "no," the heart rate usually slows down. My understanding of this is that it's simply a signal that some part of them is quite excited about what's going on.

Dick: I was also aware of a pulsating in my hands, but the eye tension seemed more dramatically different than the hand sensations, so that's why I mentioned the eye tension.

OK, let's check this, too. This time go in and thank the part that gave you the hand signals. Then ask the same question "Do you have any objections?" and ask for an increase for "yes" and a decrease for "no."

Dick: Decrease in sensation.

Decrease, so that part also doesn't have an objection. If there had been an objection at this point, you would simply recycle back to step three. You have a new "yes-no" signal—the pulsating in the hands. Now you make a distinction between this part's objection and its intention. You continue cycling through this process until you have integrated all objections.

We usually hold the first set of three choices constant and ask any part that objects to find alternative ways of doing what it needs to do without interfering with the first set of choices. But you could also ask both parts to form a committee and go to the creative part and select new alternatives that are acceptable to both.

The ecological check is very important. Many of you have done elegant work, and the client is congruent in your office. When he leaves, another part of him emerges which has concerns that are contextually bound. When he gets home, suddenly he doesn't have access to what he had in your office or in the group. There are other parts of him that know that if he goes home and simply changes in the way that he was going to change, he would lose the friendship of this person, or blow that relationship, or something like that. This is a way of checking to make sure that there are no parts whose positive contribution to him will be interfered with by the new pattern of behavior. Of course the only *real* check is in experience, but this is a way of doing the best you can to make sure that the new choices will work.

OK, now, Dick, what happens if six or seven weeks from now, you discover yourself doing the old pattern of behavior X? What are you supposed to do, then? ... You can accept that as a signal that the new choices that you came up with were not adequate to satisfy the intention. And you can go back to your creative part and give it instructions to come up with three more choices. The pattern of behavior is a barometer of how effective the new choices are. If the old behavior emerges after a test period, it's a statement that the new choices were not more effective than the old pattern. It's a signal for you to return to this process and create better choices.

Regression to previous behavior isn't a signal of failure, it's a signal of incompetency, and you need to go back and fix it. *Reframing will work.* I guarantee his behavior will change. *If* his behavior changes back, that's a signal that the new kinds of behavior were not as effective at getting something for him as the old pattern. Then he goes back through the process, finds out what other secondary gain is involved, and creates new ways to take care of that as well.

If you don't explicitly make the symptom a signal to negotiate, the person's conscious mind will call it a "failure" if the symptom comes back. When the symptom is identified as a signal, the client begins to pay attention to it as a *message*. It probably always was a message anyway, but they never thought about it that way. By doing this, they begin to have a feedback mechanism. They discover that they only get the signal at certain times.

For example, somebody comes in with migraine headaches and I reframe, and all parts are happy, and the client goes along for two weeks and everything's fine. Then they are in a particular context and suddenly they get a headache. That headache triggers off the instruction that the negotiations weren't adequate. The person can drop inside and ask "Who's unhappy? What does this mean?" If a part says "You're not standing up for yourself like you promised to," then they are faced with a simple choice of having a migraine headache or standing up for themselves.

I had a woman who got such severe migraine headaches that she was flat on her back. There was a part of her that wanted to be able to play ∟very so often, and if it wasn't going to get to play, then the other parts weren't going to get to do *anything!* Whacko! It would give her a headache. So she made an arrangement that she would spend a defined amount of time in playing activities. After the session, when the weekend came and it was time to play, she decided to do her taxes instead! That part just laid her out. She called on the phone and said "Well, I didn't keep up my end of the bargain, and I got another migraine headache. What should I do?" I said "Don't ask me; ask the part. It's not my problem. My head doesn't hurt."

So she went in and found out what she was supposed to do. That part said "Go out, get in the car, and go somewhere and have fun *or else!*" As soon as she got in the car, the headache was gone. So her headache no longer became something that was a burden; it became an indicator that she had better respond. She learned that getting a headache was a signal to go out and have some fun.

OK. Any questions about the process we went through with Dick?

Woman: Am I understanding that Dick doesn't need to be aware of what those choices are?

We prefer that he not be. That could just get in his way.

Woman: Dick, you're not aware of your three alternatives specifically?

Dick: I'm not. In some ways I feel a failure because of it, you know, because I can't *think* it.

Woman: Well, how does he know he has them?

He got a signal from his unconscious, namely the kinesthetic feeling of relaxation. He doesn't consciously know what the new alternatives are.

Dick: But it feels OK down here.

His unconscious mind knows what they are, and that's all that counts. That's the one that runs the show in this area of behavior, anyway. Let's make a demonstration for your purposes here. Would you go inside, Dick, and ask this same part down here, using the same "yes-no" signal, if it would be willing to allow your conscious mind to know what *one* of those new choices is, just as a demonstration to you that it knows things that you don't.

This is called a convincer. It's wholly irrelevant for the process of change, but it can settle people's conscious minds a little bit.

Dick: He won't do it.

And rightfully so. If I were Dick's unconscious mind, I wouldn't tell him either. He'd try to interfere. What *did* he do earlier? His unconscious part wouldn't release specific information, and he immediately had a feeling of failure! I wouldn't communicate with his conscious mind if it were going to behave like that either. It's just as convincing to have your unconscious say "No, I won't tell you what any of the new choices are," if it's an involuntary signal. Right?

Dick: Right.

Now let me mention in passing the paradoxical nature of the request that we made in step two. The question is "Would you be willing to communicate with me in consciousness?" *Any* signal that he detects has to be a response in consciousness. Even if the part says "No, I would not," that's still a communication in consciousness.

If he had gotten a "no" response, I would understand that in the following way: the intent of that part is *not* to not communicate with him in consciousness. It's a statement that it doesn't trust him. That is, it's not willing to release content information to his conscious mind. And I respect that. I really believe that unconscious minds should have the freedom, and in fact have the duty, to keep out of awareness material which would not be useful for the conscious mind to deal with.

We had a period when we did nothing but deep, deep trance hypnosis. A man came in once and said that there were all kinds of things standing in the way of his being happy. I said "Would you like to tell me wnat those things are?" And he said "No, I want to go into a trance and change it all, and that's why I came for hypnosis." So accepting all behavior, I did an induction, put him into a deep trance, sent his conscious mind away, and said "I want to speak privately with your unconscious mind." I have *no* idea what that means. However, when you tell them to, people do it. They talk to you and it's *not* the one you were talking to before, because it knows things the other one doesn't know. Whether I created that division or whether it was there already, I have no idea. I asked for it, and I got it.

In this particular case, his conscious mind was, to put it as nicely as I can, inane. His unconscious resources, however, were incredibly intelligent. So I said "What I want to know from you, since you know much more about him than I do, is what change is it that he needs to make in his behavior?"

The response I got was "He's a homosexual."

"What change does he need to make?"

"He needs to change it, because it's all based on a mistake."

"What mistake?"

The explanation that I got from his unconscious mind was the following: The first time he had ever asserted himself physically, in terms of trying to defend himself against violence, was when he was five years old in a hospital to have his tonsils out. Someone put the ether mask on his face, and he tried to push it away and fight back as he went under the anesthetic. Anesthesia became anchored to the feeling of being angry. After that, every time he began to feel angry or frightened and started to strike out, his body went limp. As a result of this, his conscious mind decided that he was a homosexual. He had lived as a homosexual for about twenty-five years.

His unconscious resources said "You must not let his conscious mind know about this mistake, because knowing that would destroy him." And I agreed with that. There was no need for him to know that he had goofed in all of his relationships for twenty-five years. The only important thing was that he make a change, because he wanted to get married. But he couldn't marry a woman because he *knew* that he was a homosexual. His unconscious mind would not allow him in any way to become conscious of the fact that he had made this mistake, because it would have made his whole life a mistake and that knowledge would have utterly destroyed him. It wanted him to have the illusion that he grew out of it and grew into new behavior.

So I arranged with his unconscious mind to have him blossom as a heterosexual person and to make the changes as a result of a spiritual experience. His unconscious mind agreed that that was the best way to go about it. He changed without any conscious representation of either the hypnotic session or where the changes came from. He believes it came as a result of a drug experience. He smoked marijuana and had a cosmic experience. He assumed that it was the quality of the grass, and not a post-hypnotic suggestion. That was adequate for him to make the changes that he wanted.

There are many parts of people that do that same kind of thing. A part doesn't want the conscious mind to know what's going on, because it believes the conscious mind can't handle it, and it may or may not be right. Sometimes I've worked with people and I've made a deal with a part to allow the conscious mind to slowly become aware of something a little at a time, to discover if in fact the conscious mind can handle it or not. And usually the part discovered that the conscious mind could accept the information. At other times I've gotten an emphatic "No, there's no way I will do that. I don't want the conscious mind to know. I will change all behaviors, but I will not inform the conscious mind of anything." And people do change. Most change takes place at the unconscious level anyway. It's only in recent Western European history that we've made the idea of change explicit.

If Dick's part had said that it was unwilling to inform his conscious mind what the intention was, we would have just gone ahead anyway because it isn't relevant. We would have just told that part to go directly to his creative part and get the new choices. In fact, informing his conscious mind is probably what made it take so long. I'm serious. Being conscious, as far as I can tell, is never important, unless you want to write books to model your behavior. In terms of face-to-face communication, either internally or with other people, you don't need consciousness. We essentially limit his conscious participation to receiving and reporting fluctuations in his signal system, and asking the questions which stimulate those responses.

It's quite possible—not only possible but quite *positive*—for him *not* to know what the intention of his unconscious part is, as well as for him *not* to know what the new choices are. The changes will still be as profound and as effective as if he knew all that. In fact, in some ways the changes will be more effective.

Man: What if you get no response at all at the beginning?

Well, if you get no response at all, your client is probably dead. But if he doesn't get a response that convinces him, I'd ally myself with his unconscious mind and say "Look, this part is unwilling to communicate with you and I agree with it, because I wouldn't want to communicate with you either. What you haven't realized yet is that this part has been doing something vitally important for you. It's been doing you a service and you've spent all this time fighting your own internal processes when they've been trying to do something positive for you. I want to salute them and compliment them. And I think you owe them an apology." I'll literally tell people to go inside and apologize for having fought with the part and having made it that much harder for that part to do what it's trying to do for them.

If that doesn't work, you can threaten them. "And if you don't start being better to your parts, I'm going to *help* them destroy you. I'm going to help them give you a terrible headache and make you gain twenty-five pounds." Then typically I begin to get really good unconscious communication. The person will be saying "Well, I don't think this is really accurate" at the same time that their head is nodding up and down in response to what I've said.

Woman: In step three you ask the part what it is trying to do—what its intention is by that pattern of behavior. Do you need to do that if it doesn't matter whether you know about it or not?

No. It's just that most people are interested. If the unconscious doesn't want to reveal the intention, we'd just say something like "Even though X is a pattern you consciously want to change, are you willing to believe that this is a well-intentioned unconscious part, and that what it's trying to get for you by making you do X is something in your behalf as a total person? If you're willing to accept that, let's keep all the content unconscious, saying 'OK, I trust that you're well-intentioned. I don't need to review and evaluate your intentions because I will make the assumption that you're operating in my best interests.'" Then we'd just go ahead with step four.

A few years ago we were doing a workshop and there was a woman there who had a phobia of driving on freeways. Rather than treating it as a phobia, which would have been much more elegant, I did a standard reframing to demonstrate that you *can* work with phobias with reframing, even though it's much faster to use the two-step visual/kinesthetic dissociation pattern. I said "Look, there's a part that's scaring the pants off you when you go near freeways. Go inside and tell this part that we know it's doing something of importance, and ask if it is willing to communicate with you." She got a very strong positive response. So I said "Now go inside and ask the part if it would be willing to tell you what it's trying to do for you by scaring the pants off you when you go near freeways." She went inside, and then said "Well, the part said 'No, I'm not willing to tell you.'"

Rather than go to unconscious reframing, I did something which may sound curious, but it's something I do from time to time when I have suspicions, or what other people call intuitions. I had her go inside and ask if the part *knew* what it was doing for her. She closed her eyes, and then she came back outside and said "Well, I ... I don't ... I don't believe what it said." "Well, go inside again, and ask if it's telling the truth." She went inside again, and then said "I don't want to believe what it said." "Well, what did it say?" "It said it *forgot!*"

Now, as amusing as that sounds, I always thought that was a *great* response. In some ways it makes sense. You are alive for a long time. If a part organizes its behavior to do something and you really resist it and fight against it, it can get so caught up in the fight that it forgets why it organized its behavior that way in the first place. How many of you have ever gotten into an argument and in the middle of it forgotten what it was that you were intending to do in the first place? Parts, like people, don't always remember about outcomes.

Rather than going through a lot of rigamarole, I said "Look, this is a very powerful part of you. Did you ever think about how powerful it is? Every single time you go near a freeway, this part is capable of scaring the pants off you. That's pretty amazing. How would you like to have a part like that on your side?" She went "Wow! I don't have any parts like that!" So I said "Go inside and ask that part if it would like to do something that it could be appreciated for, that would be worthwhile, and that would be worthy of its talents." And of course that part went "Oh, yeah!" So I said "Now go inside and ask that part if it would be willing to have you be comfortable, alert, breathing regularly and smoothly, being cautious and in sensory experience when you go onto a freeway on ramp." The part went "Yeah, yeah. I'll do that." I then had her fantasize a couple of freeway situations. Earlier she was incapable of doing that; she would go into a terror state because even the fantasy of being near a freeway was too scary. When she went through it this time she did it adequately. She then got in a car, went out to the freeway, and did fine. She enjoyed it so much that she drove for four hours and ran out of gas on the freeway!

Man: At one point it looked like there was strain showing on Dick's forehead. I just wondered if he really was bothered or just concentrating.

If you were working with someone and you had a serious doubt about that, then you owe it to yourself to verify your suspicion or deny it. The easiest way, of course, is the same methodology. I would look at

Dick and say "I noticed a furrowed brow. That sometimes indicates tension, or sometimes simply concentration. I don't know which." It only takes an extra thirty seconds to have him go inside and ask the part of him that's wrinkling his brow to increase the tension there if it has some input to this process that it would like to make manifest, and decrease the tension there if not. That would give you an immediate verification, without any hallucination. You don't have to hallucinate, and he doesn't have to guess. You've got a system which allows you to get direct sensory signals in order to answer your questions.

I hope those of you who are hypnotists recognize a couple of patterns going on here. One is fractionation: alternating from turning inward and coming back to sensory experience—in and out of trance.

Whether you are hypnotists or not you've probably heard of finger signals or ideomotor signals. A hypnotist will often make arrangements with the person in a trance that s/he will lift the right index finger with honest unconscious movements for "yes" responses, and the left index finger for "no." What we did here is nothing more than a system of natural finger signals. Finger signals are a wholly arbitrary imposition by the hypnotist. Reframing leaves much more freedom on the part of the client to choose a response signal system which is most congruent with what they need at the time. It's a naturalistic technique that also makes possible signals that can't be duplicated by consciousness. However, it's the same formal pattern, the same principle, as finger signals. Using natural signals also allows different parts to use different channels instead of having them all use the same system.

Now, what if at some point he had gotten increased sweating in the palms, sensations in the front of the leg, visual images, a sound of a racing car—all these signals as responses? I would have said "I'm glad there are so many parts active in your behalf. In order to make this thing work, go inside and thank them all for the responses. Ask all those parts to be exquisitely attentive to what happens. First we'll take the perspiration in your hands; we'll work with that part. I guarantee all the other parts that no behavioral changes will occur until we do the ecological check and I have verified that they all accept the new behaviors.

Or you could ask all those parts to form a committee and ask them to choose one signal. Then have the committee make its collective needs known to the creative part, and so on.

Man: What if in step five the part doesn't agree to take the responsibility?

Well, then something went wrong earlier. If the part that says "No, I won't take responsibility" is the same part that selected three patterns of behavior which it believes are more effective than the original pattern, that doesn't make any sense at all. That's an indicator that your communication channels got crossed somewhere, so you go back and straighten them out.

Man: Backing up one step, what if it doesn't help you select? You ask "Will you select from all these possibilities?" and it says "No, I won't."

You can say "Stupid, I'm offering you ways which are more effective than your present pattern and you're saying 'No'! What kind of a jerk are you?" I'm serious. That works really well. You get a response then! However, that's only one possible maneuver. There are lots of other maneuvers. "Oh, then you are entirely satisfied with all the wasted energy that is going on inside?" Use whatever maneuvers you have in your behavior that are appropriate at that point to get the response you want.

Woman: What kind of reports do you get about what happens when your new behavior occurs?

Usually people behave differently for a week before they notice it. Conscious minds are really limited. That's the report we get a lot. I used reframing with a woman who had a phobic response to, curiously enough, going over bridges, but only if they had water under them. She lived in New Orleans where there are a lot of bridges with water under them. There's one bridge in New Orleans called the Slidell Bridge, and she would always say "Especially the SLIDEell Bridge," accented that way. After I had done reframing with her, I said "Are you going to cross any bridges on the way home?" And she said "Yes, I'm going over the SliDELL bridge." That difference was enough of an indication for me that I knew that the reframing was going to work.

She was in that workshop for three days and never said a word. At the end of the workshop, I asked her about the work we had done on Friday. "You've been driving over bridges this weekend, and I want to know if you had any of that phobic response." She said "Oh, I really hadn't thought about it." A few days earlier she had been working on it as a problem. Two days later she was saying "Oh, yeah, they are just expressways over water." That's very, very close to the response that

Tammy offered us yesterday. When Tammy fantasized doing it, she went "Well, it was driving across a bridge." It no longer had that incredible impact, that overwhelming kinesthetic response. People have the tendency not even to think about it. They have a tendency to discover it afterwards, which to me is really much hipper anyway than if they are surprised and delighted with it.

That same woman in New Orleans also said "Well, it's a really amazing thing. Actually I wasn't phobic of bridges!"

"If you weren't phobic of bridges, how come you freaked out when you got on them?"

"Because they go over *water.* You see, the whole thing had to do with almost drowning when I was a little kid; I was underneath a bridge, drowning."

"Do you have a swimming pool?"

"Now that you mention it, no."

"Do you swim very often?"

"I don't swim at all. I can't swim."

"Do you like showers or baths?"

"*Showers.*"

She made a generalization somewhere in her past that said "Don't go near water; you'll drown." When that part noticed that she was going over a bridge, it said "Bridges go over water, and water's a good place to drown, so now is the time to be terrified."

We always have follow-ups. People come back or telephone, so we make sure that the changes they want did occur. Typically we have to ask for a report—which seems to me really appropriate. Change is the only constant in my experience and most of it occurs at the unconscious level. It's only with the advent of official humanistic psychotherapies and psychiatry that people pay conscious attention to change.

In Michigan, I worked on a phobia that a woman had. I didn't know what the content was at the time, but it turned out that she had a phobia of dogs. After we had done the work, she went to visit a friend who had a dog. What was really amusing to her as she walked in and saw the dog, was that the dog looked so much *smaller.* She said to her friend "My God! What happened to your dog? It's *shrunk!*"

Man: Dick's signal system gave a positive response that it received three new choices from his creative part. What if he got a negative?

It doesn't matter if you get a "yes" or "no." It only matters that you get one or the other. The "yes-no" signals are just to distract the conscious mind of the person you are working with. If you get a "no," then you offer it another way to go about it. "Then you go to your devious part and tell it to ally itself with your creative part and trick this part of you into having new choices." It doesn't matter how you do it.

I probably would have had him construct a creative part. I wouldn't have been satisfied that he had access to his creativity. I know there are *lots* of ways to accomplish the same thing. You can say "Do you know anyone else who is able to do this? I want you to review with vivid detail in picture and sound and feeling what *they* do, and then have this part of you consider *those* possibilities." That's just a way of doing what we call "referential index shift."

What if you say to the person "Do you have a part of you that you consider your creative part?" And they say "No." What are you going to do? Or they hesitate; they say "Well, I don't know." There's a really easy way to create a creative part, using representation systems and anchoring. You say "Think of the five times in your life when you behaved in a very powerfully creative way and you didn't have the faintest idea how or what you did, but you knew it was a positive and creative thing that you did." As s/he thinks of those five in a row, you anchor them. You then have a direct anchor to the person's creativity. You've assembled one. You've organized their personal history. Or you can ask "Do you have a part of you that makes plans? Well, have it come up with three different ways you can plan new behavior." The word "creative" is only one choice out of a myriad ways of organizing your activities.

The only way you can get stuck in a process like this is if you try to run it rigidly. You say to a client "Well, do you have a part of you that you consider your creative part?" If they look you straight in the eye and say "No," then start making up other words. "Do you realize that you have a part of you that is responsible for all *glunk* activities? And the way you contact that is by touching your temple!" You can make up *anything,* as long as the result is that they generate new ways of accomplishing the intention. That is as limitless as your own creativity. And if *you* don't have a creative part, create one for yourself!

There are a lot of other ways that this could have *not* worked, too. Do you realize that that's what people in here are doing again? You all saw it work. And you're asking "What are all the ways it could have *not* worked?" I'm sure you could manufacture a hundred ways to make this not work. And in fact many of you will. The point is, when you do

160

something that doesn't work, do something *else*. If you keep doing something else, something will work. We want you to make it work with each other so that you have a reference experience. Find someone you don't know to be your partner and try reframing. We'll be around if you get stuck.

Reframing Outline

(1) *Identify the pattern* (X) to be changed.
(2) *Establish communication* with the part responsible for the pattern.
    (a) "Will the part of me that runs pattern X communicate with me in consciousness?"
    (b) Establish the "yes-no" meaning of the signal.
(3) *Distinguish between the behavior,* pattern X, *and the intention* of the part that is responsible for the behavior.
    (a) "Would you be willing to let me know in consciousness what you are trying to do for me by pattern X?"
    (b) If you get a "yes" response, ask the part to go ahead and communicate its intention.
    (c) Is that intention acceptable to consciousness?
(4) *Create new alternative behaviors* to satisfy the intention. At the unconscious level the part that runs pattern X communicates its intention to the creative part, and selects from the alternatives that the creative part generates. Each time it selects an alternative it gives the "yes" signal.
(5) Ask the part "Are you willing to *take responsibility* for generating the three new alternatives in the appropriate context?"
(6) *Ecological check.* "Is there any other part of me that objects to the three new alternatives?" If there is a "yes" response, recycle to step (2) above.

* * * * *

Once at a workshop for a TA institute, I said that I believed that *every* part of *every* person is a valuable resource. One woman said "That's the stupidest thing I ever heard!"

"I didn't say it was true. I said if you believe that as a therapist you'll get a lot further."

"Well, that's totally ridiculous."

"What leads you to believe that that's ridiculous?"

"I've got parts that are not worth a dime. They just get in my way. That's all they do."

"Name one."

"I have a part that no matter what I do, all the time I'm trying to do anything, it just totally tells me I can't do it, and that I'm going to fail. It makes everything twice as hard as it needs to be."

She said that she had been a high school dropout. When she decided to go back to high school, that part said "You'll never be able to do it; you're not good enough; you're too stupid. It'll be embarrassing. You won't be able to do it." But she did it. And even when she did that, when she decided to go on to college, that part said "You're not going to be able to do it."

So I said "Well, I'd like to speak to that part directly." That always gets TA people, by the way. They don't have that in their model. Then I look over their left shoulder while I talk to them and that really drives them nuts. But it's a very effective anchoring mechanism, because from that time on, every time you look over their left shoulder, only that part can hear.

"I know that that part of you is doing something very important for you, and it is very sneaky about how it does it. Even if you don't appreciate it, I do. I'd like to tell that part that if it were willing to tell *her* conscious mind what it's doing for *her,* then perhaps it could get some of the appreciation that it deserves."

Then I had her go inside and ask the part what it was doing for her that was positive. It came right out and said "I was motivating you." After she told me that, she said "Well, I think that's weird." I said "Well, you know, I don't think it would be possible for you to come up here right now and work in front of this entire group." She stood up defiantly and walked across the room and sat down. Those of you who have studied strategies and understand the phenomenon of polarity response will recognize that this part was simply a Neuro Linguistic Programmer that understood utilization. It knew that if it said "Aw, you can go to college, you can do it," she'd say "No, I can't do it." However, if it said to her "You're not going to be able to cut the grade," then she would say "Oh, yeah?" and she would go out and do it.

Now what would have happened to that woman if we had somehow gotten that part to stop doing that, but without changing anything else? ... She wouldn't have had any way to motivate herself! That's why we have the ecological check. The ecological check is a way of being sure that the new behavior fits with all the other parts of a person. Up to step six we have essentially created a communication system between the person's consciousness and their unconscious part that runs the pattern of behavior they are trying to change. And we have succeeded in finding more effective alternative behaviors in that area. I don't know, of course, when I've finished that, whether this is going to be beneficial for them as a *total* person.

Let me give you another example of this. I've seen mousy little people who went to assertiveness training and became aggressive—so aggressive that their husband or wife left them and none of their friends will talk to them anymore. They go around yelling at people and being extremely assertive, so abrasive that they no longer have friends. That's sort of a polarity flip, or a swing of the pendulum. One way to make sure that doesn't happen is to have some device like the ecological check.

When you have completed communication and created alternative new behaviors for the part that originally ran the problem behavior, you ask for all other parts to consider the repercussions of these new patterns of behavior. "Is there any other part of me that has any objection to the new choices in my behavior?" If another part objects, it will typically use a distinctive signal. It may be in the same system, but it will be distinctive as far as body part. If suddenly there's tension in the shoulders, you say "Good, I have a limited conscious mind. Would you increase the tension in my shoulders if it means 'Yes, there is an objection,' and decrease it if it means 'No.'" If there is an objection, that's a delightful outcome. That means there is another part, another resource, that's active in your behalf in making this change. You are at step two again, and you recycle.

One of the things that I think distinguishes a really exquisite communicator from one who is not, is to be precise about your use of language: use language in a way that gets you what you want. People who are sloppy with language get sloppy responses. Virginia Satir is precise about her use of langauge, and Milton Erickson is even more precise. If you are precise about the way you phrase questions, you will get precise kinds of information back. For example, somebody here said "Go inside and ask if the part of you responsible for this behavior is willing to change?" And they got a "No" response. It makes perfect sense! They didn't offer it any new choices. They didn't say "Are you willing to communicate?" They said "Are you willing to change?"

Another person said "Will you, the part of me that is responsible for this pattern of behavior, accept the choices generated by my creativity?" And the answer was "No." And properly so. Your creativity doesn't know a thing about your behavior in this area. The part that's got to make a selection is the part that is responsible for your behavior. It's the one that knows about that.

Man: What if the unconscious creative part refuses to give any choices?

It never happens if you are respectful of it. If you as a therapist are disrespectful of people's creativity and their unconscious, it will simply cease communicating with you.

Woman: My partner and I found that our conscious minds were most unaccepting of change.

I totally agree with that. That's very true of therapists, especially if the choices were left unconscious. It's not necessarily true of other groups in the population. And it figures, because therapists have very nosy conscious minds. Almost every modern humanistic psychotheology I know implies that it is necessary to be conscious in order to make changes. That's absurd.

Woman: I'm confused about awareness and consciousness. Gestalt therapy talks about the importance of awareness, and—

When Fritz Perls said "Lose your mind and come to your senses," and to have awareness, I think he was talking about experience. I think he suspected that you could have sensory perception without intervening consciousness. He wrote about what he referred to as the "DMZ of experience," in which he said that talking to yourself was being as far removed from experience as you could be. He said that making visual images was a little bit closer to having experience. And he said having feelings was being as close as you could get to having experience, and that the "DMZ" is very different than behaving and acting in the real world.

I think what he was alluding to is that you can have experience without reflexive consciousness, and he called that "being in the here and now." We call it "uptime." It's the strategy we've used to organize our perceptions and responses in this workshop with you. In uptime, you don't talk to yourself, you don't have pictures and you don't have feelings. You simply access sensory experience and respond to it directly.

Gestalt therapy has an implicit rule that accessing cues are bad, because you must be avoiding. If you look away, you are avoiding. And when you are looking away you are in internal experience, which we call "downtime." Fritz wanted everybody to be in uptime. However, he was *inside telling himself* that it was better to be in uptime! He was a very creative person and I think that's what he meant, but it's really hard to know.

Woman: You said we'd see when reframing doesn't work.

I certainly did as I walked around the room! You will try it and it won't work. However that's not a comment on the method. That's a comment about not being creative enough in the application of it, and not having enough sensory experience to accept all the cues that are there. If you take its "not working"—instead of a comment about how dumb and stupid and inadequate you are—as a comment about what's there for you to learn and begin to explore, then therapy will become a real opportunity to expand yourself, instead of an opportunity for self-criticism.

This is one of the things I've discovered teaching hypnosis. I think it's one of the main reasons that hypnosis has not proliferated in this society. As a hypnotist you put somebody into a trance and present them with some kind of a challenge such as "You will be unable to open your eyes." Most people are *unwilling* to put themselves to that kind of test. People say this to me all the time in hypnosis training seminars: "What happens if I give them the suggestion and they don't carry it out?" And I say "You give them *another* one!" If they don't get exactly what they intended, they think they must have failed, instead of taking that as an opportunity for responding creatively.

There's a really huge trap there. If you decide before you begin a communication what will constitute a "valid" response, then the probability that you'll get it is reduced severely. If, however, you make a maneuver, some intervention, and then simply come to your senses and notice what response you get, you'll realize that *all responses are utilizable.* There's no particularly good or bad response. Any response is a good response *when* it's utilized, and it's the next step in the process of change. The only way you can fail is by quitting, and deciding you are not willing to spend any more time with it. Of course you can just continue to do the same thing over and over again, which means you'll have the same failure for a longer period of time!

There was a research project that I think you all are entitled to know about. Out of a group of people, one third of them went into therapy, one third of them were put on a waiting list, and one third of them were shown movies of therapy. The people on the waiting list had the same rate of improvement! That is a comment about that research project, and that's *all* it's a comment about. That finding was presented to me as if it were a statement about the world. When I made a comment that the only thing I could discern is that it was a statement about the incompetency of the people doing therapy in the project, it struck them as a novel idea that actually that might be a possibility.

I came to psychology from mathematics. The first thing that made sense to me as I entered the field of psychology is that what they were doing was not working, at least with the people who were still in the hospitals and still in the offices—the other people had gone home! So the only thing that made sense to me is that what they were doing with their clients was what I *didn't* want to do. The only things *not* worth learning were what they were already doing that wasn't working.

The first client that I saw was in somebody's private office. I went in and watched this therapist work with a young man for an hour. She was very warm, *very* empathetic, very sympathetic with this guy as he talked about what a terrible home life he had. He said "You know, my wife and I really haven't been able to get together, and it got so bad that I really felt I had strong needs and I went out and had this affair," and she said "I understand how you could do that." And they went on and on like this for a full hour.

At the end of the hour she turned to me and she said "Well, is there anything that you would like to add?" I stood up and looked at the guy and said "I want to tell you that I think you're the biggest punk I have ever met! Going out and screwing around behind your wife's back, and coming here and crying on this woman's shoulder. That's going to get you nothing, since you aren't going to change, and you're going to be as miserable as you are now for the rest of your life unless you grab yourself by the bootheels, give yourself a good kick in the butt, and go tell your wife how you want her to act with you. Tell her in explicit enough words so that she will know exactly what you want her to do. If you don't do that, you're going to be as miserable as you are now forever and *no one* will be able to help you." That was the exact opposite of what that therapist had done. He was devastated, just devastated. He left the office and went home and worked it all out with his wife. He did all of the things I'd told him to do, and then he called me up on the telephone and told me it was the most important experience of his life.

However, during the time he did that, that therapist utterly convinced me that what I had done was wrong! She explained to me all these concepts about therapy and about how this wouldn't be helpful, and convinced me that what I had done was the wrong thing.

Man: But she didn't stop you from doing it.

She *couldn't!* She was paralyzed! But she was right. It wouldn't have worked with *her.* However, it was *perfect* for *him.* If nothing else, it was just the opposite of what she had been doing all that time. It wasn't that what I did was more powerful than what she did, it was just more appropriate for him, given that all those other things hadn't worked. That therapist didn't have that flexibility in her behavior. She did the only thing that she could do. She couldn't do gestalt therapy because she couldn't yell at anybody. It wasn't a choice for her. She was *so* nice. I'm sure there were some people who had never had anybody be nice to them, and that hanging around her was such a new experience that it had some influence on them. However, that would still not help them make the specific changes that they came to therapy for.

Woman: What we did was to ask the conscious mind of the partner "Will you agree not to sabotage, not to try to—"

Oh, there's a presupposition there that the conscious mind *can* sabotage! You can ignore the conscious mind. It can't sabotage the unconscious. It couldn't sabotage the original choice that it didn't want, and it's not going to be able to sabotage the new ones either.

What you're doing with reframing is giving requisite variety to the unconscious. The unconscious previously had only one choice about how to get what it wants. Now it's got at least *four* choices—three new ones and the old one. The conscious mind still hasn't got any new choices. So given the law of requisite variety, which is going to be in control? The same one that was in control before you got here, and that is *not* your conscious mind.

It's important for some people to have the illusion that their conscious mind controls their behavior. It's a particularly virulent form of insanity among college professors, psychiatrists, and lawyers. They believe that consciousness is the way they run their lives. If you believe that, there is an experiment you can try. The next time somebody extends their hand to shake hands with you, I want you to consciously *not* lift your hand, and find out whether your hand goes up or not. My guess is that your conscious mind won't even discover that it is time to interrupt the behavior until your hand is at least half-way up. And that's just a comment about who's in control.

Man: How about the use of this method in groups?

I *hope* you notice how we have used it here! While you are doing reframing, you spend about seventy to eighty percent of the time alone, waiting for the person to get a response. While you are doing that you can start with someone else. Each of us used to do ten or fifteen people at a time. The only limitation on how many people you can do at one time is how much sensory experience you are able to respond to. You set your limitations by the refinement of your sensory apparatus.

I know a man who does it with groups, and he takes them all together through each step. "Everybody identify something. Everybody go inside. What did you get?" "I got a feeling." "Intensify for 'yes.'" "What did you get?" "I got sounds." "Have them get louder." "What did you get?" "I got a picture." "Have it brighten." He makes everybody *else* wait instead. That's another approach. It's easier if you have a homogeneous group of people.

Man: I'm kind of curious. Did you ever do this with somebody who had cancer—have them go inside and talk to the part that is causing the cancer?

Yes. I worked as a consultant for the Simontons in Fort Worth. I had six people who were terminal cancer patients, so I did them as a group, and that worked fine. I had enough sensory experience, and there was enough homogeneity in them as a group, that I could do it that way. The Simontons get good responses *just using visualization.* When you add the sophistication of all representational systems and the kind of communication system we develop with reframing, I don't know what the limits are. I would like to know what they are. And the way to find out is to assume that I can do anything and go out and do it.

We had a student who got a complete remission from a cancer patient. And he did something which I think is even more impressive: He got an ovarian cyst the size of an orange to shrink away in two weeks. According to medical science, that wasn't even possible. That client reports that she has the X-rays to prove it.

Those of you who went through medical school were done something of a disservice; let me talk about that for a moment. The medical model is based on a scientific model. The scientific model does the following: it says "In a complex situation, one way to find out something about it scientifically is to restrict everything in the situation except one variable. Then you change the value of that variable and notice any changes in the system." I think that's an excellent way to figure out cause-effect relationships in the world of experience. I do *not* think it is a useful model in face-to-face communication with another human being who is trying to get a change. Rather than restrict all behavior in a face-to-face communication, you want to vary your behavior *wildly,* to do whatever you need to do in order to elicit the response that you want.

Medical people for a long time have been willing to admit that people can psychologically "make themselves sick." They know that psychological cognitive mechanisms can create disease, and that things like the placebo effect can cure it. But that knowledge is not exploited in this culture in a useful way. Reframing is one way to *begin* to do that.

Reframing is the treatment of choice for *any* psychosomatic symptom. You can assume that any physiological symptom is psychosomatic, and then proceed with reframing—making sure that the person has already made use of all medical resources. We assume that all disease is psychosomatic. We don't really *believe* that's true. However, if we act as if that's true, then we have ways of responding appropriately and powerfully to people who have difficulties that are not recognized as psychosomatic by medical people. Whether it's aphasics that we've worked with, or people with paralysis that had an organic base, that wasn't hysterical according to the medical reports, we still often get behavioral changes. You can talk about it as if the people were *pretending* to be changed, but as long as they pretend effectively for the rest of their life, I'm satisfied. That's real enough for me.

The question for us is not what's "true," but what is a useful belief system to operate out of as a communicator. If you are a medical doctor and somebody comes in with a broken arm, then I think the logical thing for you to do is to set the broken bone, and not play philosophical games. If you're a communicator and you take the medical model as a metaphor for psychological change, then you've made a grave error. It's just not a useful way of thinking about it.

I think that ultimately the cures for schizophrenia and neurosis probably will be pharmacological, but I don't think that they have to be. I think they probably *will be,* because the training structures in this country have produced a massive amount of incompetence in the field of psychotherapy. Therapists just aren't producing results. Some people are, but what they are doing isn't being proliferated at a high enough rate. That's one of the functions that I understand us to have: to put information into a form that allows it to be easily learned and widely disseminated.

We also treat alcoholism as a psychosomatic process—like allergies or headaches or phantom-limb pain. The alcohol is an anchor, just as any other drug is. What an alcoholic is saying to you by being an alcoholic is essentially "The only way I can get to certain kinds of experiences which are important and positive for me as a human being—camaraderie, escape from certain kinds of conscious process, or whatever it is—is this anchor called alcohol." Until the secondary gain is taken care of by some other behavior, they will continue to go back to that as an anchor. So there are two steps in the treatment of alcoholism. One is making sure the secondary gain gets picked up by some other activity: they can have camaraderie but they don't have to get drunk in order to get it. You have to find out what *their* specific need is, because it's different for everyone.

Once you have taught them effective ways to get that secondary gain for themselves without the necessity of alcohol, then you anchor something else to take the place of the alcohol stimulus so they don't have to go through the alcohol state to get to the experiences that they want and need. We've done single sessions with alcoholics that stick really well, as long as we make sure that those two steps are always involved.

Man: Do you make the basic assumption that an individual is consciously able to tell you what the secondary gain is?

Never! We make the assumption that they can't.

Reframing in the six-step format we did here has certain advantages that we talked about. For example, this format builds in a program which the person can use by themselves later to make change in any area of their life.

You can also do this behaviorally. In fact, this is a strategy and outline for behavioral therapy as well as what we've been doing here. In the more usual therapeutic relationship, the therapist takes responsibility for using all his verbal and non-verbal behavior to elicit responses, to get access to resources in parts of the person directly, and to communicate with those parts. The client in the normal therapeutic process will, in turn, become those parts. S/he will cry, become angry, delighted, ecstatic, etc. S/he will display with all output channels that s/he has altered consciousness and has become the part that I want to communicate with.

In reframing we take a step back in that process and ask that s/he create a part that will have the responsibility for maintaining an efficient, effective internal communication system between parts. However, the same six-step format can be used as an organizing principle for doing more usual kinds of therapeutic work. Step one, identifying the pattern, is equivalent in a normal therapeutic context to saying "What specific change would you like today?" and getting a congruent response.

In usual therapeutic work there are a lot of ways of establishing communication with a part, as long as you are flexible. There's playing polarity, for instance. Suppose that I'm with someone who is really depressed. One way for me to contact the part in him that is really depressed is to talk directly to him. If I want to contact the part that *doesn't* want him to be depressed, I can say "Boy, you are depressing! You are one of the most depressing—I'll bet you've been depressed your whole life. You've never had *any* experience other than being depressed, never at all."

"Well, not my whole life, but for the past—"

"Oh no, I'll bet it's been your *whole* life."

"No, not my whole life, last week I felt pretty good for about an hour. .."

In other words, by exaggerating the position that is offered to you, you get a polarity response if you do it congruently. And as soon as the person accesses the polarity, you can anchor it.

Woman: I have a client who will say "This is ridiculous! I don't want to do it."

Fine. So what?

Woman: Do you laugh at that point? Or do you, you know ...

No. Well, first of all, I've never had anybody tell me that. And I think that's because I do a lot of "set-ups" before I get into this. I do a lot of pacing, matching, mirroring. So you might take this as a comment that you didn't set up this person sufficiently well.

Or you might take it as a signal that you just accessed the part that you need to communicate with. Their behavior gives one set of messages and the verbalization gives another. If you recognize that the part which is now active and just told you that this is ridiculous is the part you need to communicate with anyway, then you don't do it in the six-step format. You immediately move into the usual therapeutic format. You've already established communication with the part. Reach over and anchor it in the same way we were talking about earlier. That will always give you access to that part whenever you need it. That response is a successful response in the usual therapeutic format.

Whether you do it in the six-step format or in the format of more normal therapeutic encounters, such as I just talked about, you now have established a communication channel. The important thing here is to accept only reports—not interpretations from the person's conscious mind. If you accept interpretations, you're going to fall into the same difficulties that they are already in: the communication between their conscious understanding and the unconscious intent is at variance. If you take sides you are going to lose—unless you take sides with the unconscious, because the unconscious always wins anyway.

If your client refuses to have anything to do with exploring unconscious parts, you can say "Look, let me guarantee that the part of you that you are attacking consciously, the part of you that keeps you doing X, is doing something useful for you. I'm going to side with *it* against your conscious mind until I am satisfied that this unconscious part of you has found patterns of behavior that are more effective than what you are presently doing." Now, with that it's very hard to get any resistance. That's been my experience.

Step three of reframing is the major component of what most people do when they do family therapy. Let's say that you have a father who loses his temper a lot. Virginia Satir waits until he has expressed quite a bit of anger. Then she says "I want to tell you that in my years of doing family therapy I have seen a lot of people who are angry, and a lot of people could express it. I think it's important for every human being to be able to express what they feel in their guts, whether its happiness, or anger like you just felt. I want to compliment you, and I hope all the other members of this family have that choice." Now, that's pacing: "accept, accept, accept." And then she gets in real close to the father and says "And would you be willing to tell me about those feelings of loneliness and hurt underneath that anger?"

Another form of behavioral reframing is to say "Do you yell at everyone like that? You don't yell at the paper boy? You don't yell at your mechanic? Well, are you trying to tell her that you care about what she does? Is that what this anger is about? I mean, I notice you don't do it with people you don't care about. This must be a caring message. Did you know that this was his way of expressing that he cares what you do?"

"Well, how do you feel about knowing that now?" How many of you have heard Virginia Satir say that? That's a weird sentence; it doesn't actually have any meaning. But it works! That's another example of behavioral reframing. It's the same principle, but it involves content. That's the only difference.

Carl Whittaker has one nice reframing pattern that is apparently uniquely his. The husband complains "And for the last ten years nobody has ever taken care of me. I've had to do everything for myself and I've had to develop this ability to take care of myself. Nobody ever is solicitous toward me." Carl Whittaker says "Thank God you learned to stand on your own feet. I really appreciate a man who can do that. Aren't you glad you've done that?" That's a behavioral reframe. If a client says "Well, you know, I guess I'm just not the perfect husband," he says "Thank God! I'm so relieved! I've had three perfect husbands already this week and *they are so dull.*" What he does is to reverse the presupposition of the communication he's receiving.

We originally developed reframing by observing Virginia Satir in the context of family therapy. We have developed several other systematic models of reframing that will appear in a book titled *Reframing: NLP and the Transformation of Meaning.* In that book we also apply reframing to alcoholism, family therapy, corporate decision-making, and other specific contexts.

One aspect of reframing was introduced years ago in the process called "brainstorming," a situation in which people simply free-associate and explicitly suspend their usual judgemental responses. When brainstorming is conducted in an effective way, people generate a lot more ideas than they do in other modes of working together.

The primary way in which that works is that a really fine distinction is made between *outcomes*—what we are going to use this material for—and the *process* of generating ideas with other human beings. Reframing is the same principle applied more generally.

What I've noticed over and over again in corporate work, in arbitration, or in family therapy, is that there will be a goal toward which a number of members in the system want to move. They begin to discuss some of the characteristics or dimensions, or advantages or disadvantages, of this future desired state. As they do this, other members involved in that negotiation behave as if they feel compelled to point out that there are certain constraints that presently exist in the organization which make it impossible to do that.

Now, what is missing is the time quantifier. Indeed they are correct. There are constraints on the organization or the family which make it impossible, concretely speaking, to engage in that proposed behavior *now.* If you work as a consultant for an organization or a family, you can teach people to distinguish between responses they are making that are congruent with the description of the *future* state, and responses that are a characterization of the *present* state. Once that is done, you avoid about ninety-five percent of the bickering that goes on in planning sessions. You convince the people in the organization that it is useful for them to feel free to restrict themselves to discussing the future state, the desired state, propositions entirely distinct from present state constraints. This is an example of sorting out certain dimensions of experience, dealing with them in some useful way, and then later re-integrating them back into the system.

You also need a monitor. All of you have had the following experience. You're in an organizational meeting or a family system. And no matter what anyone says, there's one person who takes issue with it. No matter what the proposal is, there is someone who behaves as if it were their function in that system to challenge the formulation that has just been offered. It's a useful thing to be able to do, but it can also be very disruptive. What techniques do you have to utilize what's going on at that point? Does anybody have a way of dealing with that effectively?

Woman: You can escalate it; ask them to do it more.

So you would use the gestalt thing of exaggerating. What's the outcome you typically get?

Woman: Ah, they stop.

They stop doing it. That's a nice transfer from therapy. She's using one of the three patterns which are characteristic of Brief Therapy therapists, the pattern of *prescribing the symptom*. For instance, when somebody comes to Milton Erickson and asks for assistance in losing weight, typically he demands that s/he *gain* exactly eleven pounds in the next two weeks. That might seem to be irrational behavior on his part. However, it's quite effective, because one of two things will happen. Either the person will lose weight—a polarity response— which is the outcome he is working toward anyway, or they will gain eleven pounds. Typically they don't gain ten or twelve, they gain *eleven*. Since they were able to accomplish that, the behavioral presupposition is that they can control what they weigh. In either case it unstabilizes the situation. I've never heard of people stabilizing. Something always happens. It's the same kind of maneuver that Salvador Minuchin makes when he allies himself with a member of the family to throw the system out of kilter. This is a really nice example of a transfer of a therapeutic technique to the organizational context.

Let me offer you another utilization. As soon as you notice that the challenging behavior is disruptive, you can interrupt the process, and say "Look, one of the things I've discovered is that it's useful to assign people specific functions in a group. In my experience of consulting and working with organizations, I have found that this is a useful way of organizing meetings.One group member keeps track of the ideas, and so on." Then you can assign this person the function of being the challenger. When a well-formed proposition is brought before the group by anyone, or by a sequence of suggestions, his job is to challenge that formulation at some point. You explain that by challenging the formulation, he will force the people making the proposal to make finer and finer distinctions and to hone their proposal into a form that will be effective and realistic. You've prescribed the symptom, but you have also institutionalized it. I've had the experience of simply prescribing the symptom, and at the next meeting the same thing happens, and I have to do it again. One way to make sure that you don't have to make that intervention over and over again is to institutionalize it by assigning the function of challenger to that person.

You've essentially taken over the behavior. Now you can control *when* the challenges will be made. This is an example of utilization. You don't try to stop the problem behavior, you utilize it. The primary metaphor for utilization is the situation where I never fight *against* the energy offered me by anyone, or any part of them. I take it and use it. Utilization is the psychological counterpart of the oriental martial arts, such as Aikido or Judo. This is a parallel strategy for psychological martial arts. You always accept and utilize the response, you don't fight or challenge the response—with one exception, of course. If the person's presenting problem involves their running over people then you clobber them, because the presenting problem involves the very pattern that they are using: namely, they get their way. But, of course, that's a paradox, because if they were *really* getting their way, they wouldn't be in your office.

So let's say that Jim here makes a proposal and Tony is the guy I have assigned to be the challenger. When Tony begins to interrupt, I say "Excellent! Good work, Tony! Now, listen, Tony, what I think you ought to be sensitive to is that we haven't yet given Jim enough rope to hang himself. So let him make a more complete proposal and get responses from other people, and *then* I'll cue you and you jump right on it. OK?" So I've essentially delivered the message "Yes, but not yet."

Woman: That works if you are the outside consultant coming in, but what if you are already in the system?

If you are an inside consultant or you are a member of the system at the same level of functioning, there may be people who would resent or

resist if you state it as *your* proposal. So you have to frame it
appropriately. It's not a proposal coming from *you*. It's a proposal you
are offering that comes from outside, which you think might be useful
for you and the rest of the members of the group. You can do it
metaphorically. You can say "I spent a fascinating evening the other
night with a corporate consultant in Chicago. I went to a conference
and the leader told us the following:" Then you present all the
information that I just presented to you. If you do that congruently, it
will be an acceptable proposal. You can always suggest an experiential
test to find out whether it's worth doing. You can ask people to try it for
two hours. If it works, people will continue it. If it doesn't, you haven't
lost much, and you don't want to continue it anyway.

I would like to point out that discussions where antagonistic
positions are being presented are the life blood of any organization *if*
they are done in a particular context. That context is that you establish
a frame around the whole process of argument, so that the disputes, the
discussions of antagonistic proposals, are simply different ways of
achieving the same outcome that all members agree upon.

Let me give a content example. George and Harry are co-owners of a
corporation; each owns fifty percent of the stock. I've been brought in
as a corporate consultant. Harry says the following: "We've got to
expand. You grow or you die. And specifically we've got to open
offices in Atlanta, Chattanooga, and Miami this year." And George
over here says "Look, you know as well as I do, Harry, that last year
when we opened the Chicago and Milwaukee offices, we opened them
on a shoestring. And as a matter of fact, they still are not yet self-
sufficient. They are still not stabilized to the point that they are turning
over the amount of business that gives me the confidence to know that
we can go ahead and expand into these other offices. Now how many
times do we have to go through this?"

So there's a content difference between these two human beings
about the next thing they should do as a corporate entity. One strategy
that always works effectively in this situation is to reframe the two
responses that they are offering as alternative ways of getting an
outcome that they *both* agree is desirable. So first you have to find the
common goal—establish a frame. Then you instruct them in how to
dispute each other's proposals effectively, because now both proposals
are examples of how to achieve the same outcome that they both have
agreed upon.

So I would do something like the following: "Look, let me interrupt you for a moment. I just want to make sure that I understand you both. Harry, you want to expand because you want the corporation to grow and realize more income, right?" I then turn to George and say "My understanding is that your objection to the expansion at the moment, and your focusing on the fact that the Milwaukee and Chicago offices are not quite self-sufficient yet, is your way of being sure that the quality of the services that you offer as a corporation are of a certain level. You are offering a quality product and you want to maintain that quality, because otherwise the whole thing won't work anyway." And he'll say "Of course. Why do you ask these things?" And then I say "OK, I think I understand now. *Both of you agree* that what you want to do is expand at a rate congruent with maintaining the high quality of services your corporation offers." And they'll both say "Of course." You've now achieved the agreement that you need; you've now got the frame. You say "Good. *Since we agree* on the outcome that we're all working toward, let's find the most effective, efficient way to get that outcome. Now you, George, make a specific, detailed proposal about how you will know when the Chicago and Milwaukee offices are stabilized at a quality of operation that allows you to feel comfortable about turning resources elsewhere to continue expanding. Harry, I want you to come up with the specific evidence that you can use to know when it is appropriate to open new branches. What will you see or hear that's going to allow you to know that it is now appropriate to open a new office in Chattanooga, and still maintain the quality of the services you're going to offer?"

First I use language that generalizes, to establish the frame. Then I make sure it is anchored in. "*Since we all agree* about the outcome, ..." Then I challenge them to take the proposals they've been fighting over—now embedded in a context of agreement—back to the level of sensory experience. I demand that each of them give specific evidence to support that their proposal is more effective in achieving the outcome that they have both agreed upon. Now they will have useful disputes. And I will monitor their language to be sure that they are being specific enough to make a good decision. You can always figure out what would constitute evidence that one proposal is more effective than another.

Let me give you a specific strategy for doing this. You listen to both complaint A and complaint B. Then you ask yourself "What are A and B *both* examples of? What is the class or category that they are both examples of? What is the outcome that both of these two people will share? What common intention lies behind or underneath both these two particular proposals?" Once you discover that, then you interrupt and state the obvious in some way. You get an agreement between these two people, so that they can then begin to usefully disagree *within* the context of agreement.

Now that has the same formal properties of what I did with Dick in the six-step reframing. We found a point where his conscious mind and his unconscious mind could agree about a certain outcome that was useful for him as an individual.

Harry and George now agree that whatever they end up doing— either one of their proposals, both, or some alternative to those—the outcome they are working toward is to benefit the corporate entity as a unit. So I ignore the specific behaviors, and I go after an outcome that the two parts of the corporation—or the two parts of the human being—can agree upon. Now, having achieved the frame of agreement, it becomes trivial to vary behavior in order to find a behavior that achieves the outcome that both partners can agree to.

If you have more than two people involved—which is usually the case—you can simplify the situation by organizing the discussion. Just say "Look, I'm getting very confused by the way we're discussing things. Let me organize it a little bit in the following way: I want the rest of you to be exquisitely attentive. You have the job of watching and listening to exactly what these two people are going to propose, and assisting me in the process of finding what's common about what they want to do. You can reorganize it into pairs, and then work with one pair at a time. And as you do that, of course you are teaching the pattern to the observers at the same time.

People have strange ideas about change. Change is the only constant in my thirty-some years of experience. One of the weird things that's happened—and this is a really good example of natural anchoring—is that change and pain are associated. Those ideas have been anchored together in western civilization. That's ridiculous! There's no necessary relationship between pain and change. Is there Linda? Tammy? Dick?

There is one class of human beings in which you may have to create pain in order to assist them in changing, and that's therapists. Most therapists intrinsically believe—at the unconscious level as well as the conscious level—that change has to be slow and painful. How many of you at some point during the demonstrations have said to yourself "That's too easy; it's too fast." If you examine the underlying presuppositions that cause you to respond that way, you'll discover that they are associated with pain and time and money and stuff—some of which are really powerful and valid economic considerations. Others are just junk that have been associated—like change and pain. So you might examine your own belief structure, because what you believe will come out. It will be in your tone of voice, in your body movement, in the hesitation as you lean forward to do this work with someone.

All the tools that we offer you are very powerful and elegant. They are the minimum that I think you need to operate, no matter what psychotheology you were previously trained in.

If you decide that you want to fail with this material, it's possible to. There are two ways to fail. I think you ought to be aware of what those are, so that you can make a choice about how you are going to fail if you decide to.

One way is to be extremely rigid. You can go through exactly the steps that you saw and heard us go through here, without any sensory experience, without any feedback from your clients. That will guarantee that you will fail. That's the way most people fail.

The second way you can fail is by being really incongruent. If there's a part of you that really doesn't believe that phobias can be done in three minutes, but you decide to try it anyway, that incongruency will show up in your non-verbal communication, and that will blow the whole thing.

Every psychotherapy that I know of has an acute mental illness within it. Each one thinks that their theory, their map, *is* the territory. They don't think that you can make up something totally arbitrary and install it in someone and change them. They don't realize that what they believe is also made up and totally arbitrary. Yes, their method does elicit a response from people, and sometimes it works for the problem you're working on. But there are a thousand *other* ways to go about it, and a thousand other responses.

For example, TA has a thing called "reparenting" in which they regress a person and give him a new set of parents. And if it's done appropriately, it will work. The TA *belief* is that the person is messed up *because* when they were a kid they didn't get certain kinds of experiences, so you *have* to go back and give them those experiences in order for them to be different. That's the TA theology, and accepting that belief system constitutes the mental illness of TA. TA people don't realize that you can get the same result a thousand other ways, and that some of them are a *lot* quicker than reparenting.

Any belief system is both a set of resources for doing a particular thing, and a set of severe limitations for doing anything else. The one value in belief is that it makes you congruent. That part is very useful; it will make other people believe you. But it also establishes a huge set of limitations. And *my* belief system is that you will find those limitations in yourself as a person as well as in your therapy. Your clients are going to end up being a metaphor for your personal life because you are making the ultimate tragic mistake. You believe that your perceptions are a description of what reality actually is.

There is a way out of that. The way out of that is to not believe what you're doing. That way you can do things that don't fit with "yourself," "your world," etc. I recently decided that I want to write a book titled, *When you discover your real self, then buy this book and become someone else.*

If you simply change your belief system, you will have a new set of resources and a new set of limitations. Having the choice of being able to operate out of different therapeutic models is very valuable in comparison to only being able to operate out of one model. If you *believe* any of them, you will remain limited in the same way those models are limited.

One way to get out of that is to learn to go into altered states in which you *make up* models. Once you realize that the world in which you're living right now is completely made up, you can make up new worlds.

Now if we're going to talk about altered states of consciousness, we first have to talk about states of consciousness. You are at this moment in time conscious, true or not true?

Woman: I think so.

OK. How do you *know* that you're conscious at this moment? What are the elements of your experience that would lead you to believe that you are in your normal state of consciousness? I want to know what it is about *this* state of consciousness that allows you to know that you are here.

Woman: Ah, I can hear your voice.

You can hear my voice, so you have auditory external. Is anyone talking on the inside at this moment?

Woman: I may have some internal voices.

Do you? While you're listening to me talk, is anyone else speaking? That's what I want to know. And I'm going to continue to talk so that you can find out.

Woman: I ... yes.

Is it a he or a she or an it?

Woman: A she.

All right. So you have some external and internal auditory experience. All TA people have that. They have a "critical parent," saying "Am I doing this right?" No one else does, though—until they go to a TA therapist, and then they have a critical parent. That's what TA does for you. OK, what else have you got? Are you visualizing while I'm speaking to you?

Woman: No, I'm seeing you on the outside.

OK, so you have some visual external experience Are you having any kinesthetic experience?

Woman: Not until you mentioned it.

OK. What was it?

Woman: Ahhhhmmmm ... I can feel a tightness in my jaw.

Another way to get this would be to say "What are you aware of?" And you would tell me about your state of consciousness at that moment in time. So we have specified auditory, visual, and kinesthetic. You weren't perceiving any smells or taste, were you?

Woman: No.

OK, I didn't think you were. Now, *my* definition of altering your state of consciousness is to change it from *this* to *any other possible combination of these things*. For example, *if* you were to only hear my voice and not your internal dialogue, that would constitute an altered state for you because you don't usually do that. Most of the time you talk to yourself while other people are talking. If, instead of seeing externally, you were to make clear, rich, vivid, focused images of anything inside, that would be an altered state. For example, if you were to see the letters and numbers of the alphabet, an orange, yourself sitting on the couch with your hand on your ear in an auditory accessing position, the nodding of your head....

Another thing is that your kinesthetics are proprioceptive. Tightness in the jaw is a lot different than the feeling of the couch, the warmth where your hand touches your face, the feeling of your other hand ... against your thigh, ... the beating of your own heart, ... the rise and fall of your chest ... as you breathe deeply. The intonation patterns of my voice, ... the changing tonality, ... the need to focus your eyes ... and the changing focus of your pupils, ... the repeating blinking movements, ... and the sense of weight.... Now, can you feel your state of consciousness alter?

That to me constitutes an altered state of consciousness. The way to do it is to first find out what's there, and then do something that makes something *else* come into consciousness. Once you are directing an altered state of consciousness, you can begin to make maneuvers that add options, add choices.

Woman: I think at that point I was aware of what was happening and I could stop it if I had wanted to, so—

But you *didn't*.

Woman: That's right, but I don't know about this argument of whether you can make somebody go into an altered state or not. I'm still not—

Well, it's a stupid argument to begin with, because the only people who are going to resist you are people who *know* that you are doing it. And then I can get somebody to resist me right into a trance, because all I have to do is to instruct them to do one thing and they'll do the *opposite*. They'll enter an altered state immediately. An example of that is a thing that mothers often say to children: "Don't laugh." They induce altered states in their children by playing polarity. Kids don't have a choice about that until they have requisite variety.

Who can make *whom* do *what,* is a function of requisite variety. If you have more flexibility in your behavior than your hypnotist, then you can go into a trance or you can stay out of a trance, depending upon what you want to do. Henry Hilgard made up *one* hypnotic induction and administered it to ten thousand people. Sure enough, he found out that only a certain percentage of them went into a trance. The percentage that went into a trance were the ones that were either pre-adapted or flexible enough to adapt to that hypnotic induction. The rest of the people who were *not* flexible enough to adapt to that particular hypnotic induction could not go into a trance.

Going into an altered state is nothing weird. *You all do it all the time.* The question is whether you *use* the altered state to produce change, and if so, *how* are you going to use it? *Inducing* it is not that difficult. All you have to do is talk about parameters of experience that the person isn't aware of. The question is "How will you do it with whom?" If you have a person who's very visual, you're going to do something that's very different than with someone like this woman here who talks to herself a lot and pays attention to the tightness in her jaw. For her, entering a state of consciousness where she makes rich, focused images would be altered. But for a visual person that would be the normal state. In an altered state a person has more and different choices than she does in her normal conscious waking state. Many people think that going into a trance means losing control. That's where this question "Can you make somebody go into a trance?" comes from. What you're *making* them do is to go into a state where they have *more* choices. There's a huge paradox there. In an altered state of consciousness you do not have your usual model of the world. So what you have is an *infinite* number of possibilities.

Since I can represent states in terms of representational systems, I can use this as a calculus to compute what else must be possible. I can *compute* altered states that have never existed and achieve them. I didn't find that possibility available to me when I was a gestalt therapist or when I did other forms of therapy. Those models didn't offer these alternatives. If you want to learn in detail how to induce and utilize altered states, read our book *Trance-formations: NLP and the Structure of Hypnosis.*

I have a student now who I think is pretty good. One of the things that I appreciate about him is that instead of "working on himself," he takes the time to enter altered states and give himself new realities. I think most of the time when therapists work on themselves, all they do is *confuse* themselves utterly and completely. Once a woman hired me to do a workshop. She called me up three weeks before the workshop and said that she had changed her mind. So I called my attorney and sued her. She had months and months and months to plan the workshop and do what she had said she would do. She had spent all that time "working on" whether she was ready to do this or not. Her therapist called me up to try to persuade me to not sue her. He said "Well, it's not like she hasn't spent time on it. She's been working on this for months about whether she was ready to do this workshop."

It seems to me that there was one obvious thing she could have done: she could have called me up months and months earlier and told me that she was unsure. But instead of doing that, she tried to work out external experience *internally and consciously.* And I think that's a paradox, as we've said over and over again. When people come for therapy, if they had the resources consciously available they would have changed already. The fact that they haven't is what brings them there. When you, as a therapist, consciously try to change yourself, you're setting yourself up for confusion, and you're likely to go into all kinds of interesting, but not very useful, loops.

One student of mine came to me first as a client. He was a junior in college at the time, and he said "I have a terrible problem. I meet a girl, things go really fine, and then she comes and sleeps with me and everything is great. But the next morning as soon as I wake up, I think 'Well, either I have to marry her or kick her out of bed and never see her again.'"

At that moment in time I was sort of amazed that a human being had actually said that to me! I will never cease to be amazed about how people can limit their world of experience. In his world there were only those two choices!

I was working with John at the time, and John looked at him and said "Has it ever occurred to you to just say 'Good morning'?" and the student went "Uhhhhhhhhh!" I think that stunk as a therapeutic maneuver, because now what's he going to do? He's going to say "Good morning," and *then* either put his foot in the center of her back and kick her out of bed, or propose marriage. There are more possibilities than that. But as he entered that state of confusion and went "Uhhhhhhhhh!" I reached over and said "Close your eyes." And John said "And begin to dream a dream in which you learn just how many other possibilities there are, and your eyes will be unable to open until you find them *all.*" He sat there for *six and a half hours!* We went out in the other room. Six and a half hours he was there coming up with possibilities. He couldn't leave because his eyes wouldn't open. He tried standing and walking, but he couldn't find the door. All of the possibilities that he thought of in that six and a half hour period had been available to him all along, but he had never done anything to access his own creativity.

Reframing is a way of getting people to say "Hey, how else can I do this?" In a way it's the *ultimate* criticism of a human being, saying "Stop and think about your behavior, and think about it in the following way: *Do something new; what you're doing doesn't work!* Tell yourself a story, and then come up with three other ways of telling the story, and suddenly you have differences in your behavior.

There's an amazing thing about people: when they find something that doesn't work, they do it harder. For example, go to a junior high school and watch kids on the playground. One kid comes up to another one and pushes him. So the other kid sticks his chest out. The next time the kid pushes him he can push him even better because he has a firm chest to put his hand against.

One thing that really hasn't been understood is what's possible if instead of approaching a problem directly, you approach it indirectly. Milton Erickson did what I think was one of the shortest cures that I've ever heard about. The story that I heard was that he was at the VA hospital in Palo Alto in 1957, and psychiatrists were waiting in line with patients out in the hall. They were coming in one at a time, and Milton was doing a little magic, doing this and doing that. Then they went back out in the hall and talked about how Milton wasn't really doing these things and he was a charlatan.

A young PhD psychologist, who was about as straight as you could get, brought in a seventeen-year-old adolescent who had been knifing people and doing anything he could possibly conceive of that was damaging. The kid had been waiting in line for hours and people had been coming out in somnambulistic trances; the kid was going "Ahhhhhhhh ... What are they going to do to me?" He didn't know if he was going to get electric shock or what. They brought him in and there was this man with two canes standing there behind the table, and an audience in the room. They walked up in front of the table. Milton said "Why have you brought this boy here?" And the psychologist explained the situation, gave the case history as best he could. Milton looked at the psychologist and said "Go sit down." Then he looked at the young boy and said "How surprised will you be when all your behavior changes completely next week?" The boy looked at him and said "I'll be *very* surprised!" And Milton said "Get out. Take these people away."

The psychologist assumed that Milton had decided not to work with the boy. Like most psychologists, he missed the whole thing. Next week, the boy's behavior changed completely, from top to bottom and from bottom to top. The psychologist said that he could never figure out what it was that Milton did. As I understand it, Milton only did *one* thing. He gave that boy the opportunity to access his own unconscious resources. He said "You will change, and your conscious mind won't have anything to do with it." Never underestimate the usefulness of just saying that to people. "I know that you have a vast array of resources available to you that your conscious mind doesn't even suspect. You have the ability to surprise yourself, each and every one of you." If you really congruently act as if people have the resources and are going to change, you begin to induce impetus in the unconscious.

One of the things that I noticed about Milton when I first went to see him, was the incredible respect that he has for unconscious processes. He is always trying to get demonstrations back and forth between conscious and unconscious activity.

In linguistics there is something called "the tip of the tongue" phenomenon. Do you all know what that is? That's when you know a word and you even *know* that you know the word, but you can't say what it is. Your conscious mind even knows that your unconscious mind knows what the word is. I remind people of that as evidence that their conscious mind is *less* than the tip of the iceberg.

I once hypnotized a linguistics professor and sent his conscious mind away into a memory. I asked if his unconscious mind knew what the "tip of the tongue" phenomenon was—because he had demonstrated it in many of his classes. His unconscious mind said to me "Yes, I know what it is." I said "Why is it that if you know a word, you don't present it to his conscious mind?" And he said to me "His conscious mind is too damn cocky."

In our last workshop we were doing some things with strategies, and we programmed a woman to forget what her name was. A man there said "There's *no way* that I could possibly forget my name." I said "What is your name?" And he said "*I don't know!*" I said "Congratulate your unconscious mind, even though you don't have one."

It is amazing to me that hypnosis has been so systematically ignored. I think it's been ignored mostly because the conscious minds who practice it don't trust it. But every form of therapy I've studied has trance experiences available in it. Gestalt is founded on positive hallucination. TA is founded on dissociation. They *all* have great verbal inductions.

At the last workshop we did there was a guy who was skeptical through most of the day. As I walked by, during an exercise, he was saying to his partner "Can you *allow* yourself to make this picture?" That's a *hypnotic* command. He had asked me downstairs if I believed in hypnosis! What I believe is that it's an unfortunate word. It's a name given to lots and lots of different experiences, lots of different states.

We used to do hypnotic inductions before we did reframing. Then we discovered that we could do reframing without having to put people into trance. That's how we got into Neuro Linguistic Programming. We thought "Well, if that's true, then we should be able to reframe people into doing every deep trance phenomenon that we know about." So we took a group of twenty people and in one evening we prorammed all the people in that group to do every deep trance phenomenon we could remember having read about anywhere. We found that we could get any "deep trance phenomenon" without doing any ritualized induction. We got amnesia, positive hallucination, tone-deafness, color blindness—everything. One woman negatively hallucinated Leslie for the entire evening. Leslie would walk over and pick up the woman's hand; her hand would float up and she had no idea why. It was like those cartoons about ghosts and stuff. That's as good as any negative hallucination we ever got doing hypnosis.

In the phobia technique where you see yourself standing there, and then float out of your body and see yourself there watching the younger you—that's a deep trance phenomenon. It requires positive hallucination, and getting out of your own body. That's fairly amazing. Yet all you have to do is give somebody the explicit instructions, and out of a hundred people, ninety-five can do it quickly and easily as long as you don't act as if it's hard. You always act as if you're leading up to something else that's going to be difficult, so they go ahead and do all the deep-trance phenomena and alter their state.

Neuro Linguistic Programming is a logical step higher than anything that has been done previously in hypnosis or therapy *only* in the sense that it allows you to do things formally and methodically. NLP allows you to determine exactly what alterations in subjective experience are necessary to accomplish a given outcome. Most hypnosis is a fairly random process: If I give someone a suggestion, that person has to come up with a method of carrying it out. As a Neuro Linguistic Programmer, even if I use hypnosis, I would describe exactly what I want that person to do in order to carry out the suggestion. That's the only important difference between what we're doing here and what people have been doing with hypnosis for centuries. It's a very *important* difference, because it allows you to predict outcomes precisely and avoid side-effects.

Using reframing and strategies and anchoring—all the tools of Neuro Linguistic Programming—you can get any response you can get through hypnosis. But then that's only one way to go about it. Doing it through official hypnosis is also interesting. And *combining* NLP and hypnosis is even more interesting.

For instance there is the "dreaming arm" technique that works great with children—and adults, too. First you ask "Did you know you have a dreaming arm?" When you have their interest, you ask "What is your favorite TV show?" As they access visually, you notice which side their eyes go to. As they do that, you lift up their arm on the *same* side, and say "I'm going to lift your arm, and your arm will go down *only as fast* as you watch that whole TV show, and you can begin *right now*. So the kid watches his favorite TV show. You can even reach out and stop their arm for a moment and say "It's time for a commercial" and install messages.

I'll tell you the extremes you can take this to. I had a client who had a severe hallucination that was *always* with him. I could never discern quite what it was. He had a name for it which was a word I'd never heard. It was a geometric figure which was alive and that followed him everywhere. It was his own sort of personal demon, but he didn't call it a demon. He could point to it in the room, and he interacted with it. When I asked him questions, he would turn around and ask "What do you think?" Before he came to me he had been convinced by a therapist that this was a part of him. Whether it was or not, I don't know, but he was convinced that this was a part of him that he had alienated. I reached over and said "I'm going to lift up your arm, and I want you to put it down *only* as fast as you begin to integrate this." Then I pulled his arm down quickly, and that was it. The integration occurred—whammo, slappo—because I had tied the two together with words.

I once asked a TA therapist which part had total control over his conscious ongoing behavior. Because it didn't seem that people had a choice about being their "parent," or their "child." So he named some part; TA has names for everything. I said "Would you go inside and ask that part if it would knock your conscious mind out for a while?" And he went "Ah, well ... " I said "Just go in and ask, and find out what happens." So he went inside and asked the question ... and his head fell over to one side and he was gone! It is amazing how powerful it is to use language. I don't think people understand the impact of verbal and non-verbal language at all.

At the beginning of therapy sessions very often I'll say to people "If anything begins to occur to your conscious mind which is too painful in any way, I want to say to your unconscious mind that I think it has the *right* and the *duty* to keep from your conscious mind anything that is unpleasant. Your unconscious resources can do that and they should do it—protect you from thinking about things which are unnecessary in that way, and make your conscious experience more pleasant. So if anything unpleasant begins to arise in your conscious experience, your unconscious mind can slowly allow your eyes to flutter closed, one of your hands to rise up, and your conscious mind can drift away into a pleasant memory, allowing me to speak privately with your unconscious mind. Because I don't know what the worst thing that ever happened to you was...."

I'm saying when X occurs, respond *this* way, and then I'm providing X. I'm not saying "*Think* about the worst thing that ever happened." I'm saying "I don't know ..." This is the same pattern that's in *Changing with Families,* the pattern of embedded questions. Virginia never says "What do you want?" She says "Gee, I ask myself why a family would travel six thousand miles to see me. And I don't know, and I'm curious." When I say "I don't know exactly what the most *painful* and *tragic* experience of your whole life was," it'll be right there in consciousness.

People *do not* process language consciously. They process language at the unconscious level. They can only become conscious of a very small amount of it. A lot of what is called hypnosis is using language in very specific ways.

It's one thing to alter someone's state of consciousness and to give them new programs, new learnings, new choices. Getting them to *know* that they've been in an altered state is something else entirely. Different people have different strategies by which they convince themselves of things. What constitutes somebody's belief system about what hypnosis is, is very different from being able to use hypnosis as a tool. It's much easier to use trance as a therapeutic tool with people who *don't* know that they've been in a trance, because you can communicate so much more eloquently with their unconscious processes. As long as you can establish unconscious feedback loops with that person, you'll be able to alter their state of consciousness and they are more apt to have amnesia.

My favorite case of this was a guy named Hal. He came to a seminar that a student of mine had set up and at the last minute she decided that she was an inadequate human being and left the State. The people all showed up at the seminar and someone called me and said "All these people are here, what should I do?" It was nearby, so I went over and I said "Well, I'll spend the evening with you. I don't want to teach a seminar, but I would like to know what you all hoped to get." Hal said "I have been to *every* hypnotist I've ever found; I have gone to *every* seminar I could ever find on hypnosis, and I have volunteered myself *every* time, and I have not gone into a trance."

I thought that was dedication for somebody who had failed over and over again. And so I thought "Well, wow! This is really interesting. Maybe this guy really is an 'impossible,' and maybe there's something interesting here." So I thought I'd try it. I did a hypnotic induction and the guy went right through the floor! He went into deep trance and he demonstrated all the most difficult hypnotic phenomena. Then I aroused him and said "Did you go into a trance?" And he said "No." I said "What happened?" And he said "Well, you were talking to me and I sat here and listened to you talk, and I closed my eyes, and I opened my eyes." I said "And did you X?" and I named one of the trance phenomena he had just demonstrated. And he said "No." So I thought, "Ah! well, it's just a function of his amnesia."

I hypnotized him again and gave him implicit hypnotic commands to *remember* doing all the things he did. He still had no memory whatsoever. All the people in the room, of course, were going crazy because they've seen him do all these things. I tried things like saying "Tell Hal what you saw" and they all told him. And he said "That's not going to work on me. I didn't do that. I would know if I did that." The interesting thing about Hal was there was more than one of him, and they had no connection with one another, no means of communicating with one another. So I thought well, I'm going to have to mix it up a little bit. I said "While you remain in the conscious state, I'd like to ask your unconscious mind to demonstrate to you that it can do things by lifting your hand so that only your right arm is in trance." His arm began to involuntarily float up. I thought "Now this is going to convince this guy," because only his arm was in trance. And he looked me straight in the eye and said "Well, my arm is in trance, but the rest of me can't go in."

By the way, I have a rule which says I have to succeed. So I tried videotaping him and showing him the videotape. He couldn't see it! We'd turn on the videotape, and he'd just go into a trance and that was it. He could not watch the videotape. I told him that if he had not been in a trance, he would be able to watch the videotape. So he sat there with the videotape machine, and he would turn it on and drop out. We'd turn it off and he'd come back. He'd turn it on again and drop out again. He sat there for the rest of the evening trying to watch himself go into a trance. He couldn't do it. So he became convinced that he had been in a trance, but he didn't understand it.

This taught me a lesson. I stopped worrying about whether people knew they were in trance or not and only noticed the results that I could get, utilizing it as phenomenon of change. Hypnotists do a terrible thing to themselves. Hypnotists are always worried about convincing people that they have been in trance, and it isn't important. It is not essential to their changing; it is not essential for *anything*. Whether they know that they've gone into trance or not, they will notice that they have the changes.

The same is true of anchoring and reframing. As long as you use sensory experience to check your work, it's irrelevant whether your clients believe that they have changed. They will find out in experience—if they bother to notice at all.

The information and patterns that we have been presenting to you are formal patterns of communication that are content-free. *They can be used in any context of human communication and behavior.*

We haven't even begun to figure out what the possibilities are of how to use this material. And we are very, very, serious about that. What we are doing now is nothing more than the investigation of how to use this information. We have been unable to exhaust the variety of ways to put this stuff together and put it to use, and we don't know of any limitations on the ways that you can use this information. During this seminar we have mentioned and demonstrated several dozen ways that it can be used. It's the structure of experience. Period. When used systematically, it constitutes a full strategy for getting any behavioral gain.

We are very slowly tapering off teaching and doing therapy because there's a presupposition common in the field of clinical psychology which we personally disagree with: that change is a remedial phenomenon. You find something that is wrong and you fix it. If you ask a hundred people "What would you like for yourself," ninety-nine will say "I want to *stop* doing X."

There is an entirely different way to look at change, which we call the *generative* or *enrichment* approach. Instead of looking for what's wrong and fixing it, it's possible simply to think of ways that your life could be enriched: "What would be fun to do, or interesting to be able to do?" "What new capacities or abilities could I invent for myself?" "How can I make things really groovy?"

When I was first doing therapy a man came in and said "I want to have better relationships with people." I said "Oh, so you have trouble relating to people?" He said "No, I get along *fine* with people. I *enjoy* my relationships a lot. I'd like to be able to do it even *better*." I looked into my therapy bag to see what to do for him, and there wasn't anything there!

Very rarely do people come in and say "Well, I'm confident but, boy, you know, if I were twice as confident things would be *really* wonderful." They come in and say "I'm *never* confident." I say "Are you sure of that?" and they say "*Absolutely!*"

The idea of generative change is really hard to sell to psychologists. Business people are much more interested, and they're more willing and able to pay to learn how to do it. Often we do groups in which about half of them are business people, and half of them are therapists. I say "Now, what I want you to do is to go inside and think of three really different situations." The business people go inside and sell a car, win a lawsuit, and meet somebody they really enjoy. The therapists go inside and get beaten up as a child, have a divorce, and have the worst professional failure and humiliation of their life!

We are currently investigating what we call generative personality. We are finding people who are geniuses at things, finding out the sequence of unconscious programming that they use, and installing those sequences in other people to find out if having that unconscious program allows them to be able to do the task. The "cloning" thing we did for the ad agency is an example of doing that at the corporate level.

When we do that, things which were problems, and would have been meat for therapy, *disappear.* We completely bypass the whole phenomenon of working with problems, because when the structure is changed, everything changes. And problems are only a function of structure.

Man: Can that present new problems?

Yes, but they are interesting, evolutionary ones. Everything presents problems, but the new ones are much more interesting. "What are you going to evolve yourself to become today?" is a *very* different way of approaching change than "Where is it wrong?" or "How are you inadequate?" I remember once I was in a group with a gestalt therapist and he said "Who wants to work today?" Nobody raised their hand. And he said "There's really no one in here that has a pressing problem?" People looked at each other, shook their heads, and said "No." He looked at the people and said "What's wrong with you? You are not in touch with what's really going on if there's no pain here." He really made that statement; I was flabbergasted. Suddenly all these people went into pain. They all said "You're right! If I have no pain, I'm not real." Boom, they all went into pain, so then he had something to do therapy with.

That model of change does not produce really generative, creative human beings. I want to make structures that are conducive to creating experiences which will result in people who are interesting. People come out of therapy being lots of things, but rarely interesting. I don't think that it's anybody's fault. I think it's a result of the whole system and the presuppositions that underlie the system of psychotherapy and counseling. Most people are totally unconscious of what those presuppositions are.

As I walked around watching and listening to you practicing reframing, I saw a lot of you reverting to other patterns that I'm sure are characteristic of your habitual behavior in therapy, rather than trying something new. And that reminded me of a story:

Some fifteen or so years ago when the Denver zoo was going through a major renovation, there was a polar bear there, which had arrived at the zoo before a naturalistic environment was ready for it. Polar bears, by the way, are one of my favorite animals. They are very playful; they are big and graceful and do lots of nice things. The cage that it was put in temporarily was just big enough that the polar bear could take three nice, swinging steps in one direction, whirl up and around and come down and take three steps in the other direction, back and forth. The polar bear spent many, many months in that particular cage with those bars that restricted its behavior in that way. Eventually a naturalistic environment in which they could release the polar bear was built around this cage, on-site. When it was finally completed, the cage was removed from around the polar bear. Guess what happened? ...

And guess how many of those students at that university are still going down the maze, still trying to find the five-dollar bill? They sneak in at night and run down the maze to look and see if it just *might* be there *this* time.

We have been deluging you with information for three days now, totally overloading your conscious resources. And we'd like to offer you a couple of allies in this process which we have discovered are helpful to some people. Do people read Carlos Castenada here? He's a whacko multiple personality with an Indian friend. There's a section in book two or three in which Don Juan gives a piece of advice to Carlos. We would not give this piece of advice to any of you, but we will repea it for whatever it's worth.

You see, what Juan wanted to do to Carlos—which we wouldn't, of course, want to do to you—was to find some way of motivating him to be congruent and expressive in his behavior at all times, as creative as he could be as a human being. He wanted to mobilize his resources so that each act that Carlos performed would be a full representation of *all* the potential that was available to him—all the personal power that he had that was available to him at any moment in time.

Specifically what Juan told Carlos was "At any moment that you find yourself hesitating, or if at any moment you find yourself putting off until tomorrow trying some new piece of behavior that you *could* do today, or doing something you've done before, then all you need to do is glance over your left shoulder and there will be a fleeting shadow. That shadow represents your death, and at any moment it might step forward, place its hand on your shoulder and take you. So that the act that you are presently engaged in might be your very last act and therefore fully representative of you as your last act on this planet."

One of the ways you can use this constructively is to understand that it is indulgent to hesitate.

When you hesitate, you are acting as though you are immortal. And you, ladies and gentlemen, are *not*.

You don't even know the place and the hour of your death.

And so one thing you can do . . . to remind yourself that not to bother to hesitate is not to act unprofessional . . . is to just suddenly glance over your left shoulder and remember that death is standing there, and make death your advisor. He or she will always tell you to do something representative of your full potential as a person. You can afford no less.

Now, that's a little bit heavy. That's why we wouldn't tell that to you. We noticed that Juan told Carlos. We offer you an alternative.

If at any point you discover yourself hesitating, or being incongruent, or putting off until tomorrow something you could try now, or just needing some new choices, or being bored, glance over your *right* shoulder and there will be two madmen there, sitting on stools, insulting you.

And as soon as we finish the insults, you may ask us any question.

And that's just *one* way that your unconscious can present to you all the material that it has learned and represented during these three days.

Now, there's only one other thing that we like to do at the end of a workshop. And that is to say. . . .

Goodbye!

Bibliography

Bandler, Richard. *Using Your Brain—for a CHANGE.* Real People Press, 1985 (cloth $10.00, paper $6.50).

Bandler, Richard. *Magic In Action.* Meta Publications, 1985 (cloth $14.95).

Bandler, Richard; and Grinder, John. *Frogs into Princes.* Real People Press, 1979 (cloth $10.00, paper $6.50).

Bandler, Richard; and Grinder, John. *The Structure of Magic I.* Science and Behavior Books, 1975 ($8.95).

Bandler, Richard; and Grinder, John. *Patterns of the Hypnotic Techniques of Milton H. Erickson, M.D. I.* Meta Publications, 1975 (paper, $6.95).

Bandler, Richard; Grinder, John; and Satir, Virginia. *Changing with Families.* Science and Behavior Books, 1976 ($9.95).

Cleveland, Bernard F. *Master Teaching Techniques.* Connecting Link Press, 1984. (paper $12.50.).

Dilts, Robert B. *Applications of Neuro-Linguistic Programming.* Meta Publications, 1983 (cloth $22.00).

Dilts, Robert B. *Roots of Neuro-Linguistic Programming.* Meta Publications, 1983 (cloth $22.00).

Dilts, Robert B.; Grinder, John; Bandler, Richard; DeLozier, Judith; and Cameron-Bandler, Leslie. *Neuro-Linguistic Programming I.* Meta Publications, 1979 ($24.00).

Farrelly, Frank; and Brandsma, Jeff. *Provocative Therapy.* Meta Publications, 1978 ($9.95).

Gordon, David. *Therapeutic Metaphors: Helping Others Through the Looking Glass.* Meta Publications, 1978 ($9.95).

Gordon, David; and Meyers-Anderson, Maribeth. *Phoenix.* Meta Publications, 1981 (cloth $14.00).

Grinder, John; and Bandler, Richard. *Trance-formations: Neuro-Linguistic Programming and the Structure of Hypnosis.* Real People Press, 1981 (cloth $10.00, paper $6.50).

Grinder, John; and Bandler, Richard. *The Structure of Magic II.* Science and Behavior Books, 1976 ($8.95).

Grinder, John; and Bandler, Richard. *Reframing: Neuro-Linguistic Programming and the Transformation of Meaning.* Real People Press, 1982 (cloth $10.00, paper $6.50).

Grinder, John; Delozier, Judith; and Bandler, Richard. *Patterns of the Hypnotic Techniques of Milton H. Erickson, M.D. II.* Meta Publications, 1977 ($17.95).

Jacobsen, Sid. *Meta-cation.* Meta Publications, 1983 (cloth $12.00).

Lankton, Stephen R. *Practical Magic: The Clinical Applications of Neuro-Linguistic Programming.* Meta Publications, 1979 ($12.00).

Moine, Donald J; and Herd, John H. *Modern Persuasion Strategies.* Prentice-Hall, 1985 (cloth $16.95).